18 Sept.

1995

LONDON'S RIVER

PHILIP HOWARD

LONDON'S RIVER

HAMISH HAMILTON
LONDON

First published in Great Britain 1975
by Hamish Hamilton Ltd
90 Great Russell Street London WC1B 3PT

Copyright © 1975 by Philip Howard

SBN 241 89237 6

Printed in Great Britain by
Western Printing Services Ltd, Bristol

For Myrtle

CONTENTS

ILLUSTRATIONS

Illustration 2 is reproduced by kind permission of B.O.A.C.; 3a and 4c by kind permission of the British Museum; 1a, 7a, 9a, 9b, 10a, 10b, 11a, 12, and 16a by kind permission of the British Museum/Crace Collection; 5, 14b and 16b by kind permission of the Greater London Council; 1b, 4a, 4b, 6a, 6b and 7b by kind permission of the National Portrait Gallery; 8 and 15 by kind permission of Photo Pace; 3b, 11b, 13a and 13b by kind permission of *The Times.* 14a is reproduced by courtesy of the Institution of Civil Engineers.

ACKNOWLEDGEMENTS

Anybody who seeks to augment the copious flood of literature about London's River owes his greatest debt, after the primal one to old Father Thames himself, to his predecessors on the river. A selection of the most recent books about the Thames is given in the bibliography. But the names of two great Thames watermen and waterscribes have to be singled out: John Taylor, the water poet; and Sir Alan Herbert, whose devotion to the river was a dominant interest in a life crowded with important and varied interests. Their names are linked indissolubly to that of the river they loved and wrote about.

I give great thanks for books, documents, information, and advice to the archivists, librarians, and press and public relations officers of the riparian London Boroughs. Working down-stream, they are: Hounslow, Kingston-upon-Thames, Richmond-upon-Thames, Hammersmith, Wandsworth, Kensington and Chelsea, the City of Westminster, Lambeth, Southwark, the Corporation of the City of London, Tower Hamlets, Lewisham, Newham, Greenwich, Barking, Havering, and Bexley.

Archivists and public relations officers of the great institutions connected with the river have given generous help with information and documents: the Thames Water Authority; the Port of London Authority; the Greater London Council; the City of London; Trinity House; the Thames Division of the Metropolitan Police; the Company of Watermen and Lightermen; the Worshipful Company of Fishmongers; and other organizations connected with the tideway or situated beside it.

Finally I thank Jamie Hamilton heartily for publishing the book; and Christopher Sinclair-Stevenson, whose idea it was, for being the most imaginative, punctilious, and amiable of editors.

PHILIP HOWARD

CHAPTER ONE

The Thames and London

PHYSICALLY the Thames is by no means one of the great rivers of the world. Giants like the Amazon and the Nile are twenty times as long and roll down many times as much water. Even such comparatively unknown rivers as the confluent Ob and Irtysh in the Soviet Union (3,461 miles long) and the Amur in China (2,802 miles long) make the Thames's length of something more than two hundred miles look an insignificant trickle.

The length of the Thames, like so much else concerning the London River, is a matter of nice calculation and dispute, depending on where you start measuring. The nicest calculation seems the one made by that devoted and learned Thames waterman, Sir Alan Herbert: from the source at Thames Head in Gloucestershire to Teddington, where the tidal flow is halted, $146\frac{1}{2}$ miles; from Teddington to the Nore, the sandbank that is reckoned the mouth of the Thames, $68\frac{1}{2}$ miles; total, 215 miles.

The Thames Water Authority assumed control of the entire water cycle of the Thames and its catchment area of 5,000 square miles on April 1, 1974. Until then the river from its source to Teddington, eighteen miles above London Bridge, had been controlled and regulated by the Thames Conservancy, an admirably progressive Victorian institution formed in 1857. One explanation for the disproportionate importance of this small river is the huge population of twelve million that live in its basin.

The Port of London Authority, created in 1909 to replace the private dock companies that had previously disorganized the traffic of the tidal reaches, still controls navigation on the Thames from Teddington to the Authority's seaward limit north of Margate, delineated by the Barrow Deep and Tongue light vessels.

The average volume of flow to Teddington, calculated over the years since 1883, is 1,443 million gallons a day, averaged over the whole year. This figure is brought up to that level by a few periods of heavy spate in the winter and spring. Consequently a more realistic flow for the statistically-minded to expect on most days is less than a million gallons.

In length and volume, therefore, the Thames is comparatively small beside the great rivers of the world. Even in Britain the Severn is longer; and

Britain is a relatively small island. Nor is the natural scenery of the Thames
sufficiently spectacular to compel its inclusion without question in a table of
great rivers of the world. The Thames valley is green and gentle, wooded and
rich, epitomizing the soft and small-scale attractions of the southern English
countryside. But there are no mighty cataracts, no reaches miles wide, no
jungles, no great confluences staining the current a different colour for a
hundred miles.

The closest things to mountain scenery on the banks of the Thames are
the modest protuberances of the Cotswolds, the steep woods of the Goring
Gap, and the urbane slopes beneath Cliveden's proud alcove. It is significant
that the emblematic vessel of the great Mississipi is a paddle-boat with as
many tiers as a wedding-cake; of the Nile, a dhow; of the Amazon, a steamer;
and of the Thames, a punt.

Nevertheless, in spite of these defects of size, the Thames is generally
accepted as one of the great rivers of the world. It figures repeatedly and with
remarkable eulogy in European literature from Julius Caesar, Tacitus, and
the Venerable Bede onwards. Edmund Spenser built his great 'spousal verse'
Prothalamion around the haunting incantation: 'Sweet Thames, run softly,
till I end my song.' Dryden, writing of London resurrected after the Great
Fire, prophesied that the Thames would soon once again outshine with
buildings and traffic the Tagus, the Seine, the Rhine, and all the other rich
rivers of Europe:

> The silver Thames, her own domestic flood,
> Shall bear her vessels like a sweeping train,
> And often wind, as of his mistress proud,
> With longing eyes to meet her face again.

Gray complimented the hoary Thames for wandering along his silver-
winding way. Pope chose the same implausible but honorific epithet by
launching Belinda and her companions in *The Rape of the Lock* on the bosom
of the silver Thames. A lesser poet, Sir John Denham, was more explicit in
his flattery:

> Oh, could I flow like thee, and make thy stream
> My great example, as it is my theme:
> Though deep yet clear, though gentle yet not dull,
> Strong without rage, without o'erflowing full.

Herrick selected the elegant variation of 'silver-footed' and wished,
charmingly:

> May all clean *Nimphs* and curious water Dames,
> With Swan-like state, flote up and down thy streams.

'Silver-streaming', 'Parent of London' and so on: a collection of the poetry published down the centuries about the Thames would make an anthology of several volumes. It probably already has done. The Thames is a prolific source of anthologies, novels, and other river literature as well as of poetic inspiration.

Modern poets are no less provoked to composition by the river than their predecessors. But their adjectives and images these days tend to be less conventionally stylized in silver, more accurate. Alan Ross, in a marvellous piece about the Embankment before snow, wrote evocatively about phlegm-coloured waves slap-slapping stone wharves. And Richard Church said that the cranes and derricks of Hay's Wharf, which used to hang over the dark water of the Pool, looked as though some Frankenstein had taught his monster to delight in fishing.

Part of the explanation for the literary fame may be simple propinquity. Poets are inspired to write about rivers; and the Thames is the biggest and nearest river to southern England, a district notoriously fertile with poets. Part may be the nationalism that Addison satirized when he made that endearing chauvinist, Sir Roger de Coverley, reflect 'that one *Englishman* could beat three Frenchmen; that we cou'd never be in danger of Popery so long as we took care of our fleet; that the *Thames* was the noblest river in *Europe*; that *London Bridge* was a greater piece of work than any of the Seven Wonders of the World; with many other honest prejudices which naturally cleave to the heart of a true *Englishman*'.

But Sir Roger and the poets also recognized a fundamental historical and geographical truth. London came to be where it is because of the river and the port it provided. The maritime and commercial skills and acquisitive instincts of the English combined with the accidents of history made it for centuries the greatest port in the world, and the centre and market-place of the British Empire. The very long, very successful history of a numerically small race, isolated from the rest of the world on an off-shore island to the north-west of Europe, was to a great extent based on its chief river, its port, and the traffic to and from the Thames from and to every corner of the world. That is why the Thames became the greatest river in the world, the home port of traders, soldiers, and administrators from China to Peru.

If the slate was wiped clean of history and a tidy-minded committee of wise men was set up to select a site for the capital of England, it would be unlikely to hit on London. The situation in the middle of tidal swamps, flooded twice a day at high tide and surrounded by thick forest, was unhealthy and inaccessible by foot. Its position down at the south-east corner of the island is eccentric, still having an unbalancing gravitational pull on the people and resources of the rest of the country, and consequently being partly responsible for the notorious regional and class divisions of Britain. The primitive cultures of prehistory clearly felt that way. The centres of their activity were such dry, unwooded uplands as Salisbury Plain, or coast-lands such as Colchester, the chief city of the dominant tribal confederation at the time of the Roman invasions. The Romans adopted Colchester, *Camulodunum*, as their capital.

Many early civilizations, as in Mesopotamia, China, and India, were riverine, because of man's constant need for fresh water. There was no such tendency in Britain, where until this century the popular geographical and meteorological problem was too much rather than too little fresh water.

The committee would probably rule London out to be capital as unsuitable administratively, militarily, and from the point of view of communications. But then capitals like Canberra and Brasilia chosen by tidy-minded committees are notably unsatisfactory.

The early sea travellers before the Romans recognized the Thames as the conspicuous geographical feature of southern England. Caesar already knew it as *Tamesis*, which makes it the second oldest place-name in England still in use. The onomasticians derive the word from an Indo-European word meaning 'dark', probably related to the Sanskrit *Tamasa*, a tributary of the Ganges. The dark river, opening through its wide estuary to the Continent such a deep and convenient road into the heart of the mysterious island, must have been a prime piece of navigational and strategic information for those early travellers. The same root, implying 'dark water', is quite widely dispersed around British waterways, as in Thame, Teme, Tamar and Taff. The superfluous 'h' in Thames was added subsequently by later generations of pretentious spellers in a typical piece of English word snobbery and unhelpful spelling.

Pytheas, the great Greek astronomer and voyager from *Massilia* (Marseilles), circumnavigated Britain in the third century B.C., discovering *ultima Thule* (probably the Shetlands) on his journey. His writings have been lost, but echoes of them survive in quotation and commentary by later Greek and Roman authors such as Strabo and Pliny. No mention of *Tamesis* by him has come down to us. But Pytheas said that the south-eastern corner of Britain was called *Kantion*, which makes Kent the oldest extant place-name in Britain.

Thicker darkness obscures the origins of the name of London. It is reasonably certain that there was no significant settlement there at the time of the Roman invasions. The evidence for this reasonable certainty is partly archaeological. There are traces of only casual occupation of the banks of the Thames in the prehistoric period. Such traces as there are have been found thicker upstream from the City, at Battersea and Brentford, where the river was easier to ford.

Negative evidence to support this view that London did not come into existence as a trading post until the Roman period is found in the *Commentarii* of Julius Caesar. Caesar records that in 54 B.C. on his second expedition to

Britain he led his army across the Thames to march against the capital of
Cassivellaunus on the hill-top beside Wheathampstead, a little north of St
Albans. It is now generally agreed that the Romans crossed the river somewhere in the neighbourhood of Brentford, though there has been support for
a lower crossing at Westminster. No mention is made of any settlement at
London in Caesar's commentary on this campaign. Caesar was far too
punctilious a strategist to ignore the existence of a settlement and another
crossing downstream from his ford. We can therefore infer from Caesar and
archaeology that any pre-Roman settlement on the twin hills rising out of the
swamps that became the City was negligible.

In the ninety years between Caesar's invasions and the Claudian conquest
there was vigorous trade between Romanized Gaul and the Belgic tribal
confederation of southern Britain. A mint was set up at the centre that the
Romans were to call *Verulamium* and started coining British coins with
Roman inscriptions. There is other evidence of Roman influence and trade.
It is a reasonable assumption that London emerged as a trading post during
this period, quite possibly as the port of *Verulamium*.

The name London is Celtic, Romanized to *Londinium*. Its etymology is
disputed. The majority agree that it comes from the root *Londo*, meaning
'wild' or 'bold'. If that is correct, the name of the settlement was probably
derived from a personal name like *Londinos*, originally belonging either to a
tribal leader or a local deity. It could even have been the name of the original
Celtic farmstead or trading post. Another theory suggests that the termina-
tion *-dun* is the Celtic for 'hill fort', as in *Verdun*; another that the name was
imported from *Londinières* in Belgium by the Belgic invaders; and another,
the most appropriate to the future of London, that the name comes from the
Celtic *Llyn-Din*, 'the hill by the pool'.

A hill by a pool, which is flooded at high tide into an arm of the sea and at
low tide forms a vast marsh through which the river and its tributaries
meander, may not seem the ideal place to found a city. But it had considerable advantages. Two low, flat-topped hills, rising steeply from the
north bank to a height of about fifty feet above high water, were the first dry
land that touched the main stream of the river. Here was good gravel, not
liable to flooding and well supplied with fresh water, fish, and food from the
forest. The river Walbrook separated the east hill from the west hill. On the
south bank opposite at Southwark there was also the first patch of dry gravel
on the journey upstream. A crossing of sorts was probably practicable at low
tide.

Defensively the position was very strong. In addition to its natural moat,
it was protected on the east by the deeply trenched valley of the Fleet, and
on the west by the Shoreditch and the lagoons of the Thames and the Lea.
Being sixty miles from the open sea it was to some extent secluded from
pirates. To the north beyond the swamp the heights of Highgate and

Hampstead, crowned with the great Middlesex Forest, formed an impregnable and virtually impenetrable barrier. The position conveniently faced
Europe, from which trade came. The river was by far the best road to the
interior of the country or to the sea, and its tidal ebb and flow supplied
locomotive power for traffic. The crossings at Brentford, Westminster/
Lambeth, and possibly London itself were a link for commerce and passengers to the southern tribes and ports.

The line of Watling Street, the first road that the Romans built in Britain,
to connect their bridgehead at *Dubrae* (Dover) with *Verulamium*, appears to
cross the Thames at Westminster. Once their conquest was secure, the
Romans moved the main crossing a mile downstream to London. They
bridged the river at London, almost certainly early in their occupation. Their
unification of the tribes above and below the barrier of the Thames into a
single nation made London, the lowest crossing of the barrier, the most
important junction of communications. Ships from the Continent came up
river to the Pool of London. Their trade fanned out from there on the roads
north and south, and on the river west into the interior.

The exports for which Britain was principally noted at the time of the
Roman invasion were corn, wool, and slaves. Imports included wine, resin,
timber, pottery, and other Mediterranean luxuries, for which the Romans
also imported the taste. As early as Boudicca's rising against the invaders in
61 A.D. Tacitus could describe London as 'a colony much frequented by
merchants and trading vessels'. Unlike the other cities that the Romans
founded in Britain for Imperial reasons of strategic importance or administrative convenience, London was founded purely on trade. When Napoleon
said, if he did say it: 'L'Angleterre est une nation de boutiquiers' or, possibly,
the more precise attribution: 'Sono mercanti', he had greater historical
precedent to support the assertion than he realized.

During the three centuries of the Roman occupation *Londinium*, with its
bridge and its trade, grew to be the biggest and wealthiest city in the land.
The Romans changed its name to *Augusta*, possibly to celebrate the triumph
of the Emperor Theodosius over the rebel Valentinus. The natives, with
characteristic conservatism about nomenclature and tradition, stuck to the
old name of London.

After the Romans were withdrawn from Britain by the disintegration at
the centre of their Empire, successive waves of Teutonic invaders swept over
the island from the east, washing away much of its Roman civilization and
unity. But they did not wash away *Londinium* as they did many of the other
Roman towns and camps. A flash of lightning from the *Historia Ecclesiastica
Gentis Anglorum* of the Venerable Bede in the seventh century briefly
illuminates London in the Dark Ages as the capital of the East Saxon
kingdom of Essex and 'a market for many nations coming to it by land and sea'.

The Norman Conquest reoriented London's main trade routes towards

Normandy to the south and away from the Scandinavian Empire to the east, to which they had tended during the preceding three centuries. The Normans contributed to the dominance of London as a centre of communications by rebuilding London Bridge of stone. This bridge lasted for 655 years, for nearly six hundred of them as the only bridge across the Thames at London. The stone bridge obstructed traffic headed up stream to the Upper Pool and beyond more than the wooden bridges that preceded it. Larger cargo ships were forced to dock and unload in the Lower Pool.

The Normans introduced the feudal system to England and with it a potent stimulant to the predominance of London. Other ports like Bristol, Liverpool, Plymouth, and Southampton had feudal lords who taxed and restricted their growth and commercial enterprise in other ways. London was already the greatest city when the Normans arrived, and they confirmed its status as the capital, superseding such predecessors as Colchester and Winchester. As capital London had no overlord except the King, and fought a long and successful struggle for commercial independence in return for political and financial support. The supreme prerogative of the Sovereign over the Thames was first partially surrendered to the City by Richard I. His cession was chiefly concerned with fishing rights. One clause of the charter ran 'that all Kidels that are in the Thames shall be removed, wheresoever they may be'. A kidel was a weir with fish nets put across the river by such magnates as the Constable of the Tower, spoiling the fishing for private fishermen.

All the early records speak of the Thames as full of fish. The legend affirms that a salmon fisherman witnessed the supernatural dedication of Westminster Abbey. Henry VIII's polar bear was allowed out from the Tower on a collar and chain to fish for salmon in the Thames. As late as the middle of the seventeenth century James Howell in *London and Westminster* could write that Thames water 'useth to be as clear and pellucid as any such great river in the world'; that beer made from it was priced as highly as wine in foreign parts; 'and the Portugalls have found of late such virtue in that water that they carry it away by whole tuns to Lisbon'.

Subsequent charters between Kings and their richest city whittled down the water rights of the Sovereign and obtained fresh rights and commercial privileges for the City. By the time of Edward IV the Corporation had won the exclusive right to weigh, measure, and warehouse all wools brought to London, to pack woollen cloths, skins, and all other goods, to examine all merchandise liable to Customs dues, to undertake porterage for foreign merchants, to garble all spices (sc. to separate good from bad), to gauge wine, and many other rights and duties that increased both the power and the wealth of the City. London's wide and growing powers of self-government, which included jurisdiction over wide territories up and down the river, were the envy of any German 'free city'.

A third way in which the importance of the Thames and its port was increased during the Middle Ages was by the influx from all over Europe of foreign merchants, who were attracted to set up shop beside the Thames by the notorious independence, freedom, and devotion to trade of London. The fraternity of German merchants known as the Easterlings was busy in the Thames as early as the tenth century. In its heyday the Hanseatic League, which the Easterlings combined to found in the twelfth century, had trading links with eighty of the richest cities of Germany and Sweden. Other foreign merchants from Normandy, Flanders, Spain, Venice, Genoa, and other great medieval trading centres established enclaves by the Thames and opened new two-way channels for commerce and wealth to Europe.

It was to meet the competition of these powerful foreign trading combinations that the native Londoners began to establish the trade guilds and livery companies of the City. This commercial competition was bitter and frequently degenerated into riots against aliens. The apprentices of London were notoriously quick to pour out into the streets with cudgels and stones hunting for foreigners. For one example out of many, in 1493 an angry mob attacked the Steelyard, the headquarters of the Easterlings in Thames Street, and sacked it.

Nevertheless the foreign merchants were a source of wealth and growth for London. William Fitz-Stephen, the chaplain and biographer of Thomas à Becket, was clearly laying it on a bit thick, but his picture of the trade of the port in the twelfth century is interesting:

'To this City merchants bring in wares by ships from every nation under Heaven. The Arabian sends his gold, the Sabean his frankincense and spices, the Scythian arms and oil of palms from the plentiful wood; Babylon her fat soil and Nilus his precious stones; the Seres send purple garments; they of Norway and Russia trouts, furs, and sables; and the French their wines.'

Throughout the Middle Ages these influences combined to increase the traffic of the port, making it unquestionably the most important highway for merchandise from the provinces and from abroad. It was the quickest and safest road in the kingdom. London Bridge connected the port to the southern trade routes. The merchants of London were among the freest in Europe to concentrate on profit.

History does not move along the tidy tram-lines and junctions that ideologues and some philosophers and historians would like to drive it down. The growth of the port and its satellite, the City, has a majestic and imperturbable but untidy flow down the transient generations and centuries that makes it impossible to date each particular change. But it is possibly useful to identify a significant change in the sixteenth century. In the same way that the answer to the question, when did the Middle Ages end in England, is generally taken to be: 'If you insist on a simple answer to such an over-simplified question, with the arrival of the Tudors', so under the Tudors there were important changes in shipping, the pattern of trade, and the port.

Before the Tudors the trade of London River ran on medieval channels along the coasts of northern Europe and into the Mediterranean to link at its extremity with the Arab caravan trade of the Middle East. That pattern was completely changed by the discovery of the New World and the ocean trade routes to the Far East. The discoveries coincided with and inspired an astonishing growth of enterprise among London merchants and shipowners, which is generally taken to have come to full flower in the reign of Elizabeth I. Seamen from the Port of London competed with the rich argosies of the old maritime empires of Spain, Portugal, and the Low Countries for a share in the new wealth of the Americas and the Indies; and competed with formidable unscrupulousness and success. Merchant adventurers from the Thames and the West of England, statesmen, and sometimes the Queen herself, in secret, financed a series of expeditions to open new trade routes and stake a claim in the enormous new wealth. Willoughby and Chancellor's expedition from Deptford in 1553 to look for a north-east passage to the Orient opened the road to Moscow and led to the formation of the Muscovy Company. Similar expeditions, inspired by the prospect of a monopoly for the first to open up communications and trade with a new country, founded the Africa and Turkey Companies, and, most pregnant with historical consequence, the East India Company.

This portentous expedition, which led eventually to India being annexed as the brightest jewel of the British Empire, was initiated by a thing as small as a peppercorn. For centuries the Dutch had monopolized the lucrative trade in spices, a more essential commodity than today to preserve food in the winter and make it palatable. In 1599 they raised the price of pepper from three to eight shillings a pound. The Lord Mayor called a meeting of indignant merchants, and Queen Elizabeth signed the charter of the East India Company on the last day of the sixteenth century. In the following year James Lancaster sailed from Woolwich with a fleet of five ships. He returned two and a half years later with a cargo of more than a million pounds of pepper. Trading stations were established at Surat, Fort St George, Madras, and Hooghly, and Britain's Indian connexion was tied, with immense consequences for both countries.

The rise of English nationalism in the new era, stimulated by the trade wars and the shooting wars, led to the expulsion of the foreign merchants from London. This did not in itself increase the trade of the port, but at least it ensured that the profit went into English pockets and so provoked English enterprise and avarice. The Dissolution of the Monasteries and the end of the feudal comity, in which each man knew his station, encouraged the ambitious to fly high.

The growth in the size of shipping made rival English ports such as Hull and Boston inadequate and contributed to the supremacy of London.

The final collapse of the feudal world abroad also benefited London. The long and terrible revolt of the Low Countries against their Spanish overlords and the eventual triumphant rise of the Dutch Republic nullified the great financial and trading skills of the Dutch for much of the sixteenth century. The Duke of Parma sacked Antwerp in 1576, destroying its predominance as the financial and commercial capital of the old world. London merchants, personified and led by Sir Thomas Gresham, the founder of the Royal Exchange, took advantage of the vacuum and ensured that London captured the gold and the credit that had belonged to Antwerp. From this period the entrepôt and transhipment trades, which were to grow so important and profitable to the City, brought new activities to the Thames.

The Port of London at the beginning of the sixteenth century was just one of the important ports, away on the perimeter of the known trading world. By the end of the century it had been reoriented at the centre of the trade routes of the world, and London was becoming the greatest trading city in the world.

Londoners recognized how much they owed to their river. They treated it, as it deserved, as their chief highway and ornament, the great necklace of their City. The magnificent houses of the great men were built along the Strand, looking out over the magnificent Thames. The river was crowded with craft of all sorts, for private transport, for pleasure, and for ceremonial as well as for commerce and fishing. The engravings and paintings of the period show a Thames thick with sails and oars of all shapes and sizes. Visiting foreigners note in their reports their passage on the river in wherries to shoot the Bridge and admire the decapitated heads of traitors impaled on poles above it, or in a royal barge to Richmond, or Greenwich, or Hampton Court, to stare at the tourist attraction of the Queen having dinner or going to chapel: the contemporary equivalent of taking a coach to watch the Changing of the Guard. James Howell in the seventeenth century commented on the good use that London had made of its river and 'the stately palaces that are built on both sides of her banks so thick, which made divers foreign ambassadors to affirm that the most glorious sight in the World (take water and land together) was to come upon a high Tide from Gravesend, and shoot the Bridge to Westminster'.

The political struggles that led to the Civil War were not conducive to trade. London, that ancient stronghold of freedom, was the headquarters, bank, and fortress of the Parliamentarians. In spite of the troubles, the extraordinary impulse to adventure for trade persisted. In 1606, fourteen years before the Pilgrim Fathers sailed from Plymouth in the *Mayflower*, Captain John Smith led an expedition from Blackwall sponsored by a company of London Merchant Adventurers. None of his tiny fleet, the

Susan Constant, Godspeed, and *Discovery,* weighed more than a hundred tons. They founded the state of Virginia, with all the commercial and colonial consequences that flowed from it.

Another such expedition in 1668 had even more momentous effects on the Thames, London, and Britain. Two ships, the *Nonsuch* and *Eaglet,* sailed from the Thames to explore the territory around Hudson Bay. Only the *Nonsuch* came back, bringing a cargo of furs. Charles II signed the charter of the Hudson Bay Company, so opening a gateway from the Thames to yet another huge and wealthy region of the world. The phenomenal flowering of English prosperity depended on a handful of enterprising merchants prepared to take a risk, and a handful of sailors who put out from the Thames to the farthest corners of the world to bring its riches home by hook or by crook.

The plague of 1665 halted the trade and killed at least 100,000. The Great Fire of the following year almost completely destroyed the medieval City and its port. A tax of a shilling a chaldron was levied on coal brought into the port to help to pay for the cost of rebuilding London. The new City was built on the congested street plan of the old, retaining the maze of medieval streets and missing the opportunity of Wren's plan of a great, spectacular, and symmetrical piece of town planning modelled on Paris. The trouble was that his ambitious plan would have involved pooling all private freeholds in the charred City and redistributing them according to the plan adopted. This proved to be too complicated and too controversial for property-loving Londoners. The port was rebuilt on the pattern of the medieval one, with quays and wharves lining the banks, particularly the north bank, of the Pool; though warehouses and other accommodation were improved and enlarged.

Thomas Babington Macaulay, Great Tom, wrote a description of London of the period, marvellously evocative of the small City beside the Thames as well as of his high Victorian London:

'Whoever examines the maps of London which were published towards the close of the reign of Charles the Second will see that only the nucleus of the present capital then existed. The town did not, as now, fade by imperceptible degrees into the country. No long avenues of villas, embowered in lilacs and laburnums, extended from the great centre of wealth and civilization almost to the boundaries of Middlesex and far into the heart of Kent and Surrey. In the east, no part of the immense line of warehouses and artificial lakes which now stretches from the Tower to Blackwall had even been projected. On the west, scarcely one of those stately piles of building which are inhabited by the noble and wealthy was in existence; and Chelsea, which is now peopled by more than forty thousand human beings, was a quiet country village with about a thousand inhabitants. On the north, cattle fed, and sportsmen wandered with dogs and guns, over the site of the borough of

Marylebone, and over far the greater part of the space now covered by the boroughs of Finsbury and of the Tower Hamlets. Islington was almost a solitude; and poets loved to contrast its silence and repose with the din and turmoil of the monster London. On the south the capital is now connected with its suburb by several bridges, not inferior in magnificence and solidity to the noblest works of the Caesars. In 1685, a single line of irregular arches, overhung by piles of mean and crazy houses, and garnished, after a fashion worthy of the naked barbarians of Dahomy, with scores of mouldering heads, impeded the navigation of the river.'

Macaulay's majestic tide of eloquence overflows into hyperbole here. Heads of traitors were no longer exhibited on London Bridge by 1685 and the houses on either side of the Bridge were mostly regular modern blocks with balustrades and dormer windows built after the Fire. London has changed as much again in the century since he wrote.

The volume of trade and the size of ships continued to grow through the eighteenth century, fluctuating with the periods of war and peace. By the end of the century they had grown so large that there was a chaos of congestion on the river. In the Upper Pool, 1,775 vessels were allowed to moor simultaneously in a space intended for 545. At a busy period the river was so thick with shipping that it was difficult for a ship to thread its way through. Hundreds of lighters and other small craft, employed to ferry cargoes from the moorings to the shore, confounded the confusion. Goods waited for weeks before they were unloaded, at the mercy of the weather and organized pilfering. Gangs of river thieves did a roaring trade, operating under such names descriptive of their methods as Night Plunderers, Light Horsemen, Heavy Horsemen, and Scuffle-Hunters. Patrick Colquhoun, a founder of the first Thames Marine Police Force, described it accurately as 'a bold, audacious system of plunder'.

To escape the congestion from the end of the eighteenth century private companies began to build enclosed, protected wet docks downstream from the Pool. By the 1860s Macaulay's immense line of warehouses and artificial lakes stretched along the banks of the Thames for the six miles from the Tower to Blackwall. It was a landmark in the development of the river like the building of the Bridge or the foundation of the East India Company.

Westminster, the second bridge over the Thames, was opened in 1749. Other bridges followed at an increasing momentum, eventually allowing Victorian megalopolis to spill its sprawling suburbs all over the south bank. By 1850 London was a city around both banks of the river, no longer, as it had been for the preceding eighteen centuries, a city straggling along the north bank.

Unfortunately the Victorians were so carried away by the vast impetus of the industrial revolution that they generally neglected social and environmental considerations. They had a great chance to redevelop the riverside of the Pool as the port slipped downstream. They had a chance to make large-scale, rational, balanced plans for the great expanse of riverside east of the old City that the port was about to occupy.

Instead they left it to *laissez-faire*. In that Gadarene rush the fields and marshes of the East End were covered with black industrial enterprises and hideous slums to house those who worked in them: slums that were a blot on the civilized world. The Elizabethans had grown rich on trade; but they had always respected the London River and used it as an embellishment of the City as well as its main artery. The Victorians were the first generations to turn the face of London away from its river, using the banks for factories and commerce instead of for stately houses and great public buildings. London still suffers from their lost opportunity.

The water of the Thames suffered, along with everything else. It was no longer the pellucid water that foreigners imported for its purity. The salmon had given up the struggle early in the nineteenth century. The Thames had become so filthy that anybody who fell in was in danger of dying of poisoning before he drowned. Charles Dickens, as perceptive about pollution as he was about the human degradation of the slums, wrote an imaginary dialogue with the Thames in his weekly periodical *Household Words* of 1851:

'How black and solid stands the forest of shipping on each side!—how large and black lie their shadows on the water!— . . . but, what is that floating by?—pah! it's a dead dog, or something— . . . How very thick the water is hereabouts, Father Thames; and, pray, may I inquire what that black, sluggish stream may be which I see pouring into you from a wide, bricked archway, yonder?'

'Oh, that's one of my sewers,' replied the Father of Rivers . . .

'But what are those smaller mouths that send forth strange party-coloured currents to mingle with your waters?'

'That one belongs to a soap-boiler—a particular friend of mine; the next to it, is from a slaughter-house, kept by a very estimable friend indeed, who wouldn't allow a particle of the refuse and drainage of his yards to run anywhere else, on any account . . . Those other agreeable little outlets you are looking at, or will shortly see, on both sides of my banks, are from gas-factories, brewhouses, shot-factories, coal-wharfs, cow-houses, tan-pits, gut-spinners, fish-markets, and other cheerful and odoriferous tributaries; while the inky flood yonder which your eyes are now fixed upon is from a very populous grave-yard, which produces so large a quantity of liquid every four-and-twenty hours, that it has to be drained off by regular arrangement, and made to flow into my convenient, all-embracing bosom.'

Since the Second World War people have begun to take other matters beside profit into account to an extent that would have gratified Dickens and shocked sterner Victorians. There has been a marked improvement in the condition of the water of the Thames, which is as perceptible as the reduction of air pollution and the dispersal of the London particular, pea-soup fog. The river is no longer black, but the colour of Brown Windsor soup. Every year the colour grows paler, the dissolved oxygen content increases, and foolhardy fish of different species penetrate farther upstream.

The world commercial supremacy of the Port and City of London, begun by the Elizabethans and brought to a culmination by the Victorians, has gradually and inevitably declined during this century. Other countries, mostly from the north-western quarter of the world as seen from Greenwich, have caught up with and overtaken Britain in the industrial and techno-logical revolutions. The 1914-18 War, that mountainous watershed of his-tory, ended the extraordinary situation by which the Thames, as if by some divine right, took the lion's share of world trade. Britain's trading might and her naval blockade of Germany were largely responsible for Britain finishing on the nominally winning side in that Armageddon. But the losses to U-boats and in capital were crippling to trade, and the terrible loss of life on the Western Front educated and civilized national morale. The survivors were less single-mindedly dedicated to winning at all costs, to coming top, to acquiring, to making money.

The Great War also brought America from isolation into the modern world and woke Russia, another future industrial giant. The British Empire dwindled to a Commonwealth of Nations, and when, on January 1, 1972, Britain acceded to the Treaty of Rome and joined the European Economic Community, the special trading links of the Thames with the Common-wealth countries were generally so attenuated as to be almost invisible. Europe was clearly politically and geographically a more rational trading connexion for Britain than the far-flung Empire on which the sun had finally set.

Many Britons were discontented about this return to reality after their astonishing centuries of predominance; and suffered accordingly from a bad attack of nostalgia for the grand old days when the Thames was the home port and trading headquarters of the world. But even if their discontent were one day to drive Britain to leave the European Economic Community, the old Commonwealth links could never be refastened. The emergent countries of the world want to be industrialized themselves and to sell their produce to the highest buyer; not to have 'special relationships' with a faraway country just because, in the sixteenth and seventeenth centuries, a few adventurers in small sailing-ships from a comparatively small river happened to arrive at their shores before anyone else, or more aggressively than anyone else.

The historical, cultural, and sentimental links between the Thames and places as distant and diverse as the Hooghly, Hudson Bay, Jamestown, and

Sydney will, of course, subsist, for as long as people read history, as one of the most remarkable happenings in history.

Although the Thames is still one of the great rivers of the world, its relative importance has declined. It is no longer unquestionably the headquarters of world trade. Rotterdam passed it as the greatest port in Europe in the 1960s. London retains the dubious pre-eminence of having the busiest airport in Europe at Heathrow, twenty miles upstream from the City in the London borough of Hounslow.

Britain, although proportionately to its population still one of the wealthiest countries of the world, is painfully reorienting itself yet again to a new and more realistic position as a member of Europe, the greatest trading combination in the world. The Thames, with its deep and vast port, is, as usual, conveniently placed, at the apex of the golden triangle that encompasses the heaviest concentration of industry and wealth of the European Economic Community. The indications are that it will continue to be one of the great trading rivers of the world.

During the past century the ancient process of moving the port farther downstream to meet the vast modern bulk-carriers and tankers has continued. Large new docks were opened at Tilbury as early as 1868. In 1909 the Port of London Authority, a self-governing public trust, was created to take over the running of the port from the unrestricted and ultimately unprofitable private enterprise of the Dock Companies. This was a satisfactorily tidy reversion to the earlier arrangement by which the Sovereign and then the Lord Mayor and Corporation were responsible for administering the River and Port for the public good. The Port of London Authority's long-term strategy of the 1960s and 1970s, by far the most ambitious development of the London River ever proposed, was to construct a deepwater port at Maplin Sands in Essex, beyond Southend at the mouth of the estuary. If Britain's economic situation allowed the vast expenditure needed to make Maplin and the concomitant communications to it, there would be obvious advantages of convenience, speed, and safety for the big ships of the future. The diversion of the biggest ships from central London would improve the environment of the East End, though not that of the inhabitants and wild life of Foulness. Whether Maplin is ever built or not, the centre of gravity of the Port of London will continue to move down river to Tilbury; and the business of London and the prosperity of the country as a whole will continue to depend, as they always have done, on the London River.

The Blitz by the *Luftwaffe* in 1940 concentrated, with sound strategy, particularly on the Port and East End of London. The London River is Britain's life-line and, if it could have been cut, Britain would have strangled. The devastating German bombardment laid waste large areas of dockland. This destruction combined with the gradual movement of the port downstream gave the best chance since the Great Fire to rebuild a large area of

London. As in the case of the Great Fire, there is little evidence so far that the chance will be taken to build a brave new City that embraces its river as Venice its canals or Paris the Seine. The dreadful Victorian slums of Tower Hamlets and Newham have been replaced by modern housing estates with a high percentage of squat tower blocks, which have none of the dramatic and soaring grandeur of the congeries of true skyscrapers on Manhattan. There is evidence that many who live in these vilely-named 'high-rise' blocks find them lonely and less congenial than the village life in the pre-war slums. Nevertheless, at least in places, the chance is being taken to turn the face of London back to its river. Such great housing estates as Thamesmead and Rotherhithe and, upstream of the City, Brentford are putting houses for people instead of industrial buildings on the banks of the river.

That the buildings do not seem conspicuously beautiful may be partly the fault of architecture, which is not at present enjoying a period of great efflorescence. But, of course, to build beautiful riverside houses for hundreds of thousands is quite different and a much harder project than building great houses beside the Thames for a few wealthy patrons.

Whatever political and social changes occur, whatever decisions are taken, the decades until the end of the century are certain to alter the physiognomy and character of the London River more than any period since the mid-Victorian or even the Elizabethan. This is the last generation that will be able to talk to a London docker who lifted cargo by hand and, consequently, has a permanent list to the shoulder on which he carried timber. Thames watermen, that enduring race, will no doubt persist whatever happens. As the port and the big ships and the pollution move farther from the City, perhaps Londoners will begin to enjoy their river again. When the barrage gets built, we might even see a renaissance of the great days when the river was full of little boats and Samuel Pepys, Samuel Johnson, and all the generations of Londoners who have left no name behind them called for 'oars' and gloried in their river.

CHAPTER TWO

Hampton to Richmond

SOME forty-two miles of the Thames flow through Greater London, where seven and a third million people live and four and a half million people work. In character the London River is divided into three parts. The upper reaches of the eighteen miles from Hampton to Putney Bridge are still predominantly rural and wooded. The river is never more than a hundred yards wide, the banks are almost level with the water, and there are many small islands known in the old Thames vernacular as eyots. Medieval villages and Georgian terraces survive on the banks. Ten bridges span these upper reaches, each bridge distinctive, most of them handsome and Richmond Bridge, two hundred years old, being a listed building of historical and architectural importance.

From Putney to Tower Bridge the Thames flows beneath seventeen more bridges through the heart of London. Throughout these central reaches the river is about two hundred and fifty yards wide and bounded along most of its length by embankment walls. Many of London's most famous and important buildings are on the banks of the river, the historically and architecturally important tending to the north bank, and the great commercial and industrial buildings tending to the south bank.

From Tower Bridge the river runs for seventeen miles through one of the world's great congeries of docks and industry, until it leaves Greater London at Crayford Ness for the estuarine marshes of Kent and eventually the North Sea. There are no bridges over these lower reaches, which widen from three hundred and fifty yards at Tower Bridge to a thousand yards at Crayford Ness.

The Thames acts as the boundary of Greater London at its south-western corner, beside Kempton Park race-course and such relatively unspoilt and pleasant old riverside villages as Hampton and Thames Ditton. They lie about fourteen miles from Charing Cross as the London pigeon flies, and twice as far as the river meanders. Some of these exclusive dormitory suburbs in what is scornfully and enviously called 'the stockbroker belt' of Surrey were horrified to find themselves included in London by the reorganization of local government that came into effect on April 1, 1965. Many of their

residents had removed there in the ancient progress of moving out of London
and becoming the modern equivalents of country gentlemen.

'Merry Hampton' was the home of David Garrick, the friend and pupil of
Samuel Johnson. They came from Lichfield to London together, and while
Johnson went on to become the Great Cham of literature, Garrick became
the king of the London stage as actor, manager, and author of sprightly
farces. He made his reputation in the part of Richard III, and his portraits
by Reynolds, Hogarth, and Gainsborough are instinct with the emotional
power and self-confidence of one of England's greatest actors, who set the
standard in so many of the greatest parts.

Garrick bought Hampton House in 1754 at the height of his triumph,
when he was working his way steadily through Shakespeare's choicest parts
at Drury Lane. Robert Adam altered it twice for him. Between Garrick's
house and the river stands his grateful temple to Shakespeare, to whom he
owed much of his success. The pretty little octagonal temple with its Ionic
portico was probably designed by 'Capability' Brown. It shelters a fancifully
pious statue of the bard by Louis-François Roubiliac.

Tagg's Island, the first serious island upstream in the London River,
indicates with its shoals of great, gleaming, basking yachts and launches that
this is still a preserve of the rich and successful successors to Garrick. The
seedier house-boats and converted barges, in which genuine watermen and
women actually live, still cling to the decreasing moorings around the island.
They are continually harassed and evicted by property developers and local
authorities, who seem to look on them as untidy and unprofitable water
gypsies. The water gypsies in turn look down on the week-end boatmen with
professional scorn, and call their floating gin-palaces 'jelly-moulds'.

Tagg's Island itself has a notable history. Until 1971 it was the site of The
Karsino, which was a strong contender for inclusion in a list of the ten
strangest buildings in Britain. This excessively ornate pleasure-dome,
decorated with more gilt goddesses and painted ceilings than an average man
could aspire to meet elsewhere in a life-time, was built as a theatre, hotel,
restaurant, dance-hall, and casino in 1913 by Frederick Westcott, better
known by his pseudonym of 'Fred Karno'. Fred, an oppressed boy from a
rough, tough, working-class home in Nottingham, was the founder of
English slap-stick as an art form. He found everything funny, so long as it
happened to somebody else. His disciples, who learned their business on
Tagg's Island, included Charlie Chaplin, Stan Laurel, Bud Flanagan,
George Robey, Will Hay, Max Miller, Bobby Howes, and an army of other
soldiers with two left feet, whose talents, like Garrick's, still kindle the gaiety
of nations and have augmented the public stock of harmless pleasure. The
isle is full of noises, sounds and sweet guffaws as a melancholy comedian
stumbles jackass over wit on life's banana-skin. It was the original stage for
much seminal ancient knock-about comedy, where custard pies and mud-

packs once flew through the air with the first, fine, greasy rapture of a new art form.

Karno, whose stock-in-trade on the stage was the misfortune of others, spent £70,000 building his palace of comedy on Tagg's Island. The enterprise was ruined by the First World War and some miserably wet summers in the years after the war. Karno became bankrupt in 1927. By a suitably malevolent irony of fate he was reduced to keeping an off-licence at a place called Lilliput in Dorset.

The Karsino was finally demolished in 1971 by an American property developer and entrepreneur, who proposed to replace it with a luxury hotel and marina club. His plan, like so many others for Tagg's Island, foundered. But it will always be Fred Karno's island, haunted by the ghosts of comedians whose defiant reply to the tragedy of life was to cock a snook and blow a raspberry-tart.

At Thames Ditton the river turns north through a sharp bend of more than a right angle and enters London. The next eight miles, running sinuously north to Kew Bridge, are the setting, as they have been for many centuries, for some of the most agreeable and expensive residential suburbs of London.

Before the London and South Western Railway Line was laid from Clapham Junction and Waterloo a century ago, so making it possible to commute to work in Central London, only rich Londoners could afford to have their country houses beside the Thames. They tended to build their mansions here rather than downstream from London because it is obviously prudent to be up-river from the drains and docks of a city. In any case the broad river valley above London, extending majestically through wooded parkland to the blue line of the Surrey hills on the horizon, used to be the most admired landscape in the south of England, before the giant pylons and the dual carriageways marched across it. Foreign visitors in previous centuries continually commended the 'sweet, clean, and pleasant river', the rich pasture of the Thames Valley, and the prodigious flocks of sheep grazing at it. For instance, Paul Hentzner, a jurist from Brandenburg who visited England in 1598 as the companion and tutor of a young Silesian nobleman, wrote of the sheep: 'Upon these [hills] wander numerous flocks extremely white, and whether from the temperature of the air or goodness of the earth, bearing softer and finer fleeces than those of any other country. This is the true Golden Fleece, in which consist the chief riches of the inhabitants, great sums of money being brought into the island by merchants, chiefly for that article of trade.'

This reference to the excellence of English sheep-breeding and its importance to the economy had become a commonplace among unoriginal foreign visitors who kept journals. It was regularly repeated in parrot fashion by unimaginative diarists from Polydore Vergil onwards. Polydore was an Italian who became a naturalized Englishman and the Tudor historian and propagandist. He noticed the sheep in his *Anglica Historia*, published in 1534, the first attempt at a modern history of England.

The history and architecture of these upper reaches of the Thames in London is excessively concerned with the rich and the regal. Kings and their magnates built their palaces here when London was small and white and clean, and the clear Thames bordered by its gardens green.

Like the short and simple annals of the poor, their humbler houses have generally been forgotten. As Henry Hallam, the author of the *Constitutional History of England* to the death of George II, truly and sadly wrote: 'We can trace the pedigree of princes, fill up the catalogue of towns besieged and provinces desolated, but we cannot recover the genuine history of mankind. It has passed away with slight and partial notice by contemporary writers, and our most patient industry can hardly at present put together enough of the fragments to suggest a tolerably clear representation of ancient manners and social.'

Palaces and the vestiges of princes mark the banks of the Thames especially thickly on its long northern march through the outskirts of London.

The first and most conspicuous is the palace of Hampton Court, one of the great buildings of Britain and a monument to the glory and vaulting ambition of Thomas Wolsey, correctly considered by a contemporary 'the haughtiest man in all his proceedings alive'. Wolsey, the son of 'an honest poor man', probably a butcher, from Ipswich, was one of the new men promoted to the ruling class by the Tudor seizure of power. He acquired the lease of the manor of Hampton Court from the Order of St John of Jerusalem in 1514. He was the Archbishop of York and the rapidly rising man of English politics. By his accumulated plurality of bishoprics he was becoming the richest as well as the most powerful man in England. In the following year Henry VIII made him Lord Chancellor and Pope Leo X sent him the red cardinal's hat that Wolsey had long been soliciting. In 1518 he was given the unprecedented office of permanent Papal Legate *a latere* in England, which made him Vice-Pope as well as Vice-King. For the next fifteen years Wolsey held in his hands both civil and ecclesiastical power of the kingdom, as England's first Prime Minister and last resident Pope.

He was just forty. The King was twenty-three and more interested in sports, music, entertainments, and the pageantry of monarchy than in power politics. Wolsey's upstart arrogance exceeded even Tudor upstart arrogance and the snobbish arrogance of the old feudal nobility, who loathed and feared him. It was shown off in more than Tudor ostentation. Personal ostentation in clothes, servants, and architecture was one of the functions of the Renaissance Prince. Wolsey passed unpopular sumptuary legislation restricting the apparel, households, and diet of the rest of the nation. But he admitted no restriction of the splendour that was Rome, incarnate in his own person.

He extracted his tribute, perquisites, pensions, and fees with a despotic avarice that Henry was to learn from him only too well. Ludovico Falier, the Venetian ambassador, reported to the Signory that Wolsey's ordinary income just before his fall was 150,000 ducats a year, not counting his French and other pensions and his New Year's and other obligatory presents. This would be well over two million pounds in modern inflationary money. In the list of household servants assessed for subsidy in 1526, those of Henry's sister Mary, the ex-Queen of France, number forty-four; those of his daughter Mary, sixty-five; Wolsey's number four hundred and twenty-nine.

Wolsey's architectural activities were on a similarly megalomaniac scale. Christ Church at Oxford is the greatest academic monument of the age, and Wolsey founded another great school at Ipswich that never developed. He built himself palaces at York Place, the More near Rickmansworth, Tyttenhanger also in Hertfordshire, Esher, and Hampton Court. The More was his favourite country house, and Guillaume du Bellay, a French diplomatist who stayed in both, considered it more magnificent even than Hampton Court. But Henry VIII coveted York Place most, and when he took it, converted it into Whitehall, so producing the apt historical coincidence that Wolsey, who did so much unconsciously to create the modern British state, should also provide the site for the home of the British Civil Service.

Alone of the Cardinal's palaces Hampton Court survives. Wolsey, who was as strong as a horse but a hypochondriac, chose the site for its gravel soil, healthy air, distance from the plagues of London, and politically convenient proximity to the favourite Tudor palace of Richmond. He enclosed about two thousand acres around his palace. They have become the Home Park and Bushey Park, which make this still the greenest and most open suburb of London.

Typically Wolsey refused to drink Thames water, which was becoming murky even as early as the sixteenth century. Everybody else drank it, and then wondered why there were annual epidemics of typhoid and the 'sweating sickness'. Wolsey had Hampton Court's supply of fresh water brought in leaden conduits from the salubrious Coombe Springs, more than three miles away and on the other side of the Thames.

The west front of the palace still looks approximately as it did when Wolsey built it: a grandiose pile of diapered red brick, spiral chimneys, turrets, and bay windows rising beside the grey-green, duck-infested Thames that was the main road to it. Its battlements survived as ornaments in an age in which an Englishman's home had ceased to be his castle, except in a figurative sense. The great gatehouse in the centre of the west front regrettably had two storeys lopped off it in the eighteenth century, but the first courtyard called the Base Court is little altered since it was built by Wolsey. The passages surrounding it lead to rooms where the army of his household and guests was lodged. Two hundred and eighty richly furnished rooms were available for guests. When the treaty between England and France was signed in 1527, the Cardinal entertained the French ambassador and his retinue of four hundred at Hampton Court at his own expense.

The second gate-tower is known as Anne Boleyn's gateway, because it was redecorated by Henry VIII after he had occupied the palace. However, a beautifully modelled panel of Wolsey's arms above his self-confident motto *Dominus michi adjutor* remains in the east side of the gate-tower in spite of Henry's attempt to deface it. The arms are surmounted by the Cardinal's hat and supported by plump *putti*. They were obviously carved by one of the Italian workmen whom Wolsey brought over for Hampton Court, as Giovanni da Maiano modelled the terra-cotta medallions of the more dis-agreeable Roman Emperors, which appropriately decorate the gate-towers.

The inner or Clock Court was the main courtyard of Wolsey's house. The Great Hall on the north side of the courtyard, with its hammer-beam roof dripping stalactites of elaborate pendants and lanterns, was built by Henry VIII to replace the more modest hall of Wolsey's house. The panelled apartments on the south side reserved for the Cardinal's private use and the east side of the main inner court were largely reconstructed by Sir Christopher Wren and other later architects.

The main outline of Wolsey's original palace was complete by 1520. It was at least three hundred by five hundred and fifty feet in size, by far the largest house built in England in the period and larger, for instance, than Chambord, the contemporary palace built by that other magnificent Renais-sance Prince, Francis I of France. Wolsey's master mason was probably Henry Redman, who also worked for him on the building of Christ Church.

Such architectural grandeur naturally excited the envy of the satirists and the cupidity of the King. John Skelton wrote a savage poem, 'Why come ye nat to courte?', which attacked Wolsey and set forth the evil consequences of his centralizing autocracy:

> To whyche court?
> To the kynges courte,
> Or to Hampton Court?
> Nay, to the kynges court:
> The Kynges courte
> Shulde have the excellence;
> But Hampton Court
> Hath the pre-emynence.

In another powerful passage Skelton described Wolsey's contempt for the old nobility:

> For all their noble blode
> He pluckes the hode,
> And shakes them by the eare,

And brynges them in such feare;
He bayteth them lyke a bere,
Lyke an oxe or a bull:
Theyr wyttes, he saith, are dull;
He sayth they have no brayne
Theyr astate to mayntayne;
And maketh them to bow theyr kne
Before his maieste.

As a result of this poem Skelton was obliged to take sanctuary at West-minster, where he died.

Wolsey averted the growing royal jealousy and greed by formally making over the lease of Hampton Court to Henry in 1525. After that, when he remembered, he headed his letters to the King: 'From your manor of Hampton Court.' He still addressed other correspondents: 'From my manor of Hampton Court.' His gift inspired the Imperial envoy to make a sour joke: 'That having given his house and all his furniture to the King, he might say, "Here is a sucking-pig from your own sow's litter, which pray take as my humble gift."'

A suite of rooms survives in Hampton Court unchanged from Wolsey's day. The little, low rooms with their linen-fold panelling, oriel windows, and richly painted ceilings give a good impression of what life at Hampton Court was like for a guest. Wolsey himself had far grander apartments, which were replaced by Wren's redevelopment.

But the Cardinal would not have been amused by the choice of pictures in 'Wolsey's Rooms', which have a crude anti-Papist bias. They depict such propaganda themes as heroic Reformation freedom-fighters stoning capitalist Popes and their running-dogs labelled 'Hypocrisy'. Wolsey unintentionally showed England the way to the Reformation, but he was always the Pope's man, who always intended to resist the centrifugal tendencies of the Roman Catholic Church as it emerged from the Middle Ages.

The best contemporary description of life in the original palace was given by George Cavendish, one of Wolsey's regiment of ushers, who wrote *The Life and Death of Thomas Wolsey*, the classic example of a gentleman-usher's impressionable view of history. Cavendish contrasts the magnificence of Wolsey's years of triumph with his subsequent disgrace, and indicates 'the mutability of vaine honors and brittle assurance of aboundaunce . . . the uncertainety of dignities, the flattering of feigned friends, and the fickle favor of worldly princes'.

One of his purplest passages is the account of the French embassy's reception at Hampton Court in 1527. Cavendish was one of the ushers put in charge of seeing the guest-rooms 'nobly garnished'. He wrote, in contemporary permissive orthography:

'Our paines were not small nor light, but dayly travelling up and downe from chamber to chamber. Then wrought the joiners, carpenters, masons, painters, and all other artificers necessary to be had to glorify this noble feast. There was carriage and re-carriage of plate, stuffe, and other riche implements, so that there was nothing lacking to be devised or imagined for the purpose. There were also provided two hundred and eighty beddes, furnished with all manner of furniture to them belonging, too long particularly here to be rehearsed.'

The Frenchmen arrived and were duly impressed by the range of great chambers hung with rich arras and the profusion of cupboards and tables covered with gilt and silver plate. The feast was so lavish and indigestible with elaborate 'subtleties' of marzipan in the shape of St Paul's Cathedral and knights jousting that 'the Frenchmen, as it seemed, were rapt into a heavenly paradise'.

After the browsing and sluicing, and much ostentatious complaisance by Wolsey, who arrived late, booted and spurred: 'Then went the cuppes so merrily about that many of the Frenchmen were faine to be led to their beddes . . . And whilst they were in communication and other pastimes, all their liveries were served to their chambers. Every chamber had a basen and an ewer of silver, a great livery-pot of silver, and some gilt; yea and some chambers had two livery-pots with wine and beare, a bowle and a goblet, and a pot of silver to drink in, bothe for their beare and wine; a silver candlestick, bothe white and plaine, having in it two sizes, and a staffe torche of waxe, a fine manchet [best white bread], and a cheat [second-best bread] loafe. Thus was every chamber furnished throughout all the house, and yet the cupboards in the two banquetting chambers not once touched.'

When the Nemesis of power overtook the proud Cardinal in 1529, all his arras, plate, goods, and lands were declared forfeit to the King. Hampton Court at once became one of Henry's favourite palaces. He brought five of his six Queens here in succession, and the initials and arms of Anne Boleyn and Jane Seymour can still be seen in the hasty and reiterated redecorations done for Henry.

Edward VI was born in the palace and held court in it. So, regularly, did Henry's other two children, Mary and Elizabeth I.

James I presided here at the Hampton Court Conference, held in 1604 to settle matters said to be 'amiss in the Church' and other points of dispute between the Church party and the Puritans. This conference initiated the preparation of one of the most influential books in the English language, the Authorized Version of the Bible.

Charles I resided in Hampton Court both as King and then, briefly, as prisoner during the Civil War. After his execution most of the royal palaces and other possessions were sold by order of Parliament, but Hampton Court was retained as the country retreat for the Lord Protector, Oliver Cromwell. Charles II repaired the palace and, characteristically, laid out its gardens in the grandiose new style of French gardening patronized by Louis XIV and epitomized in the work of the great Le Nôtre.

William and Mary had the eastern half of Hampton Court rebuilt in the contemporary neo-classical architecture. William could not live in Whitehall, partly because of his chronic asthma and partly because of his chronic shyness. Accordingly they decided to make Hampton Court their Versailles. Sir Christopher Wren started work in 1689. Because it was a double monarchy, Wren had to build double sets of state apartments, the south front facing the river for the King and the east front facing the great Home Park for the Queen. The interior decoration was done by court artists as brilliant as the wood-carver Grinling Gibbons and the iron-smith Jean Tijou, and as pedestrian as the painter Antonio Verrio. Verrio's gods, goddesses, classical heroes, royalties, and *putti* rollick and sprawl over the ceilings in an unpersuasive portrayal of gaudy nights on Mount Olympus or, yet more unpersuasively, at the court of William and Mary. The effect of the new east end erected grandly around the Fountain Court is impressive but no rival to the Sun King's Versailles.

Decoration, furnishing, and minor work continued under Queen Anne and the first two Georges. George III abruptly abandoned Hampton Court and it has never been used as a royal residence since.

One of George's sons asserted that his father never went back to Hampton Court for the weighty and lingering reason that he once had his ears boxed there by his grandfather, George II.

Apartments were divided off and granted by 'grace and favour' ('gracious favour': one of the few true examples of hendiadys in English) to widows or children of distinguished men who had done the state some service. William IV described Hampton Court under this arrangement, in a phrase of royal ungrace and disfavour, as 'the quality poor-house'. About a thousand rooms are still used today. The State Apartments of Wolsey, Henry, William and Mary have been open to the public since 1834. On rare occasions, such as the celebration of Britain's accession to the European Economic Community, the Tudor banqueting hall is resuscitated for a state banquet: the catering facilities from the great kitchen are primitive by Wolsey's luxurious standards.

From Hampton Court the Thames, still quite narrow, flows north through country, still quite rural. Wolsey's Hampton Court Park and Bushey Park extend along the left bank, now decorated with occasional golfers and notices prohibiting feeding or touching the deer and 'behaving or being clothed in any manner reasonably likely to offend against public decency'. On the right bank, after a stretch of reservoirs and the goal-posts of playing-fields, the suburban utopia of Surbiton closes in with riverside villas, boat-houses, and

cabin cruisers moored up to three abreast. The second island inside the
boundary of Greater London is called *Ravens Ait* in one of the vexingly
chaotic spellings of the word for a small Thames island. The Ait bristles
with burgees at the yard-arm, skiffs and canoes in racks, crates of beer on
the bank, and other indications of the boating for which this part of the
Thames has always been notable. Paintings in Hampton Court by Leonard
Knyff and other court hacks depict the river even more crowded with barges
and craft of all amazing sorts than it is today.

As the playing-fields and then the large houses fence in the wilderness on
the left bank as well as the right, Kingston Bridge cuts across the river.
Beneath its balustrades the green metal railway bridge is visible and the
square tower of All Saints' parish church rises above it, though not so conspicuously as the twin smoking chimney-stacks of the London Electricity
Board's power station.

Kingston-upon-Thames is chiefly known to outsiders today as a desirable
commuters' suburb and for the by-pass around it and the traffic congestion
inside it. But it has an ancient history as the coronation place of the Saxon
Kings of all England. Their reputed coronation stone, a weathered lump of
greywether sandstone nearly three feet high, is proudly displayed, surrounded by 'an ornamental Saxon-type railing', outside the Guildhall. It
looks an uncomfortable throne.

Tradition records that on it were crowned: Edward I, the Elder, in 900
A.D.; Athelstan in 925; Edmund I, the Magnificent, in 940; Edred in 946;
Edwy, the Fair, in 956; Edward II, the Martyr, in 975; and Aethelred II,
the Unready or Redeless, in 979. Documentary support for this apt tradition
of ancient royal residence beside this royal stretch of the Thames is late. The
earliest authority is the Tudor historian, John Leland, who stated that: 'At
the fascion of coronation of kinges that were solemnised at Kingeston upon
the Tamise afore the conqueste were made apon schaffoldes yn the midle of
the market place.' John Speed wrote in his *Historie of Great Britaine* in 1627:
'At Kingston likewise stood the Chair of Majesty whereon Athelstan, Edwin
and Ethelred sate at their Coronations and first received their scepter of
Imperiall Power.'

There is, however, much older documentary evidence that Kingston was
an important town for the Saxons. A charter of 838 records that in that year
King Egbert, accounted as the first King of all England as well as of Wessex,
held a great council in 'that renowned place which is called Cyningestun in
the region of Suthregia'. His council was attended by the Archbishop and
other prominent Saxon churchmen. Suthregia is Old English for the under-
kingdom of Surrey, and Anglo-Saxon enthusiasts believe that the Saxon
sub-Kings of Surrey had their palace at Kingston from as early as the
seventh century.

A straightforward man might therefore imagine that the name Kingston means 'King's Stone', and that its etymology echoes the remote crownings of the first Kings of all England on a sacred stone beside the Thames. But a straightforward man would, as usual, be mistaken. The onomasticians can demonstrate that the name is not 'Cyninges stān' (King's Stone) but 'Cyninges tūn'. 'Tūn', the ending found broadcast all over the area of the English settlements, for instance also in Hampton, means something like a farm or settlement enclosed in a rough stockade. Therefore Kingston means 'the King's enclosure'. Its modern form, 'town', gives an entirely erroneous impression of its original meaning.

Whatever imprecisions and doubts there may be about the early Saxon settlement at Kingston, there can be little doubt why the Kings settled beside this reach of the river. They did so not primarily for the notorious beauty of the view or the freedom of the alluvial valley from the primeval forest that covered much of England, but because from earliest times there was a commercially and strategically important river-crossing at Kingston. The ford was the first easy crossing above the longer and more hazardous fords at Westminster and Brentford. Kingston Bridge is known to have existed before 1219, when there is a record that a William de Coventry was appointed Bridge Master. By then endowments for the maintenance of the bridge were already in existence. This was the first bridge over the Thames above London Bridge for five centuries, until Westminster Bridge was built between 1738 and 1749. It accordingly made Kingston an important place both socially and militarily, as a key crossing of the formidable barrier of the Thames.

There are misty and imprecise records of frequent skirmishes in Kingston during the civil wars of the thirteenth century. It is most probable that these were fought to control the river crossing. During the Wars of the Roses Kingston Bridge was a back-door to London, of vital importance several times in the long campaigns. For example, Edward IV escaped from Falconbridge's army because Kingston Bridge was impassable, either by accident or because it had been shrewdly put out of action.

Although there was no major battle fought at Kingston during the Civil War of the seventeenth century, the first and the last skirmishes between Parliamentarians and Royalists took place there, attracted to Kingston by the importance of the crossing as well as the accidents of war.

Socially the Bridge was of great importance as a crossing-place for market and other civilian traffic. History has left small record of the centuries of civilian use. As Gibbon wrote of the peaceful and prosperous principate of Antonius Pius: 'His reign is marked by the rare advantage of furnishing very few materials for history; which is, indeed, little more than the register of the crimes, follies, and misfortunes of mankind.' A bridge for which a minor skirmish is fought in a medieval power struggle, whose purpose was obscure even to most of those fighting in it, is given a mention in the history books.

Meagre memorial is left of the centuries in which generations of farmers drove their cattle and flocks peacefully to market across it.

We know that Kingston Bridge was originally wooden, and the Bridge Warden's accounts show that it was continually in need of repair, because of the heavy traffic across it. Until 1565 a toll was charged, although even with the endowments this was still inadequate to maintain the bridge, and the town had to contribute the balance.

Kingston Bridge was so narrow that it inspired one of the earliest one-way traffic regulations on record. A fine of sixpence was levied from both careless drivers if 'two cartes mete upon the Grete Bridge'.

By the nineteenth century the records show that some 25,000 people and nearly 3,000 vehicles were crossing Kingston Bridge each week, as well as unnumbered horses, cattle, and sheep. The bridge could no longer carry the traffic and it was replaced by a new stone bridge erected between 1825 and 1828. This had to be widened in due course in 1914.

In 1965 Kingston, the coronation place and enclosure of the first Kings, was amalgamated with the Boroughs of Surbiton and Malden and Coombe to form one of the thirty-two new London Boroughs. It covers 9,281 acres of some of the greenest land and most beautiful water in London. The Registrar General estimated its population in 1970 at 142,690. Lyons's tea-rooms, Boots the chemist's half-timbered palace, and suburban commuters keep the King's court, where Edmund the Magnificent gloried and drank deep of ale brewed with Thames water.

From Kingston railway bridge the river runs between the power station and then tow-path and open ground of the old village of Ham on the right bank and the closely built, respectable streets of Teddington on the left.

In the middle of the river Steven's Eyot and Trowlock Island provide moorings for flotillas of cabin cruisers with saucy names, and the massed masts sway in the current.

At Teddington there is the lowest and largest of the traditional locks. It is one of the great milestones and landmarks of the Thames, marking the beginning of the tideway and the jurisdiction of the Port of London Authority. Above Teddington swans and ducks are the symbolic birds of the river; below it gulls, the scavengers of London. The semicircular weir is the largest on the Thames and computes and records the daily flow of water into the tideway. The first weir, built in 1912, was hit and damaged by a bomb in the Second World War. It has been rebuilt with thirty-four radial gates, the latest pieces of weir furniture, which measure every gallon of the precious water that roars through them.

Kipling was evidently mistaken in his etymology in *The River's Tale*:

> Up I go till I end my run
> At Tide-end-town, which is Teddington.

Anglo-Saxon precisians have demonstrated that the name is actually descended from Tudingtune. But, whatever the scholarship, the tide does end at Teddington; and London River and the empire of the Port of London Authority begin, to be exact 265 yards below the lock.

The right bank with its tow-path continues past a wilderness of meadow and marsh, playing-fields, and the Young Mariners Basin, where canoeists and river sailors train. On the left the terraces of Teddington merge imperceptibly into the streets of semi-detached villas and 'stockbroker's Tudor' of Twickenham. The settlement of Twickenham stretches back into the Dark Ages. A charter of 704 A.D. records that the King of the East Saxons granted a piece of land at *Tuican-hom* in the province which is called *Middel Seaxon*. No royal palace is known to have been built on this stretch of Thames-side. However, a series of great houses support the theory that this has always been a part of the world where the rich and hopeful have chosen to live. In particular, above all its neighbouring villages that have become suburbs, Twickenham is remarkable for its literary associations. Artists, authors and actors were attracted to the area from the sixteenth century onwards by the beauty of the river and perhaps, more practically, by the advantage of living near royal and noble patrons. Its eighteenth-century literary fame was conspicuous:

> Twit'nam, the Muses' fav'rite seat,
> Twit'nam, the Graces' lov'd retreat.

Their houses and gardens at Twickenham were major influences bordering on obsession in the lives of Alexander Pope and, the lesser talent, Horace Walpole.

Pope appears to have loved his villa and its garden beside the Thames third only to his literary fame and his mother. He bought the lease of the villa in 1719 and spent the remainder of his life there, devoting almost as much care to making the garden picturesque as he did to polishing his heroic couplets. With Addison and 'Capability' Brown he ranks as one of the creators of that most English of art forms, landscape gardening.

He built his villa between the road now called Cross Deep and the river, but laid out most of its miniature and fragmentary garden on the far side of the road. Accordingly, he built his famous Grotto beneath the road to give access to dusky groves, the tiny lawns, and the cypresses that led up to his mother's tomb.

He described it in 1725: 'I have put my last hand to my works of this kind, in happily finishing the subterraneous way and grotto. I there formed a spring of the clearest water, which falls in a perpetual rill that echoes through the cavern day and night. From the River Thames you see through my arch up a walk of the wilderness to a kind of open temple, wholly composed of shells in a rustic manner, and from that distance under the temple you look down through a sloping arcade of trees, and see the sails on the river passing suddenly and vanishing, as through a perspective glass. When you shut the doors of this grotto, it becomes on the instant, from a luminous room, a camera obscura; on the walls of which all objects of the river—hills, woods, and boats—are forming a moving picture in their visible radiations; and when you have a mind to light it up, it affords you a very different scene. It is finished with shells, interspersed with pieces of looking-glass in angular forms; and in the ceiling is a star of the same material, at which, when a lamp (of an orbicular figure of thin alabaster) is hung in the middle, a thousand pointed rays glitter, and are reflected over the place.'

Pope considered his decorations 'in the natural taste, agreeing not ill with the little dripping murmur and the aquatic idea of the whole place'. To modern tastes they sound almost as ornately artificial as his prose describing them. Samuel Johnson's comment on these arrangements is, as usual, full of robust and nicely balanced common sense: 'A grotto is not often the wish or pleasure of an Englishman, who has more frequent need to solicit than to exclude the sun.' However, in the case of Pope's grotto, 'vanity produced a grotto, where necessity enforced a passage'. Johnson also said, in the gruff eighteenth-century manner of a man impervious to argument, that grottoes excavated out of damp hillsides were habitations fit only for toads.

But Pope lined his pretty grotto with shells, mirrors, and pieces of various exotic rocks: Vesuvian lava, Cornish metallic ores, West Indian coral, Peruvian gold ore, and Italian marbles as veined as Gorgonzola. A spring fed a little stream that trickled through the tunnel into a fern-ringed basin, giving the grotto the character of a *nymphaeum*, a natural cave sacred to a nymph. Pope hinted at this classical allusion when he referred to it as his 'Egerian grot'.

The garden and grotto physically expressed Pope's theoretical ideas of nature and art, and the beauty of variety in order and order in variety that he saw inherent in all nature. He formulated these ideas in philosophical poems such as the *Essay on Man*. His garden was a symbol for his philosophy and the setting where, with his classical busts and urns, he could lead the ideal life of the Horatian happy man: retired, contented, self-sufficient, virtuous, and looking priggishly down his nose at the outsiders whom he satirized.

The grotto only survives as the subway under the road. All the minerals and stones that his friends had given to Pope and everything else of order and variety has gone. The garden was cut down in 1760; and the villa was pulled down in 1807 by the new owner, to get rid of the frequent crowds of literary pilgrims that besieged her gates. A convent school now occupies the site. Otherwise only such place-names in the vicinity as Pope's Grove and Pope's Grotto Café preserve the memory of the strange home of Twickenham's most famous resident.

Pope's epitaph in St Mary's, the parish church of Twickenham, is a characteristically offensive piece from the vain little man who made a brilliant career of vexing dunces and former friends in exquisite verse: For one who would not be buried in Westminster Abbey:

> Heroes and kings, your distance keep,
> In peace let one poor poet sleep
> Who never flattered folks like you,
> Let Virgil blush and Horace too.

Upstream and next door to the site of Pope's villa still stands Strawberry Hill, the extraordinary neo-Gothic castle that was the masterpiece and life's work of Horace Walpole. Walpole, the fourth son of Sir Robert Walpole, the prime minister, was one of the greatest gossips, *dilettanti*, wits, *virtuosi*, and letter-writers of his or any age. He later succeeded his nephew in his father's title as fourth Earl of Orford. His prolific, catty correspondence is one of the chief sources for the political scandal and social history of the eighteenth-century upper classes.

In 1747, when he was aged thirty, Walpole removed to Twickenham in what was to be the great event of his life, and bought the house that was to become his life's obsession. He described it in a letter that June:

'It is a little plaything-house that I got out of Mrs Chenevix's shop' (a fashionable London toy-shop) 'and is the prettiest bauble you ever saw. It is set in enamelled meadows, with filigree hedges:

> A small Euphrates through the piece is roll'd,
> And little finches wave their wings in gold.*

'Two delightful roads, that you would call dusty, supply me continually with coaches and chaises: barges as solemn as Barons of the Exchequer move under my window; Richmond Hill and Ham Walks bound my prospect; but, thank God! the Thames is between me and the Duchess of Queensberry. Dowagers as plenty as flounders inhabit all around, and Pope's ghost is just now skimming under my window by a most poetical moonlight.'

In another letter of the same month he informed Sir Horace Mann, preciously, that his new house, being situated on a hill, 'descends to the Thames through two or three little meadows, where I have some Turkish sheep and two cows, all studied in their colours for becoming the view'. Mann was the British envoy at Florence for forty-six years, and his main business was to watch over the doings of the Pretender and his family in Italy. He was also Walpole's chief correspondent, more written against than writing, on a scale that Walpole remarked was not to be paralleled in the history of the post office.

Walpole spent the next thirty years converting his cottage into a battlemented castle in what he referred to as 'the charming, venerable Gothic'

---

* A couplet of Pope's, with finches substituted for eagles.

and 'venerable barbarism'. He found the site described as Strawberry-Hill-Shot in some old deeds and accordingly gave the house its now historic name of Strawberry Hill. It is not in fact the earliest example of the Gothic Revival in English domestic architecture, though it is widely and erroneously supposed to be so; but it is easily the most notorious. Walpole consulted folios of engravings of medieval work and started on addition after improbable addition until by 1776 the house was complete.

The index to his prodigiously voluminous letters is crowded with repeated references to his works at Strawberry Hill: from the Holbein Chamber, the Armoury, the Beauclerk Tower, Henry VIII's Chapel, and the State Bedroom to the Star Chamber. The Staircase Hall, with its Chippendale Gothic staircase balustrade, was said by Walpole to be wrapped in 'the most venerable gloom . . . that ever was since the days of Abelard'. The Library has elaborate brown and gold Gothic book-cases copied from the side doors to the screen of Old St Paul's. In the Holbein Chamber the screen was inspired by the gates and choir of Rouen Cathedral and the chimney-piece by Archbishop Warham's tomb at Canterbury. The Gallery has a plaster fan-vault, gilt fretwork, and pieces of mirror glass in the niches to give an ever-changing ripple of reflections.

Nikolaus Pevsner considers the total effect 'both amusing and awful, both Rococo and romantic'. At any rate it provided an eminently suitable atmosphere of gloom in which Walpole could write *The Castle of Otranto*, his Gothic novel ornate with a haunted castle, damsels in distress, and mysterious murders. The architect for much of the work was Richard Bentley, another of Walpole's correspondents and the son of the great classical scholar.

In a letter to Sir Horace Mann in 1753 Walpole sent Bentley's plan of Strawberry Hill, as it then was, and gave his fullest epistolary description of his castle and treasure house, so as to 'help to let you know whereabouts we are when we are talking to you'. After describing the grounds and gardens and delicious prospect of the Thames, Walpole wrote:

'Now you shall walk into the house. The bow-window below leads into a little parlour hung with a stone-colour Gothic paper and Jackson's* Venetian prints, which I could never endure while they pretended, infamous as they are, to be after Titian, &c., but when I gave them this air of barbarous bas-reliefs, they succeeded to a miracle: it is impossible at first sight not to conclude that they contain the history of Attila or Tottila, done about the very aera.'

The letter goes on: 'From hence, under two gloomy arches, you come to the hall and staircase, which it is impossible to describe to you, as it is the most particular and chief beauty of the castle. Imagine the walls covered

* John Baptist Jackson (died *circa* 1780) revived the art of printing in chiaroscuro. The prints mentioned by Walpole were executed in that style.

with (I call it paper, but it is really paper painted in perspective to represent) Gothic fretwork: the lightest Gothic balustrade to the staircase, adorned with antelopes (our supporters) bearing shields; lean windows fattened with rich saints in painted glass, and a vestibule open with three arches on the landing-place, and niches full of trophies of old coats of mail, Indian shields made of rhinoceros's hides, broadswords, quivers, long bows, arrows, and spears—all *supposed* to be taken by Sir Terry Robsart in the holy wars.'

Sir Terry, who was a Knight of the Garter, was an ancestor of the Walpoles, who suffered from that *pox Britannica*, snobbery, and sometimes wrote as if he was the proud father of his own ancestors.

The itinerary of Strawberry Hill rambles gloating on through interior decoration unimaginable and caverns measureless to mannerism. Here Walpole spent his life with 'my books, my *virtu*, and my other follies and amusements'.

He established his printing-press in Strawberry Hill and from it published elegant limited editions of his own works and those of his friends. Such of his books as *Catalogue of Royal and Noble Authors* and *Anecdotes of Painting in England* retain importance, but his letters and his castle are the foundation of Walpole's reputation. Unfortunately the whole phenomenal collection of Strawberry Hill bric-à-brac, bibelots, rococo oddments, and other curios in the high aesthetic line was sold in 1842. But the house itself is carefully preserved, having been restored to its original fairy-tale condition. Today it forms part of St Mary's Roman Catholic training college for teachers, and strapping young women wave jolly hockey sticks on playing fields beside the turrets and battlements, and so shatter Walpole's Gothic gloom.

Several other large and ancient houses in Twickenham support the theme that this stretch of the Thames was an upper-class ghetto for the rich and royal and those who wished to batten on them. Among those that still stand is York House, now used as municipal offices. The property was granted in 1666 to Edward Hyde, Earl of Clarendon, Charles II's chief minister and the grandfather of Queen Mary II and Queen Anne. He probably rebuilt the existing house into its present form of dignified brick with stone quoins. The last private occupant before the municipal offices moved in was Sir Ratan Tata, an Indian, who introduced the group of statuary that still dumbfounds visitors to the river gardens. Some claim that the statues represent the birth of Venus; others the Pearl Fishers; and either or both schools of sculptural interpretation could well be right.

Marble Hill with its riverside park is conspicuous among the other great houses of Twickenham. George II built this white pile, supported in the centre by giant Ionic pilasters, *circa* 1720 for his mistress Henrietta Howard, who was later promoted to Countess of Suffolk. Pope planned the gardens, and Swift and Gay arranged the interior decoration. Mrs Maria Fitzherbert was living in Marble Hill when she had the misfortune to meet the Prince of

Wales, who later became her unacknowledged husband and George IV.

Across the river on the Surrey bank, screened from the Thames by its elms and sycamores, stands yet another stately home of the stately families of England, Ham House. This massive and severe Jacobean rectangle of brick with stone dressings was originally built by Sir Thomas Vavassour in 1610. Its best-known resident was John Maitland, Duke of Lauderdale. His initial provided the 'L' of the notorious Cabal ministry of Charles II, which, among other unpopular acts, signed the treaty of alliance with France for war against Holland in 1672.

Lauderdale enlarged Ham House and decorated it with such unusual lavishness that it became a synonym for prodigality in its day. Macaulay wrote of him: 'Loud and coarse both in mirth and anger, [he] was perhaps, under his outward show of boisterous frankness, the most dishonest man in the whole Cabal.'

One of the rooms in Ham House is called the 'Cabal Room'. Unfortunately for historical accuracy the room was not in fact built until after the Cabal and the system of government by secret committee was dissolved. But Ham House, with its Great Hall, magnificently carved wooden staircase, and Long Gallery, is looked after by the Victoria and Albert Museum as a shining example of what life was like for a noble family in the Thames valley in the seventeenth century. It is a vivid reminder of the politer way of living introduced at the Restoration, which soon passed to luxury and intolerable expense.

Eel Pie Island lies in the Thames opposite Ham House and, on the other bank, Twickenham Church, and is linked to Twickenham by a hump-backed foot-bridge. Today the island is an untidy jumble of bungalows, house-boats, ramshackle shacks with corrugated iron roofs, a bird sanctuary, and a marine engineering works that builds Thames launches. It has, however, like Tagg's Island, a rowdy and raffish past as a place of popular amusement, unusual and welcome in these polite upper reaches of the London Thames. Old gazetteers describe it as 'a resort of anglers'. It was also a resort for pleasure excursions in the nineteenth century and probably earlier, but the record has perished. In real life Charles Dickens often visited it; and in *Nicholas Nickleby* he made the Kenwigs family picnic there on 'bottled beer, shrub and shrimps'.

From the 1920s bitter complaints are on record from the mainland residents of Twickenham about the vulgar noise of loud-speakers and dance music from Eel Pie Island. In the 1950s and 1960s the island's jazz club was one of the loudest and most popular in England. It then lost its drinks licence and concomitantly most of its membership.

Eel Pie Island next briefly became the home of a brave new experiment for a community development centre, where hippies shipwrecked there by the failure of the jazz club and other drop-outs dropped on their feet, and sociologists and social workers from all over Europe and the United States came to study the attempts to rehabilitate them into conformist society. Many respectable local residents were not happy about that either. In fact they have seldom been happy about activities on Eel Pie Island.

Now there are persistent plans to redevelop the island with houses, a restaurant, and a bridge to carry cars, which would finally destroy its uninhibited individuality. Fortunately this reach of the Thames is a conservation area and the island may therefore be safe from redevelopment. There has always been an atmosphere of picturesque and seedy romance about Eel Pie Island. It so moved a journalist recently that it evoked a *locus classicus* of verbless sentences to vex the grammarians: 'Eel Pie Island is like the Deep South. The same feeling of soft dereliction. The Thames green and dulled —a New Orleans bayou? The moon a silver magnolia.'

Local oral tradition explains, unsurprisingly, that the island got its name from eel-tanks, which were situated at the north end of the island before the boat-yard was built there. Thames fishermen unloaded their catches into the tanks, and an adjacent shop made the eels into pies, which were a famous delicacy for the trippers in the eighteenth and nineteenth centuries. Mrs Raffald, a precursor of Mrs Beeton, made the first recorded mention of 'An Eel Pye' in English literature, when she gave the recipe in her *English Housekeeper* of 1778.

The Thames runs north to Richmond Bridge and Richmond, which is the historic focus of this whole stretch of river. The eighteenth-century bridge with five arches and elegant balustrade is one of the most beautiful over the Thames. It replaced a horse-ferry that had existed there for uncounted years before. The residential area on the Twickenham side of Richmond Bridge is built over the site of Twickenham Park, the country home of Francis Bacon. Bacon, described by his neighbour Pope a century later as 'the wisest, brightest, meanest of mankind', is an excellent early example of the literary men, politicians, and courtiers who were attracted to the district by its beauty and adjacency to royalty.

The beauty, particularly of the view of the Thames valley from Richmond Hill, has been a famous commonplace ever since artists started to paint real landscapes and travellers to keep itineraries. From the sixteenth century onwards Richmond was as regular an excursion for tourists to England as the Changing of the Guard or an overnight trip to Stratford-on-Avon are for package tourists today. Here is the impression it made on Carl Philipp Moritz, a romantic, neurotic, and prolific German author, who wrote *Travels, chiefly on foot, through several parts of England in 1782 by a literary gentleman of Berlin*. He claimed that the evening view of the Thames valley at Richmond 'was in its kind the purest and loveliest natural prospect I have ever witnessed. The feelings it aroused in me no pen can describe.' Unfortunately his pen makes the effort: 'O Richmond! Richmond! never shall I forget that evening when from thy hills thou didst so gently smile upon me, causing me to forget all my cares, as I walked in raptures up and down the flowery banks of the Thames.'

Sir Walter Scott wrote a fictional but equally enthusiastic eulogy of Richmond Hill in the eighteenth century in *The Heart of Midlothian*. The Duke of Argyle is taking Jeanie Deans to her interview with Queen Caroline:

'After passing through a pleasant village [Richmond], the equipage stopped on a commanding eminence, where the beauty of the English landscape was displayed in its utmost luxuriance. Here the Duke alighted, and desired Jeanie to follow him. They paused for a moment on the brow of a hill, to gaze on the unrivalled landscape which it presented. A huge sea of verdure, with crossing and intersecting promontories of massive and tufted groves, was tenanted by numberless flocks and herds, which seemed to wander unrestrained and unbounded through the rich pastures. The Thames, here turreted with villas, and there garlanded with forests, moved on slowly and placidly, like the mighty monarch of the scene, to whom all its other beauties were but accessories, and bore on his bosom an hundred barques and skiffs, whose white sails and gaily fluttering pennons gave life to the whole.

'The Duke of Argyle was, of course, familiar with this scene; but to a man of taste it must be always new.'

The view is still beautiful today, with the Thames winding through parkland like a broad belt around a shaggy, green, tweed suit. But the Duke of Argyle would notice some startling innovations that make the landscape always even more new: the gas-holders of Staines, the neo-Georgian-Imperial palace of the Star and Garter Home for invalid and incurable servicemen, Richmond ice-rink on the left bank, the huge stands of the Rugby Union football ground at Twickenham, and the distant minarets and municipal tower blocks of Isleworth.

People still fish hopefully with rod and line in the Thames at Richmond, but they do not catch as much as they used to. Richmond's reputation for fishing, at least among obdurate anglers, was once almost as high as its reputation for the view. A deep pool just above the bridge, called 'the Duke of Buccleugh's hole', was famous, particularly for barbel. Pollution and over-fishing have driven the fish away. But Raphael Holinshed's *Chronicles*, published in 1577 and written by several hands, give an idea of an additional attraction of this part of the river:

'This noble river, the Thames, yieldeth not clots of gold, as the Tagus doth, but an infinite plentie of excellent, sweet, and pleasante fish, wherewith such as inhabit neere unto her banks are fed and fullie nourished. What should I speake of the fat and sweet Salmon dailie taken in this streame, and that in such plentie after the time of the smelt be passed, and no river in Europe able to exceed it? What store of Barbels, Trouts, Pearches, Smelts,

Breames, Roches, Daces, Gudgings, Flounders, Shrimps, &c., are commonlie to be had therein, I refer me to them that know by experience better than I by reason of their daily trade of fishery in the same; and albeit it seemeth from time to time to be as it were defrauded in sundry wise of these hir large commodities by the insatiable avarice of the fishermen, yet this famous river complaineth commonlie of no want, but the more it looseth at one time the more it yieldeth at another. Onelie in Carps it seemeth to be scant, though it is not long since that kind of fish was brought to England. Oh, that this river might be spared but even one yeare from nets, &c.; but alas! then should manie a poor man be undone.'

However, the main attraction of Richmond for tourists was not the fishing or even the view but the chance to peer at royalty. From the end of the Middle Ages we have records of travellers who went out to Richmond to look at the Queen or the King. For example, Samuel Kiechel, a rich young man from Ulm, visited England in 1585. He was determined not to leave London without seeing Queen Elizabeth, so he rode out to Richmond, where he had a close view of her as she gave audience on the terrace below the Palace. Among others a ship's captain from Hamburg handed her a petition:

'We were so near that we heard her asking the captain whether he could speak English, and then in French whether he could speak that language; he, however, understood neither of these tongues and shook his head, whereupon Her Majesty handed over his petition to one of her councillors.'

Kiechel noticed the customary signs of Gloriana-worship, recorded by many sixteenth-century travellers: 'A great crowd had gathered, and whenever the Queen passed by, the people fell on their knees, raised their hands and shouted: Gott save te quene.'

The royals made Richmond; and they brought in with their train the pattern of settlement of this part of the Thames. The oldest name of the district recorded in the manuscripts was Syenes, which gradually became altered to Shene and then Sheen. As early as the reign of Henry I it appears as a separate manor belonging to the Crown, and from that date there was a royal residence there. Edward III died alone in Shene Palace. Richard II enlarged it for his young wife, Anne of Bohemia, with his characteristic love of foreign luxury and elegance. The wardrobe accounts show that at Shene he introduced such conveniences into England as separate lavatories and hot and cold running water, unprecedented since the Romans left. When Anne died young, tradition reports that Richard was so enraged by grief that he had Shene Palace pulled down. Henry V restored it, and Henry VII made it his favourite residence. When it was destroyed by fire in 1497 he rebuilt it on a grand scale and, at the same time, changed the name of the palace and the settlement that had grown around it to Richmond, after the town in Yorkshire of which he was Earl.

His building was one of the great Tudor palaces. Elizabeth died in it. And it survived as a royal residence until the death of George II. The royals then removed to less grandiose, more comfortable homes in Kew.

The Tudor palace became derelict and its materials were used to build new private houses on the site. Little of it survives except the Gateway, with Henry VII's arms above the arch, the supporters emaciated by the leprosy of erosion. Inside the gate Old Palace Yard preserves one side of the outer court of the palace, now known as the Wardrobe Court. Diagonal patterns of blue diapering still show faintly in the Tudor brickwork of what used to be apartments for courtiers and have now become a terrace of extremely expensive houses.

It is not easy to reconstruct in the mind's eye the appearance of the Tudor palace. A handful of contemporary sketches and engravings, the best of them by Wyngaerde, survive, showing distant and imprecise views of a thicket of turrets with onion domes encircled with battlements and walls. There are one or two contemporary descriptions, all provokingly confused and erratic. The fullest gives an account of Henry VII entertaining a Spanish embassy at Richmond, presumably connected with the marriage of Katherine of Aragon to his eldest son, Arthur. It goes on to give a survey of 'this erthely and secunde Paradise of our region of England, and as I credeablie suppose of all the great circuyte of the world': the King's manor of Richmond.

Unfortunately the author is a colour-writer, better at admiration and striking detail than architectural precision. He records that 'His opynyngs be strong gats of duple tymbre and hert of oke, stikkyd full of nailys right thikke, and crossyd wt barres of iron'.

Immediately inside the gates was the Base Court, made of brick and timber in familiar Tudor style and providing galleries of lodgings for the court and for visitors. A broad conduit flowed through the middle of the courtyard. At the far end the middle gatehouse led into the inner quadrangle, which was built towards the river with Henry's private lodgings overlooking the famous reach.

The buildings of the Inner Court were of free-stone in the perpendicular style and the court was paved with stone. In the middle stood an elaborate fountain, decorated with lions and Tudor red dragons and issuing jets of water out of spouts set in sculptured branches of red roses. Above your right hand as you passed through the gate impended the hall, a tall building with huge windows and fan vaulting. Inside, between the windows, hung paintings of the most famous warrior Kings of England, including, by a happy coincidence, the victor of Bosworth. On the left hand of the Inner Court, in symmetry with the hall, was the chapel. It was 'weel paved, glasid, and hangyd wt cloth of golde, of arres, the body and the quere wt cloth of golde, and the autors sett wt many relikks, juells, and full riche plate'.

Its walls were hung with pictures of the most saint-like Kings of England. Surprisingly these did not include Henry.

The far end of the inner Stone Court comprised the private lodgings of the royal family, three-storeyed ranges of buildings around a third and innermost court. They looked down on the river through the gardens, which were famous for their native and exotic fruit, their frequent statues of wild animals and dragons, and their sporting facilities for every known game from chess to tennis and archery.

No less than fourteen stone towers were set about the perimeter of the central Stone Court: 'And uppon everyche of them, bothe penacles and toure a vane of the King's armys (payntid and gilte wt riche gold and asure) in such exceeding guyse and manr that as well the plesunt sight of them as the heryng in a wyndy day was right mrvellous to knowe and undrestond.' The spelling is erratic by modern conformist standards, but authentic sixteenth century.

Wyngaerd's drawings show the dramatic cluster of onion domes crowned with weather vanes. Their creaking in the wind was as common a sound in a medieval or Renaissance palace as chapel bells, as Geoffrey Chaucer noticed:

> Alofte the toweres, and golden fanes goode
> Did with the wynde make full swete armony.

The presence of this major royal palace necessarily attracted to Richmond officers of state, court officials, artists who wanted royal patronage, high society who wanted to be near the King, and other parasites on the monarchical body. By the end of the seventeenth century the royal palaces were ceasing to be communal lodgings for the large civilian army of the court. Kings and courtiers began to live something approaching private lives in something approaching private houses. These were built in increasing numbers in and around the ten acres of the Old Palace and its gardens. A conspicuous early example of such a building is Maids of Honour Row beside the Gateway to the Old Palace on the south-west side of the Green. This elegant terrace was built in 1724 for the maids of honour of the Princess of Wales, later Queen Caroline.

Discreet trade also followed the royal flag. Nevertheless Richmond remained a small town with a population of no more than 4,500 at the end of the eighteenth century. Twickenham, Hampton, Teddington and Richmond were tiny villages clustered around the walls of their great houses. In the nineteenth century the railway and the improved roads rapidly transformed the area into a sprawl of residential suburbs. The population of the Borough of Richmond is today rising towards 200,000. However the residents are still aware of their superior antecedents and touchily jealous of their village atmosphere, which, they assert, persists in spite of the fact that they are now part of Greater London.

CHAPTER THREE

Isleworth to Kew

FROM Richmond the Thames continues north-east beneath the metal and brick railway bridge and then, immediately, the three concrete arches of Twickenham Bridge, which carries a continuous stream of traffic to and from the south-western suburbs.

Next the river runs through Richmond lock with its unusual double iron footbridge. The three sluices of this lock are drawn up completely when the tide is in flood to let the water up river. But when the tide is at half-ebb they are partly lowered so that they let some water through, but retain enough to make navigation easier above the lock.

After the respectable suburbs of Richmond the riverside on the right bank reverts to its now customary scenery of park, playing-fields, golf-course, and intimations of stately homes in a statelier age. This is the Old Deer Park, which corresponds approximately to the royal park that was attached to Sheen and then Richmond Palace.

From the Normans to the Stuarts the English and then the British monarchs demonstrated their royal blood and royal blood-thirstiness by killing deer, often with insatiable ferocity. James I had an ugly superstition about the virtue of cervine blood and tried to cure his gout and arthritis by paddling his feet in the bellies of stags he had slaughtered in the hunting-field. Queen Anne followed hounds furiously, 'like Jehu' Jonathan Swift told Esther Johnson, to whom he addressed *Journal to Stella*, driving herself in a one-seated, one-horse calash when she was too fat to ride. The highest ranking man present was given a knife and invited to cut off the animal's head. Young spectators, including Anne's son, the six-year-old Duke of Gloucester, were horridly baptized all over with blood. Royal palaces regularly had an enclosure attached to them where the hunting was reserved for the monarch and severe penalties were reserved for poachers. Prince Albert revived the practice with his extremely unsporting and, in the original sense of the word, internecine *battues*; and Princess Anne's pleasure in chasing foxes and vexing the anti-blood-sports lobby baying in the public prints shows that the atavistic instinct is not quite dead.

The Old Deer Park, where the London Welsh rugby pack today hunts other game, was once, as its name indicates, the private hunting-field of kings and queens.

On the left bank, however, the scenery changes to indicate for the first time that the river is actually running into the heart of a great city. After the thick woods of Isleworth Ait, Isleworth and then Brentford and Chiswick line the Thames with cranes, warehouses, wharves, and light and heavy industry as well as with houses and gardens. These Middlesex boroughs were amalgamated to form the London Borough of Hounslow in 1965, when Middlesex ceased to exist as an administrative county, having been wholly swallowed by London.

The previous history of the left bank is in some respects similar to that immediately up-stream. Great houses were also built here because of the beauty of the Thames bank and its convenience for transport and drains. But here there survives a better record of life outside the great houses, which is often ignored by history.

Brentford, as might be guessed, derives its name from the old ford across the river Brent, which flows into the Thames here. And Brent, for those who are engaged by such derivations (and enthusiasts for place-names seem to be more numerous in Britain than elsewhere), occurs in the written records first as *Braegente*. The onomasticians or place-namers connect this with the goddess Brigantia, whose name has been found in Latin inscriptions in Britain and Gaul and seems to have meant 'the high one'.

The river here was almost certainly the site of one of the earliest military actions recorded in British history: Julius Caesar's crossing of the Thames in 54 B.C. The early skirmishing confirmed that the man behind the British resistance to the Romans was Cassivellaunus, King of the chief tribe among the recent Belgic settlers, the Catuvellauni. His capital and stronghold was north of the Thames, a fortress a hundred acres or more in extent on the hill-top beside Wheathampstead, just north of St Albans. Caesar decided to finish the running war by striking at Cassivellaunus's territory.

First he had to cross the awkward barrier of the Thames. He wrote in his *Commentarii* that the crossing-place that he found was eighty miles from the sea and the only practicable one on the lower reaches of the river. This indicates somewhere in the neighbourhood of Brentford, though Caesar was mistaken about it being the first ford on the Thames. He found the north bank of the river strongly defended and obstructed with sharpened stakes obliquely fixed above and below the water in the bed of the river. Archaeologists have discovered large numbers of oak stakes in the bed of the river and on the banks beside the confluence of the Brent and the Thames.

The Roman legionaries waded over, with the water reaching to their necks. The cavalry swam across at a distance from the ford and turned the flank of the position. The Britons fled. And Caesar marched across to victory over Cassivellaunus, but he had to abandon his original intention of wintering in

Britain, 'because of sudden disturbances in Gaul'. The trouble that caused him to retreat from his partial conquest back across the Thames and the Channel was the first movement of the rising of Vercingetorix.

The strategically important river crossings at Brentford were the scene of other ancient military engagements. Edmund Ironside defeated those sea-wolves who lived on the pillage of the world, the Danes under Canute, at Brentford in 1016. *The Anglo-Saxon Chronicle* gives an uncharacteristically lively account of the battle: 'The King [Edmund] went over at Brentford, and there fought against the army and put it to flight; and there were drowned a great many of the English folk, by their own carelessness, those who went before the force, and would take booty.'

According to unpersuasive local tradition Edmund was treacherously murdered a few days later on the spot that has since become the yard of the Red Lion Inn.

Another battle of Brentford was fought at the beginning of the Civil War in 1642, when the Royalist army led by Prince Rupert was advancing on London. They caught and defeated two regiments of the Parliamentary army in a desperate struggle through the narrow streets of Brentford. The gateway seemed open to London. But the City poured out troops and trainbands towards Brentford all night and the Parliamentarians regrouped. Skirmishing continued on the following day, culminating in the complete rout of the Royalists at Turnham Green.

John Evelyn, unfortunately for the readers of his *Diary*, arrived on the scene just too late to be an eye-witness:

'12th November, was the Battle of Braineford surprisingly fought, and to the consternation of the City, had his Majesty (as 'twas believed he would) pursu'd his advantage. I came in w'th my horse and arms just at the retreat, but was not permitted to stay any longer than the 15th by reason of the Army's marching to Gloucester.'

However, the most significant aspect of the history of Brentford and Middlesex was not its strategic but its agricultural and economic importance to London. Henry I granted the county to the City of London to farm for £300 a year, and gave the citizens the right to appoint the Sheriff of the county from among themselves. From that time London and Middlesex came to be regarded as one unit from an administrative point of view. Until it was flooded by the suburban expansion of London in the nineteenth century, Middlesex was a largely agricultural county, the granary and market-garden of London. Its industry was controlled ultimately by the City authorities and more directly by the City companies with a monopoly of the various trades.

For centuries its fertility was famous. John Norden, the great surveyor from the reigns of Elizabeth I and her successor, stated in his *Speculum*

Britanniae that its farming could compare for quality though not quantity with that of any other shire: 'For the soyle is excellent, fat and fertile and full of profite.'

Broadcasting his commendations and commas as generously as a Brentford sower his seed, Norden wrote:

'Towardes the time of Harvest, a man may beholde the fields round about, so sweetely to address themselves, to the siccle, and sith, with such comfortable aboundance, of all kinde of graine, that the husbandman which waiteth for the fruits of his labours, cannot but clap his hands, for joy, to see this vale, so to laugh and sing. Yet doth not this so fruitefull soyle yeeld comfort, to the way-fairing man in the wintertime, by reason of the claiesh nature of soyle; which after it hath tasted the Autumne showers, waxeth both dyrtie and deepe: But unto the countrie swaine it is as a sweete and pleasant garden, in regard of his hope of future profite, for—
>The deepe, and dirtie loathsome soyle,
>Yeelds golden gaine, to painfull toyle.

'The industrious and painefull husbandman will refuse a pallace, to droyle in these golden puddles.'

However Norden regretted that, in spite of the golden puddles, 'things are more confounded by ignorance and evel husbandrye in this shire then in anie other shire I knowe'. He attributes this to the large number of country seats owned by citizens of London—'prebends, gentlemen, and merchants'. Their fine houses, gardens, and orchards were ornaments of the countryside and riverside, but were less good for agriculture, the land 'being noethinge husbandlike manured'.

Above the river valley Middlesex afforded some of the best arable land in the country. But the riverine strip on the left bank in a continuous line from Teddington to London was famous for its market-gardening. The records indicate that nurseries for fruit and vegetable growing were started on this strip of flood-plain gravel soil at least as early as the seventeenth century. The osiers that grow along the bank and on the eyots were woven into baskets for the soft fruit, and the river gave convenient water carriage to the London markets.

Isleworth was noted for its staple crop of strawberries and its raspberries, which were used for distilling. In his report to the Board of Agriculture in 1794 Peter Foot recommended that vines could be successfully grown at Isleworth. He described the excellence and different varieties of the strawberries, and the careful cultivation by the gardeners beside the Thames: 'To this manure, and care of sowing seeds, the kitchen-gardeners who supply the markets at Spitalfields, who cultivate in general on a light black soil, owe their celebrity in the article of lettuces.'

In addition to its market gardens this bank of the Thames has always been notable for the traffic along its roads. The Thames itself was for centuries the quickest, safest, and most convenient highway in the kingdom. On land the main roads from London to the west and south-west have always run beside this stretch of river. Today the Great West Road, opened in 1925, and the M4, one of Britain's first motorways, cut through the riverside suburbs. The flight paths for aircraft landing at London's Heathrow airport lie close and thunderously overhead. The Bath Road, which was one of the great roads of coaching and posting days from the seventeenth century until the invention of the internal combustion engine, runs beside the river. The weight of traffic along it is shown by the huge rent of £19,000 a year that was paid in 1836 for the tolls of the Hammersmith Turnpike Trust. Five hundred vehicles a day, including seven mail-coaches, were then passing along the Bath Road.

Travellers on the early roads beside the left bank of the Thames had to endure the two notorious local hazards of mud and highwaymen. Norden, in the passage quoted above, referred to the deep and dirty nuisance of Middlesex clay to travellers in winter. The road to the south-west from Hyde Park Corner through Brentford and Hounslow was usually a foot deep in fluid mud in the eighteenth century, even though the King travelled along it to Hampton Court several times a week. A beluted sufferer on the road in the winter of 1797–8 wrote: 'The only labourers to be seen on the road were those of a neighbouring gentleman, and they were employed in carting the footpath into his inclosures.'

Highwaymen were traditionally associated with Hounslow Heath, and there are frequent records of robberies on the heath from the sixteenth century on. One reason for the prevalent association was the fact that from an early period the heath has been used as an army camp near London. When peace came, armies were disbanded and some soldiers naturally tended to turn highwaymen, as the civilian occupation that seemed nearest to soldiering. Lord Macaulay wrote in his *History of England*: 'The peace [1698] had all over Europe, and nowhere more than in England, turned soldiers into marauders . . . On Hounslow Heath a company of horsemen, with masks on their faces, succeeded in stopping thirty or forty coaches of the nobility, and rode off with great booty.'

However, many of the popular stories of Hounslow highwaymen are fabricated on foundations of painted smoke. For instance, there is no evidence that Dick Turpin ever practised on Hounslow Heath. As a discouragement to the others, the bodies of criminals were hung on gibbets by the road as late as 1801.

For many centuries the Middlesex bank of the Thames continued to be London's rural market-garden, granary, and main road to the south-west. The architecture of its main town, Brentford, has never been highly thought of. Samuel Johnson once devastatingly snubbed Dr Adam Smith, who was expatiating on the beauty of Glasgow, by cutting him short with: 'Pray, Sir, have you ever seen Brentford?' Boswell, when told of this thunderbolt, said: 'My dear Sir, surely that was *shocking*?' And the old bear crushed him with: 'Why, then, Sir, *you* have never seen Brentford.'

Later, when they were passing through Glasgow on their way to their Highland jaunt and, according to Boswell, had 'viewed this beautiful city', Boswell reminded Johnson of his Scots-baiting on the subject of Brentford. While Johnson expressed admiration of the beautiful buildings, Boswell whispered to him: 'Don't you feel some remorse?'

From the middle of the nineteenth century Middlesex rapidly developed into an important dormitory, factory, and, eventually, airport of London. An idea of the sudden transformation that the industrial revolution brought to this stretch of the river was given by Thomas Hoffland, a fisherman and artist of some celebrity. In *The British Angler's Manual* published in 1848 he wrote of the fishing in the Thames by Isleworth and Brentford:

'Salmon have been driven from the river by the gas-works and steam navigation, not one having been caught to my knowledge during the last twelve or fourteen years; although many were taken formerly of a peculiarly fine quality within my recollection at Mortlake, Isleworth, and other places. The brandling, salmon pink, or skegger, has also disappeared; the last salmon I saw taken, in a net, was opposite Twickenham meadow in the year 1818.'

In addition to its principal character, there are medieval records of some industry beside this Middlesex bank of the Thames. In 1297 the lord of the manor owned a mill 'of Isleworth' and another 'of Brentford', presumably driven by the Brent. One of the earliest industries was the manufacture of gunpowder, and there were several powder-mills still operating in the district until about 1925. It is probable that the first gunpowder made in Britain came from mills on this reach of the river. The accounts show that Edward III employed a man from these parts to manufacture the gunpowder used at the battle of Crécy in 1346, the first battle in the western world in which the ominous report of explosives signalled the end of the Middle Ages.

From 1850 the gasworks, the waterworks, Brentford Dock, and other industrial buildings spread rapidly along the bank of the Thames, cutting off the public from access to and even sight of the river. Other industry proliferated in ribbons along the main roads that run parallel to the Thames. By the middle of the twentieth century travellers to Heathrow along the Great West Road and later the M4 were barricaded from the river by large factories manufacturing razor blades, hair grease, shoe polish, motor car tyres, and other artefacts whose trade names are household words around the world. Brentford and Chiswick became to some extent places where people came to work, or hurried through on their way to somewhere else, or returned to at night, as bed-sitter-land marched steadily westward out of London.

Brentford in particular decayed into a depressed and depressing area. The long and historically notorious high street was filled with heavy traffic and barred from view of the Thames by a high wall. In the shadow of the prominent erections of North Thames Gas, the church of St George-by-the-gasholder has been deserted and converted into the British Piano and Musical Museum ('About two hundred pianos and other organs: open Saturdays and Sundays, March to November'). The riverside was congested by 'Cash and Carry' warehouses and factories manufacturing leather goods and glass fibre.

Then in 1966 the docks began to be run down. The gasworks were removed from the riverside. And, after years of indecision and neglect, the opportunity arrived to redevelop Brentford, taking advantage for the first time since the industrial revolution of its handsome situation beside the Thames. Large housing estates, with a noble prospect of the river and Kew Gardens opposite, are being built on the sites of old Brentford Dock and the waterworks. For the first time since industry arrived people will have continuous access to the bank of the Thames. Other ambitious plans further into the future include one for a modern town centre with pedestrian precincts and all the contemporary accessories, and another to seal off the long backwater behind the Brentford Aits and turn it into a non-tidal marina and boating lake.

Hounslow Borough Council states, with justice: 'Rome was not built in a day. However, a great deal of progress has been made in planning a new Brentford which will transform the sad town of yesterday into a modern, attractive community.'

One of the most engaging minor characteristics of Middlesex and Brentford was always the exuberance of their politics. The Middlesex elections were held in Brentford throughout the most boisterous and disreputable centuries of British politics. In the eighteenth-century records of Parliamentary elections Brentford is conspicuous for the violence, bribery, barratry, and intimidation of its elections. The electors were known as potwallopers because, as in other boroughs, they derived their franchises as householders from the possession of separate fireplaces to cook their food on. They tended to be venal and furiously partisan. The Middlesex mobs were customarily egged on by clergymen and were sometimes delivered by the Thames to disrupt the poll.

To take a typical example, regularly repeated by both parties at all elections: for the 1727 election Henry Barker, the Whig candidate, hired a mob 'of about a hundred . . . at 5s each, at an alehouse, where samples of their clubs were produced . . . Mr Barker was not confined to land forces only, for that the captain of a certain man of war went by water to Brentford, and there landed a great number of his ship's crew, which, he said, were there delivered for the service of Mr Barker . . . At this poll several justices of the peace appeared in the booth, and though they had no votes, made use of their authority to intimidate the friends of Mr Bertie and Mr Child [the Tory candidates] by threatening to commit some without cause further than that they polled for Mr Bertie and Mr Child, and by actually committing others upon bare suspicion of having been rioters'.

The *Annual Register* of the period declares that 'it was impossible for any but those who have witnessed a Middlesex Election to conceive the picture it exhibited; it was a continued scene of disorder, riot, and tumult'.

The outstanding figure of Brentford's disreputable politics is the disreputable and great John Wilkes, who on this bank of the Thames was responsible for asserting and securing several of Britain's most valuable political liberties. These include, for example, the freedom of the press to publish Parliamentary debates and discuss public affairs; and the right of a constituency to choose its Member irrespective of the dictates of Parliament.

Madcap Jack Wilkes, the darling of the London mob, with his squint, his symbolic and metaphorical cap of liberty and his literary, libertarian, and rakish proclivities, is familiar from William Hogarth's unkind caricature. In spite of his grotesque squint, Wilkes was London's answer to Casanova. He spent a lifetime fighting for the freedom of the press, in particular his freedom to publish what he wanted, and won the friendship of Dr Johnson, who said, handsomely: 'Jack has great variety of talk, Jack is a scholar, Jack has the manners of a gentleman.'

Wilkes's momentous connexion with Brentford began after he had been prosecuted for libel, expelled from the House of Commons, and outlawed. The offence that attracted such savage penalties was to have libelled the Government led by Lord Bute in No. 45 of *The North Briton*, which Wilkes had founded for the general purpose of libelling the Government. The offending issue as usual sarcastically congratulated the Scots on the triumph of their favourite, Bute, over their hereditary enemies, the English. It described the speech from the Throne as 'the most abandoned instance of ministerial effrontery ever attempted to be imposed on mankind'. It used other phrases that seem bland and anodyne in these more robust days.

Wilkes had also vexed the Establishment with an indelicate burlesque of Pope's *Essay on Man*, entitled *Essay on Woman*, with an appendix of blasphemies containing an obscene paraphrase of the *Veni, Creator Spiritus*.

He was outlawed and No. 45 was ceremonially given to the common hangman to burn as a seditious libel on the steps of the Royal Exchange. As could have been foreseen by anybody with any knowledge of human nature, this grossly combustible proceeding added greatly to Wilkes's growing popularity. However, Wilkes himself discreetly took refuge in Paris. While there he met the famous 'Parson of Brentford', John Horne Took, one of Brentford's prolific supply of political parsons. Took persuaded Wilkes to return to England and contest Middlesex at the next election. Took sponsored him, ran his campaign, and looked after contributions to his election fund.

Election day was March 28, 1768, and for the occasion every road from London was lined with the turbulent and partisan mobs for which Middlesex elections were renowned. Supporters of Wilkes were in the large majority and used the magic numeral '45' as their election symbol. They forced everyone who passed through Brentford to proclaim and display it. The unfortunate Austrian ambassador, who tried to maintain a proper diplomatic neutrality, was held upside down while '45' was written on the soles of his shoes.

William Whitehead, the uninspired Poet Laureate, described the new hazard of travelling through Brentford in addition to the familiar mud and the highwaymen:

> Bridges they cross, through lanes they wind,
> Leave Hounslow's dangerous heath behind;
> Through Brentford win a passage free,
> By shouting *Wilkes and Liberty*.

Not surprisingly Wilkes was elected by a handsome majority. This brought the electors of Middlesex into direct conflict with the House of Commons, for Parliament at once resolved that their chosen Member 'was and is incapable of being elected a Member to serve in this present Parliament'. Twice more in 1769 the voters of Middlesex returned Wilkes as their Member by increasingly overwhelming majorities and characteristically tumultuous polls. Twice more Parliament annulled his election. By now Wilkes was a martyr and the idol of the ordinary men in the street, who displayed his portrait in every shop window and public house in town.

After his third election was declared inoperative, a large crowd proceeded from Brentford to King's Bench Prison, where their Member was confined for yet another political libel, and congratulated him on his theoretical success. Wilkes acquired a devastating champion in 'Junius'; the Government acquired a dull and unpersuasive apologist in Johnson. Wilkes was made sheriff of London and Middlesex, but he was not allowed to take his seat in the House until 1774, having been elected yet again at Brentford, this time unopposed.

By now he had become Lord Mayor of London and, almost, respectable; and there had been a very necessary revolution in the attitude of Members of Parliament to the rights of those who elected them. Nice prudes and reactionaries tended to disapprove of Wilkes, in particular of his demagogism and his sexual morals: he was a leading and active member of 'the profane and profligate fraternity of Medmenham Abbey', the Hell-Fire Club, which followed the permissive doctrine of Rabelais, *Fay ce que voudras*. However, most of the causes he supported were eminently civilized and libertarian, ranging from opposing the Government policy of sanctions against the disobedient American colonies to pleading for more generous treatment of the British Museum.

Even worthies like Johnson and Gibbon, who disapproved in principle of Wilkes's behaviour and politics and distrusted his character, in practice found his company agreeable because of his wit and his liveliness. Entirely appropriately, a rebel to the end, John Wilkes died as he had lived, insolvent and unrepentant. He gave the undistinguished but agreeable little town of Brentford its most eminent Member of Parliament and a place in British constitutional history.

On either side of Brentford on the Middlesex bank of the Thames are two more respectable though less interesting villages that have expanded into continuous suburbs during the last century.

Upstream Isleworth still has an attractive waterfront lined with boats, warehouses and wharves and the apparatus of boat-building. Ships weighing as much as four hundred tons can tie up at the dock, and it is possible though unconventional to take a passage from Isleworth to the Continent. The view of the Isleworth bank from across the river is one of the most picturesque and peaceful in London. A green and informal square is bounded by the church, the trees of Syon Park, some fine Georgian houses and the inn called The London Apprentice, part of which was built in the fifteenth century.

The tourist guide-books, which believe, perhaps correctly, that royals are irresistible to their customers, emphasize that this old riverside pub was once a favourite port of call for the more dissolute royalties, particularly Henry VIII, Charles II, and Lady Jane Grey, the nine-day Queen. But its name suggests that it was an even more favourite landfall for the apprentices of the livery companies of the City of London, rowing up river on their rare holidays. It is also reported to have been a haunt of smugglers.

Isleworth parish church of All Saints overlooks the river on the other side of the square from The London Apprentice. Its fifteenth-century tower is built of Kentish rag with diagonal buttresses. The body of the church was burnt by vandals at the beginning of the 1939–45 war. But a smaller church and hall have been ingeniously rebuilt inside the shell of the outer walls and have become centres for local cultural and artistic as well as religious activities.

The bank between Isleworth and Brentford is dominated by Syon House, one of the most spectacular of all the palaces beside the Thames and one of the very few still lived in as a private house. It is the home of the Dukes of Northumberland and for more than three hundred and fifty years it has been occupied as a home as well as admired by visitors as a work of art. The current Duke now supports his estate by running Syon Park as a large gardening centre for selling plants and garden furniture and machinery. The selling area, the rose garden with more than four hundred varieties of rose, the camping site, the machinery hall and, more recently, the London Transport Museum of old trams and underground trains have encompassed the majestic, battlemented block with its square corner turrets.

The Bridgettine convent of Syon was founded by Henry V in 1415. According to the tradition recorded by Shakespeare, this act of piety was intended to expiate his guilt for the irregular way by which his father, Henry IV, had become King: by the deposition and subsequent murder of Richard II. Shakespeare makes Henry pray during the long night before Agincourt:

> Not today, O Lord!
> O! not today, think not upon the fault
> My father made in compassing the crown . . .
> Five hundred poor I have in yearly pay,
> Who twice a day their wither'd hands hold up
> Toward heaven, to pardon blood; and I have built
> Two chantries, where the sad and solemn priests
> Sing still for Richard's soul.

The priests and nuns of Syon, sad only by profession, were among the richest in the country, being endowed with a great many farms and manors on the north bank of the Thames, including 'the messuage, land, meadow, wood, pasture and rent in Istelworth, Twykenham, Worton and Heston, with their appurtenances aforesaid, in free and perpetual alms for ever'.

Henry V intended the present magnificent site beside the Thames for a third monastery, which was built but never occupied, for monks of the Celestine order. The monks, being French, persistently and patriotically refused to pray for Henry's success in his wars against their country. Accordingly Henry refused to endow them.

When he died, the Bridgettines of Syon moved in. The north end of their new home was the scene of Caesar's crossing of the Thames. Some of the sharpened oak stakes with which Cassivellaunus tried unsuccessfully to defend his bank against the Romans have been found during dredging and can be seen in the Great Hall of Syon House.

After the dissolution of the monasteries, the ambitious and avaricious Duke of Somerset, Lord Protector of the realm and manipulator of the boy King, Edward VI, secured the monastery and estate of Syon for himself. It was not at first a lucky house for its secular tenants. Around the middle of the sixteenth century Somerset built the shell of the present building in substantially its present shape on the site of the convent: the massive, square, crenellated block with corner turrets, which seems built for a medieval siege or a film set. Somerset's personal doctor, Dr Turner, the father of British botany, established the first botanic garden in England in the grounds.

When Somerset paid the condign penalty for his ambition and lost his

head, Syon passed to John Dudley, Earl of Northumberland. Northumberland was another greedy carnivore in the jungle power struggles of the
sixteenth century. On Edward VI's death he offered the throne to his
daughter-in-law, Lady Jane Grey, in Syon House. She was only seventeen
and sufficiently weak-minded or compliant to accept his offer, and, as a
result, shortly made the one-way journey to the Tower. On it she was
fittingly accompanied by her ambitious father-in-law and her husband, Lord
Guildford Dudley.

Syon consequently reverted to Mary Tudor. Mary's sister, Elizabeth I,
granted a lease of Syon to Henry Percy, ninth Earl of Northumberland. In
1604 the lease was converted into a gift by James I, who was grateful to
Northumberland for his support in securing the succession. During the
occupation by the Percies, Inigo Jones made repairs and alterations in the
Italian style at Syon, and the leaden Northumberland lion of the Percies was
removed from the vanished Northumberland House in the Strand and placed
above the east front of Syon House.

The direct line of the Percies came to an end. And in the eighteenth century Syon passed to Sir Hugh Smithson, later the first Duke of Northumberland. His descendant, the heir to so much turbulent history and so many
savagely ruthless and selfish magnates, still lives in the great house.

The first Duke commissioned Robert Adam to carry out extensive alterations in the 'antique' neo-classical style. Adam commended the Duke in his
Works as 'a person of extensive knowledge and correct taste'. Horace Walpole, who passed the gateway while it was being built in 1773, cattily
remarked the 'filigree' character of the screen that fringes the east front of
the house facing the London road, and objected strongly, perhaps enviously,
to it. He seldom had a good word for architecture or gardening that was not
his. Adam created inside the rectangular Tudor shell one of the most famous
suites of state rooms in the neo-classical style in England. The rooms and
their furniture remain much as they were in the eighteenth century, with
their frequent columns, entablatures, apses, and niches for Roman figures
arranged by Adam in characteristically elegant proportions. The state rooms
are opened to the public on week-days in the summer.

'Capability' Brown, the most fashionable landscape gardener of the
eighteenth century, was, naturally, called in to lay out the grounds for that
man of exquisite taste, the first Duke. William Cowper described Brown's
remarkable methods of gardening:

> Lo! he comes,
> The omnipotent magician Brown appears.
> He speaks; the lawn in front becomes a lake;
> Woods vanish, hills subside and valleys rise;
> And streams—as if created for his use—

> Pursue the track of his directing wand;
> Now murmuring soft, now warring in cascades
> E'en as he bids.

The Great Conservatory with its large glass dome, the oldest erection of such a size and type in the world, was built in the grounds in the early nineteenth century. Both it and the spacious landscapes devised by 'Capability' Brown have been much modified to meet the commercial needs of the Gardening Centre, Ltd. However, Syon House itself remains one of the least changed palaces beside the Thames, still occupied in much the same style as it was two hundred years ago.

The romance of such an unchanging and conspicuous building has been a potent inspiration of poor poetry. For example, Adrian Bury was moved by it to write:

> Here on the silent pleasances of Syon
> The centuries are gathered up as one,
> As if Time had not been
> To darken and divide . . .
> I see a spectral host of Kings and Queens,
> And noble knights in valor's armoured strength,
> Assembled on these lawns
> Under the crescent moon.

He and others expatiate on Syon at length with similar, appropriate sentiments.

Astonishingly the Bridgettine nuns of Syon still survive after a long peregrination. After the dissolution of their convent at Syon, they removed to Lisbon, where they were established from 1594 until 1861. They then came home to England, and settled at South Brent in Devon, where they remain, the oldest English religious community with an unbroken history since before the Reformation.

On the right bank, opposite Syon House and the native industry and traffic of Brentford, the most exotic and improbable landscape along the whole course of the Thames astounds the unprepared. A great Chinese pagoda protrudes a climax of ten roofs beside the bushy tops of the Maidenhair Tree, that living fossil formally called *Ginkgo biloba*, and many thousands of other alien and beautiful plants. There is an absurd profusion of small classical temples, ruined arches, Peking lions, and the other oriental exuberances with which eighteenth-century landowners used to embellish their estates. A flagstaff made from a *Pseudotsuga taxifolia*, commonly known as Douglas Fir, from British Columbia, rises two hundred and fourteen feet above the serried herbaria, the museums, the conservatories, the prodigious domes of the palm-house and other glass-houses, and the gardens.

The Royal Botanic Gardens at Kew comprise by far the greatest and most comprehensive collections of plants in the world. They contain more than 45,000 species and varieties of living plants and many millions of dried specimens. The 50,000 botanic volumes are the richest taxonomic library in the world.

The plants represented in the three hundred acres of originally rather infertile and sandy soil beside the Thames have been hunted down and transplanted there from the round earth's imagined corners, from the tropical orchid-jungles of Asia and the high, rhododendron-infested Himalaya to the summit of the Alps and the bottom of English hedgerows. No less than twenty-nine beds in one of the herbaceous gardens are devoted to exhibiting a selection of the members of the dandelion and thistle family, which contains more than 13,000 species.

This phenomenal Garden of Eden arrived at Kew in the usual way that most things arrived on this stretch of river, as a concomitant of royalty. During the eighteenth century the prolific Hanoverian royal family overflowed from the old, derelict palace of Sheen or Richmond and established a congeries of little palaces around Kew. At Kew royals come not single spies but in battalions. Some of them took an interest in the current and splendid fashion for landscape gardening. From this beginning Kew Gardens grew, one of the few public benefits brought to Britain by the Hanoverian dynasty.

The first of these royal gardeners was Queen Caroline, the consort of George II. Even before George succeeded to the throne, the couple made the Keeper's Lodge of the Old Deer Park of Richmond Palace their favourite country residence. Caroline occupied herself laying out elaborate gardens in the new fashion and building exotic garden structures that excited sarcastic contemporary comment.

There was, for instance, the Hermitage, housing a dome-headed disputation of busts of celebrated philosophers of antiquity, and an even more famous folly called Merlin's Cave. This was a delightful tripartite cottage with three tall, thatched, bee-hive roofs and a Gothic ogee-arched entrance. For no overwhelmingly apt reason it contained three pairs of waxwork figures: Merlin and his secretary; Queen Elizabeth and her nurse; and Elizabeth Tudor, the Queen of Henry VII, and the goddess Minerva. Caroline made Stephen Duck, the peasant poet, the 'Curator' of this remarkable toy, having promoted him from the plough to the royal pulpit at Kew.

Duck was born in Wiltshire and began life as a farm labourer. He was almost entirely self-educated and took to writing verses, which were brought to the notice of Queen Caroline. She gave him a pension and made him a Yeoman of the Guard and curator of Merlin's Cave. He took Holy Orders and later was promoted from Kew to become rector of Byfleet. But he drowned himself four years later in a fit of depression.

Queen Caroline's gardens and the vestiges of her follies at the Keeper's
Lodge have become the western part of the present Kew Gardens.

Meanwhile her eldest son, Frederick, Prince of Wales, and his wife
Augusta had set up house and a rival court at Kew House, otherwise called
the White House, only a few hundred yards farther downstream. Relations
between Fred and his parents were the usual ones between the generations
in their family: sabre-toothed, paranoiac, and, if opportunity had ever arisen,
probably cannibal. The asperity reached extremes in a bitter and infantile
quarrel about where the Prince of Wales's daughter should be born. George
II and Queen Caroline commanded that the birth should take place at
Hampton Court, where they were in residence at the time. Contrary Frederick
insisted on St James's Palace and nearly killed his wife by driving her head-
long there in the last stages of labour. After that they were virtually expelled
from court and so set up a court on their own at the White House.

When Fred died, Walpole recorded this unkind anonymous poem in his
Memoirs of George II:

> Here lies Fred,
> Who was alive and is dead:
> Had it been his father,
> I had much rather;
> Had it been his brother,
> Still better than another;
> Had it been his sister,
> No one would have missed her;
> Had it been the whole generation,
> Still better for the nation:
> But since 'tis only Fred,
> Who was alive and is dead,—
> There's no more to be said.

His widow, Augusta, the dowager Princess of Wales, stayed in the White
House and devoted herself to gardening and to bringing up her son George
in the deplorable way that she considered fitting for the future King George
III. Her gardening was ultimately more successful than her pedagogy. In
1759 she made over nine acres of her garden to botanical purposes, so laying
the foundation of the present Botanic Gardens. The ancient Maidenhair
Tree is a survival from her garden. She had the fashionable passion for
ornamental garden buildings and follies, with which her architect, Sir
William Chambers, encumbered her grounds. Horace Walpole described
these operations in his customary tone:

'Frederick, Prince of Wales, enlarged and ornamented the House, and
began great works in the Garden. The Princess Dowager continued the

improvements, and Lord Bute had the disposition of the ground . . . There is little invention or Taste shown. Being on a flat, Lord Bute raised hillocs [sic] to diversify the ground, and carried Chambers the architect thither, who built some temples, but they are all of wood and very small. Of his design was the round Temple in the middle . . . called the Temple of Victory on the Battle of Minden; another with a Doric portico [the temple of Bellona] . . . the Roman Ruin, the Aviary, and a Chinese building in the Menagerie. The bridge and the round Temple were each erected in a night's time to surprise the Princess.'

Chambers is best known as the architect of Somerset House and one of the founders of the Royal Academy that was originally housed therein. Most of these extravagant erections survive as elegant playthings from a vanished era to decorate the serious scientific work that is the main function of the Botanic Gardens today. The most conspicuous of them is the Pagoda, as outlandish and beautiful a creation to find beside the Thames as a pyramid or a mosque. There was, of course, also a mosque, which dilapidated early in the nineteenth century. In it Sir William Chambers said that he had 'endeavoured to collect the principal particularities of Turkish architecture'. It had a dome painted to look like a sunny day by Richard Wilson, the landscape artist. Chambers also built an Alhambra, painted red, white, and blue, and a number of Chinese pavilions. He had visited Canton three times in his youth and never recovered from the experience. He wrote an important monograph on oriental gardening in opposition to the contemporary fashion of the simple and natural in landscape gardening, of which 'Capability' Brown was the chief exponent. Chambers asserted that the Chinese theory of gardening was designed to produce 'Pleasing, Terrible or Surprising effects', and he did his best to evoke such effects at Kew.

In addition to his surviving classical temples of Bellona, Arethusa, and Aeolus, he built Graeco-Romanish temples to Military Fame, Peace, the Sun, and Pan, the elegant Orangery, and a Theatre of Augusta, named in honour of his folly-fanatical patroness. Regrettably a projected Mausoleum in memory of Pope, Swift, and Gay never proceeded further than the drawing-board.

But the Great Pagoda was Chambers's masterpiece of eccentricity. The octagonal building is one hundred and sixty-three feet high, each of its ten storeys decreasing one foot in diameter and one foot in height from the one below. Originally each of the eighty corners of the roofs was decorated with an iron dragon covered with thin glass of many colours that produced a dazzling reflection. The summit was gilt and the lower roofs were covered with iron plates varnished with different colours.

Augusta's gardening at Kew, like Queen Caroline's, excited derision. For instance, Chambers's exotic garden structures were described by a jealous contemporary philistine as 'an unmeaning falballas of Turkish and Chinese chequer-work'. A falbala is an alien word of obscure derivation meaning a flounce or trimming for women's petticoats; its obscurity aggravated the sting of the insult.

In 1760 George II died and his grandson aged twenty-two, Augusta's son, succeeded him as George III. In the following year George married Princess Charlotte of Mecklenburg-Strelitz. The Princess was allotted Richmond Lodge and its grounds as part of the marriage settlement, and the young King and Queen made it their country house. George had absorbed a love of gardens as well as a tendency to despotism from his mother.

When Augusta died, her son removed back into the White House, his boyhood home. The house was too small for his large family that increased with remorseless regularity once a year. Accordingly the children were boarded out in adjacent houses under tutors. The Prince of Wales, aged eleven, and Prince Frederick, aged ten, were transferred to the Dutch House, which is now known as Kew Palace and is the only surviving specimen of the Hanoverian palaces at Kew. It is an agreeable and persuasive theory that the Prince of Wales, later George IV, developed his passion for *chinoiserie* in the strong Chinese atmosphere constructed by Chambers and his mother and grandmother at Kew. The Great Pagoda and the other exotic pavilions may well have been the ancestors and inspirations of the Chinese Room at Carlton House and of the Royal Pavilion, Brighton, that apotheosis of the English fantasy of the mysterious Orient.

There are numerous accounts of the life of the royals at Kew, most notably that of Fanny Burney, later Madame d'Arblay, the successful author of *Evelina* and other novels who became an unsuccessful second keeper of the robes to Queen Charlotte. It was a quiet, secluded family life in the gardens: 'The Royal Family are always here in so very retired a way, that they live as the simplest country gentlefolks. The King has not even an equerry, nor the Queen any lady to attend her when she goes her airings.'

The daily routine was that the King rose at half-past seven and went to chapel. At nine the whole family went to breakfast, 'the King and Queen sitting at the head of the table, and the Princes and Princesses in order of seniority. The King rode, when the weather was favourable, with some of his children; at other times played chess with General Fitzroy or General Manners. His Majesty dined at two, the Queen and Princesses at four. The hours after dinner were usually employed with his private secretary or one of the ministers. The evening was passed in the Queen's Drawing-room, where three card-tables were set out.'

Another reverential royalty-watcher reports: 'Three card-tables were set out and a few visitors from the neighbourhood had the honour of an invitation. At ten these departed. At eleven the entire family retired to rest.'

In 1788 the King fell incontinently into the first of his recurrent bouts of insanity. It was first noticed when he shook an oak tree in the Great Park by the branch and engaged it in long conversation under the misapprehension that it was the King of Prussia. He was, with difficulty, persuaded to remove to the seclusion of Kew, where his malady would be less embarrassingly public. He was confined on the ground floor of the White House. George regained his wits shortly afterwards, and the happy event was celebrated by 'a grand transparency', painted by Biagio Rebecca, displaying 'the King, Providence, Health, and Britannia, with elegant devices', and erected in the courtyard of the house.

Fanny Burney, whose novels tended to be about the entry of inexperienced young girls into the droll, wide world, has left a lively factual account of life at this period inside the Palace at Kew.

The house had never been used as a winter residence, and was 'in a state of cold and discomfort past all imagination'. There were no carpets on the floors, and Madame Schwellenberg, Keeper of the Wardrobe, an intolerably arrogant, punctilious, and silly woman, ruled the household with a whim of iron, like a Prussian sergeant major. Fanny herself was an erratic and incompetent lady-in-waiting, described by an unsympathetic commentator as 'utterly unfit for any place requiring punctuality, neatness, and manual dexterity'. From the world outside Kew came alarming rumours of a Regency, 'a word,' wrote Fanny, 'which I have not yet been able to articulate'. The King was dosed with fumes of musk, in whose therapeutic qualities his vaguely charlatan doctors, a father and son called Willis, believed so firmly that the Palace permanently reeked of it. He suffered from a delusion that he was no longer married to the Queen, and that he was going to retire to Hanover, where he would dissolve all marriages there and in Britain by Act of Parliament. Queen Charlotte, who was now so fat that the uncharitable said that she looked as if she was bearing all her fifteen children at once, was naturally wounded by his obsession.

One day in February Fanny was walking in Kew Gardens for the sake of her health when she had an extraordinary encounter with the King. She saw a group of men through the trees, and, being very short-sighted, assumed they were gardeners. When she was almost on them, she recognized the King and turned and ran away in terror. But the King pursued her, calling hoarsely, 'Miss Burney, Miss Burney,' and was himself pursued:

'More and more footsteps resounded frightfully behind me,—the attendants all running, to catch their eager master, and the voices of the two Doctor Willises loudly exhorting him not to heat himself so unmercifully. Heavens, how I ran! I do not think I should have felt the hot lava from Vesuvius—at least, not the hot cinders—had I so run during its eruption.'

Above the pounding feet she heard shrill voices calling: 'Stop! Stop! Stop!' Then an attendant shouted: 'Dr Willis begs you to stop.'

She answered, still sprinting for her life: 'I cannot. I cannot.'

He shouted back: 'You must, ma'am; it hurts the King to run.'

So Fanny stopped and faced them as undauntedly as she was able through here terror of lunacy. When they were within a few yards of her, the King called out: 'Why did you run away?' Not knowing what to reply, she forced herself to walk up to him; 'I fairly think I may reckon it the greatest effort of personal courage I have ever made.' Fanny had a proclivity towards exaggeration and self-dramatization.

The King put his arms around her, and she felt a sudden horror that he meant to crush her like a bear. Instead he put his hands on her shoulders and kissed her cheek. Then he started talking to her in the excited, rambling way that was a symptom of his illness, about her father, Dr Burney, the rough behaviour of the household pages, Madame Schwellenberg, and the root and branch reconstruction of the Government he intended to make when he was allowed out.

The Willises, thinking he was growing too excited, proposed that Fanny should walk on. The King cried: 'No, no, no', a hundred times in a breath, and was allowed to walk through the gardens with Fanny. The conversation hopped erratically to the King's favourite subject, Handel, and George ran over most of his oratorios and tried to sing several airs and choruses, 'but so dreadfully hoarse that the sound was terrible'. Dr Willis, alarmed at this performance, again proposed a separation, but the King cried: 'No, no! I want to ask her a few questions; —I have lived so long out of the world, I know nothing.'

So they walked on, talking about acquaintances and public personalities. George said that he was very dissatisfied with his Ministers, and took a paper out of his pocket-book to show Fanny the list of names of the new Government he intended to form 'as soon as I get loose again'. He said: 'I shall be much better served; and when once I get away, I shall rule with a rod of iron.'

The doctors were again alarmed by the King's vehemence and volubility, and insisted again that the conversation must stop, this time successfully. They parted with the King shouting that he would protect Fanny against the dragon Schwellenberg, whom Fanny tends to describe in her occasionally high-flown vocabulary as 'the coadjutrix'. Fanny returned to the Palace, 'inexpressibly thankful to see him so nearly himself—so little removed from recovery'.

In 1800 George relapsed into madness again, and was brought back to his garden asylum at Kew. This time he was confined in the Dutch House opposite the White House. When he again recovered, the White House was demolished and the Dutch House, popularly known as Kew Palace, became the main royal residence at Kew.

This most modest and human of the surviving Thames palaces was built in 1631 for Samuel Fortrey, or de la Forterie, a rich London merchant of Dutch descent. It is constructed of brick, laid in Flemish not English bond, which was an innovation at the time, and has three gables on each of its main fronts. It is an unusual house. In that period the fashionable connoisseurs among the aristocracy were building their houses in the neo-classic style exemplified by the work of Inigo Jones. The wealthy conservatives of the provinces were continuing to build in the Tudor tradition. But a few gabled brick houses like Kew Palace were built around London by rich City merchants, who found the Tudor architecture too antiquated and the new Palladian architecture too plain.

The domestic life inside Kew Palace was of an unpretentious simplicity to suit the building. Because of the smallness of the house it is possible to imagine the intimate lives of its former occupants more convincingly than in the great state rooms of palaces like Hampton Court and Windsor.

Period furniture and various trivial possessions like snuff-boxes and smell-ing-bottles of George III and his family are preserved in Kew Palace as evocative bric-à-brac of the Hanoverian way of life. In the library a silver filigree rattle that was given to the infant Prince of Wales, later George IV, by his governess, Lady Charlotte Finch, is exhibited. George's brothers and sisters and later Queen Victoria's children were brought up to shake this rattle as their first toy and their first chance to assert their noisy royal wills. There is also a toy-box labelled 'Royal Playthings' and containing a set of alphabetical counters showing on one side a capital letter and on the other a picture of an object beginning with that letter: A, Apple; K, Kiln; M, Mill; U, Urn; Q, Quince.

This library, which was lined with book-cases when the Dutch House was the royal country home, was the scene for one of the endearing stories told with the intention of demonstrating that George was a human as well as that strange animal, a Hanoverian King. Apparently he was sitting in the library one day and shouted to a page in the ante-room to put some more coal on the fire. The page, who took a snobbish and hierarchical view of job demarcation in the royal household, called to an old footman to fetch coal.

The King himself at once got up, picked up the scuttle and told the page to lead him to the coal cellar. He filled the scuttle with coal and carried it back to the library, where he threw it on the fire and admonished the page: 'Never ask an old man to do what you can more easily do yourself.'

George III's chief landscape gardener at Kew and Hampton Court was Lancelot Brown. He was given the humorous sobriquet of 'Capability' because of his customary remark that the garden of any great house that he was invited to inspect showed capability of improvement. Capability, who had started life as an ordinary gardener in Northumberland, had so flourished that by 1764 he was appointed 'Surveyor to His Majesty's Gardens and Waters at Hampton Court'. At Kew he was employed to relay the gardens of Richmond Lodge, which had originally been planted by the King's grandmother, Queen Caroline of Anspach. Some of his work survives, in

particular the lake, the river and the rhododendron dell. This winding valley
was excavated in 1773 by a company of Staffordshire Militia under the
command of 'Capability' Brown.

The digging of the lake unfortunately involved the demolition of Queen
Caroline's best folly, Merlin's Cave. A contemporary verse marked its end:

> Lo, from his melon-ground the peasant slave
> Has rudely rush'd, and levell'd Merlin's Cave . . .
> And marr'd with impious hand each sweet design
> Of Stephen Duck and good Queen Caroline.

While 'Capability' Brown was redesigning what has since become the
western part of the Botanic Gardens, George III had initiated the construction of the most ambitious and grandiose folly yet attempted at Kew, that
home of lost follies: a castellated palace beside the Thames in the late
Georgian Baronial manner, with battlements, machicolation, and all the
other sham medieval trimmings. This fantastic building was designed by
James Wyatt, George's favourite new architect and the Surveyor-General
of His Majesty's Works. It was planned to consist of a large central keep set
about with round towers, and surrounded by a great courtyard enclosed by
a high curtain wall, square towers, and gatehouses. The castle was intended
to supersede the Dutch House and the White House, which was demolished
in 1802.

Contemporaries were critical, as they usually are of such royal extrava-
gances. One described it as 'a structure such as these in which Ariosto or
Spenser depicture captive Princesses detained by Giants or Enchanters'.
Another compared it to 'the Bastille Palace from its resemblance to that
building, so obnoxious to freedom and freemen. The foundation is in a bog
close to the Thames and the principal object within its view is the dirty town
of Brentford.'

The main walls had been built and many of the floors and staircases were
complete, when the King became blind and then permanently mad. Accordingly work on his medieval *folie de grandeur* was halted and the Castellated
Palace was demolished between 1827 and 1828. Pulling it down was a difficult
and dangerous operation, because it was extremely solidly constructed with
floor joists of cast iron. After several workmen had been killed in an accident,
it was decided that it would be safer to blow it up with gunpowder, and the
last and greatest of the follies of Kew went out with a bang. After Queen
Charlotte died in the Dutch House in 1818, the Palace was closed and the
royals and their courtiers departed from Kew. George IV, that exquisite
virtuoso of follies, had his own palaces to build elsewhere.

In 1841 the gardens were handed over to the nation and were developed
towards their present form by the first two Directors, Sir William Hooker
and his son, Sir Joseph Hooker. Joseph, who travelled widely in the Himalaya

in the middle of the eighteenth century botanizing and collecting, is largely responsible for the vast variety of rhododendrons in Kew and so in England, and for the vast English enthusiasm for the plant. The rhododendron, an exotic immigrant like the pheasant, has become one of the most characteristic species of southern England, as has the unfortunate pheasant. The great Botanic Gardens, the world's largest living laboratory for plants and a perennial green pleasure-ground for Londoners, survive as a memorial to the agreeable horticultural impulses of the Hanoverians and as a tract of exotic garden beside the domestic Thames.

The village of Kew was originally built for relatives, courtiers, tradesmen holding royal warrants, wicked uncles, and other satellites of the royalties in their various palaces at Kew. Although it has developed around Kew Green on the usual pattern of dormitory suburb, it is still said by its sentimental inhabitants to retain its old small village atmosphere. As dormitory suburbs go it is certainly a very spacious and exclusive place.

On the opposite side of the river, down-stream from Brentford, lies Chiswick, another riverside village that grew into a middle-class suburb during the second half of the eighteenth century, after the commuter trains had arrived. The progress of Chiswick's development is typical. In 1801 the parish had 3,275 inhabitants, most of them occupied in the market-gardening that was the traditional occupation of the district. In 1861 there were 6,500 inhabitants; in 1881, 15,600, and the village had grown up. Today Chiswick is part of the London Borough of Hounslow, which has a population of more than 205,000 living in an area covering twenty-three square miles.

However, more than most London suburbs, Chiswick has retained along its river front the appearance of what it used to look like when it was a small, independent village outside London. Strand on the Green and Chiswick Mall are ribbons of Georgian development along the river that have become intimate, riverside villages for extremely rich Londoners.

Most of the big houses by the river have gone, but Chiswick House with a vista of the Thames survives. It was built in the cool, classical Palladian style by the third Earl of Burlington, who had returned from his Grand Tour early in the eighteenth century with a learned passion for the work of Palladio. The Earl's protégé, William Kent, designed the decoration and laid out the garden in the new irregular style of the Picturesque. After Lord Burlington's death his house was inherited by his son-in-law, the fourth Duke of Devonshire; and remained in possession of the Devonshires until Chiswick Borough Council bought it in 1929. It is now opened to the public as one of the finest Palladian villas in the grand manner in the country.

Hogarth House, where William Hogarth, the painter, engraver, and satirist, who held a caricaturist's mirror up to the barbarities of the eighteenth century, lived for many years, survives as a more modest museum. As well as caricaturing John Wilkes and the malpractices of Brentford elections,

Hogarth is best known for his series of engravings on moral subjects such as *The Harlot's Progress*, *The Rake's Progress*, and *Marriage à la Mode*.

William Hazlitt, the pioneer essayist and perceptive art critic of the next generation, gave Hogarth's painting the title of epic pictures: 'Every thing in his pictures has life and motion in it. Not only does the business of the scene never stand still, but every feature and muscle is put into full play; the exact feeling of the moment is brought out, and carried to its utmost height, and then instantly seized and stamped on the canvass [sic] for ever. The expression is always taken *en passant*, in a state of progress or change, and, as it were, at the salient point.'

Zoffany House on the river in Strand on the Green is an archetype of the process that brought the rich and ambitious to live on these upper reaches of the Thames above London. Johann Zoffany, born in Frankfurt, emigrated to England as a successful portrait painter. He was elected one of the first members of the Royal Academy in 1768 and became a fashionable court artist, painting George III and members of his family; Garrick in many of his characters; and many others of the famous, the rich, and the rebarbative members of London society.

Zoffany then went to India, where he earned a fortune at the court of an Indian prince. He returned with his pile to live in the house named after him at Strand on the Green. While he was there, he painted a picture of the Last Supper intended for St Anne's Church, Kew, though he eventually gave it to St George's, Brentford, now the piano museum. Zoffany used local fishermen as his models for eleven of the apostles, and painted a self-portrait to represent St Peter.

Zoffany's career is a paradigm of the colonization of the Middlesex and Surrey banks of the Thames. From the Middle Ages Kings and wealthy nobles built their palaces beside the river here, and settlements of their dependants and servants clustered around them to service their palaces. The ordinary people lived by sheep-farming, agriculture, market-gardening, and fishing, as they had since before Julius Caesar broke the ancient peace of the Thames valley. From the sixteenth century, when the royal palaces on the upper Thames above London became favourite and regular residences of the monarch, courtiers, artists, authors, and others who depended on royal patronage found it convenient as well as agreeable and stylish to live near their patrons.

The railways built in the second half of the nineteenth century made it possible for the businessmen who worked in the City to commute to work from Kingston, Kew, Chiswick and the other villages. Although the arrival of the airport, the motor car, and industry, particularly on the Middlesex bank, have reduced the rural charm of this stretch of London's river. it remains one of the most beautiful parts of London and, as in Henry VIII's and George III's time, one of the most desirable places to live.

CHAPTER FOUR

Mortlake to Putney

THE four and a half miles of tideway from Chiswick to Putney Bridge are among the best known along the entire course of the Thames. This is by no means because many of the buildings along the banks are historically significant, beautiful, or even remarkable. But they are traditional way-marks and water-marks in one of England's old tribal rites and lunacies, the University Boat Race. Harrod's furniture depository, the old pubs called The Crab Tree and The Doves, Griffin and Mortlake breweries, and other dingy erections of suburban architecture are instinct with emotion and meaning for all muscle-bound oarsmen with hands like bunches of bananas and blurred memories of their day of triumph or disaster.

The Boat Race is an unsatisfactory contest for racing eights. The course bends around the huge northward loop of the Thames for four miles, three hundred and seventy-four yards, a distance that is far too long for modern competitive rowing. It is rowed on moving water, on the flood tide between an hour and a half and two hours before high water, from the University Stone just above Putney Bridge up-stream with the tide to the finish just below Chiswick Bridge. However, modern Olympic and other international rowing is performed in still water, generally over a distance of two thousand metres. The Boat Race is therefore poor preparation for any other race. It is not even often exciting. The extremely crooked nature of the course gives an almost insuperable advantage to the crew that can capture or hold the Surrey station by the beginning of the long bend opposite The Crab Tree. Accordingly the race is usually a procession. It is generally obvious after a few minutes' rowing who is going to win. And with monotonous regularity the winners are Cambridge.

For some reason Cambridge is more successful at persuading large numbers of outsize undergraduates to turn out on its river and at coaching them to swing, swing together in the pure old Cambridge style. Oxford has had to rely largely on Eton and recently on Harvard and Yale to supply it with ready-trained oarsmen. Cambridge's boring supremacy can be taken to imply something about the fundamental flippancy of Oxford; or something else about the fundamental earnestness of Cambridge in its ability to produce young men willing to propel their way excruciatingly through the water, panting to themselves from *The Last Chronicle of Barset*: 'It's dogged as does it. I ain't thinking about it.'

There are those who consider that it is a matter of some importance. Mr R. D. Burnell, an old Oxford rowing Blue, has gone so far as to assert that Oxford's reputation in the outside world has been gradually undermined by its lack of success on the river, and in particular in the Boat Race, which he considers the most important shop window of university sport.

Only a small fraction of Britons are educated at Oxford or Cambridge or have any connexion with either of the two ancient universities. Nevertheless a very large fraction are partisan on the day of the Boat Race and exercised about the result, though perhaps not quite so large a fraction as in the old days or as rowing Blues pretend. Large festive crowds line the tow-path or fill the terraces of The Doves and the other riverside pubs. The race is invariably televised and broadcast by the BBC, accompanied by an almost liturgical commentary. In his description of the 1949 race, one of the closest and fiercest on record, the commentator pronounced a sentence that has become immortal: 'I can't see who's ahead—it's either Oxford or Cambridge.'

Anthropologists have tried to explain the peculiar popularity of the Boat Race, without arriving at any entirely persuasive conclusion. Some say that the cult has been created by an innate English respect for routine: the race is a regular part of the revolving year for Londoners, a harbinger of summer as pointless but as calendarially satisfying as Trooping the Colour, the August bank holiday, or the illumination of the Christmas tree in Trafalgar Square, which takes place earlier each year until it will one day coincide with Midsummer Day. Others suggest that it is the last true gladiatorial contest left in a soft and decadent world: the participants spend a whole year painfully training and then put the matter to the test on the Thames to win or lose it all in about twenty minutes of excoriating agony.

Occasionally the race is exciting as a spectacle, suspending disbelief and arousing pity and terror, usually when somebody sinks. In 1859 Cambridge went down, rowing gallantly to the last, opposite the White Hart Hotel near the finish. Oxford were waterlogged opposite The Doves in 1925, but were just kept afloat by the bladders with which the boat was filled. In 1951 Oxford sank in a violent west wind after two and a half minutes. In 1912, a vintage year, both crews sank, but Oxford managed to reach the shore, empty their boat, re-embark and finish the course. The umpire, who had been busy rescuing Cambridge, then arrived and declared the race off. In 1877 the race ended in a dead heat; tradition records that 'Honest John' Phelps, the admirable waterman who had judged the race for many years, originally announced his verdict as 'dead heat for Oxford by five yards'. Apart from 1877, the closest, finest, and most satisfying race in Boat Race history was in 1952. The crews overlapped for the whole course, and Oxford forced their way to the front to win in the last few strokes. However, since the race was rowed in a raging blizzard, there were regrettably few witnesses of their famous victory.

The record time for the present course used to be seventeen minutes, fifty seconds, rowed in 1948 by a powerful Cambridge crew, with the help of exceptionally favourable tide and wind. In addition both stake-boats dragged and the crews started about a length up on the University Stone. Then in 1974, after a melancholy sequence of defeats that seemed interminable, Oxford broke all records by rowing the course in an astounding seventeen minutes, thirty-five seconds. The tide was fast. The wind was in just the right quarter. Oxford's stroke from Harvard, Dave Sawyier, was aggressive and dedicated. And all the rowing experts, who had dismissed both crews before the race as mediocre, were proved satisfactorily and resoundingly wrong. In fact the conditions after Hammersmith must have been exceptionally favourable, since even Cambridge, who finished five and a half lengths behind Oxford and looking as if they had been racked, recorded the fifth fastest time ever over the course.

As would be expected, the race has a long and curious history. The first University Boat Race was rowed at Henley in 1829. Oxford won after a foul and a restart before a crowd of twenty thousand spectators, which had made its way to Henley by the limited means of transport available in those days. Clearly the excitement roused by the event was already potent. A correspondent wrote of the race in *London Society*:

'Never shall I forget the shout that rose among the hills. It has never fallen to my lot to hear such a shout since. There was fierce applause at the installation of the Duke of Wellington a few years after, and there has been applause under a hundred roofs since; but applause that fills a valley is a different thing. I did not see the great pageant of the entry of the Princess Alexandra into London; but I had the good fortune to see her embark with the Prince of Wales at Southampton, on the evening of their marriage. The quays and the Southampton water gave back no such answer to our cheers as the Henley valley gave on 10th June, 1829.'

After this first race had shown how much prestige was attached to the performance, there was intricate and protracted negotiation about where, when, and under what precise rules subsequent races should be rowed. For many years it was disputed whether the race should be held at Easter, or after Schools at the end of the summer term, at a time of year that suited Oxford better. It was also hotly disputed whether 'bachelors', that is men who had already taken their first degrees, should be allowed to row.

As a consequence of this political manoeuvring and gamesmanship the second race was not held until 1836, when it was rowed from Westminster to Putney. This is memorable as the occasion on which Cambridge by accident acquired light blue as its emblematic colour. Oxford had worn dark blue striped jerseys and black straw hats in the original race. Just before the second race somebody pointed out that Cambridge had no colour on their bows, and an undergraduate ran to a shop by the river and bought a piece of light blue Eton ribbon, which has persisted as the Cambridge colour.

Professional Thames watermen coached and coxed the crews in those early, golden days of amateur rowing. They were the only men who knew how to row and also understood the twists, currents, and tides of the river. However, the amateurs of Oxford and Cambridge gradually evolved their long smooth stroke, quite different from the short, choppy stroke that was the most efficient propulsion for the heavier boats of the watermen. Moreover, as coxes the watermen were implacably addicted to fouling. This practice had none of the pejorative connotations that it carries today. Fair was foul and foul was fair, and obstructing one's rival was considered a legitimate and indeed an important tactic in rowing. As a result boat races were often halted and spoiled by a succession of collisions reminiscent of the livelier moments in the Battle of Salamis.

A good example of the sort of bumping and boring that went on can be found in the accounts of a race between Eton and Westminster in 1836. Noulton, the professional cox, steered the Westminster boat, the *Fairie Queen*, across the bows of the Etonians and bored them so closely inshore that they were obliged either to foul Westminster or run aground. The report concludes: 'A foul consequently took place which lasted five or six minutes, ending in the discomfiture of the *Fairie Queen*, who had her rudder struck off, an oar broken, and was turned completely round.'

Oxford and Cambridge therefore abandoned the use of watermen as coxes and coaches. At the meeting at Oxford that decided no longer to employ professionals, A. T. W. Shadwell in his speech gave a classic example of the Oxford manner that, inexplicably, so vexes outsiders.

'The committee had now a few days ago challenged Cambridge, and had proposed as a condition of the race that no watermen be employed by either party—the next consequence of this was that no watermen be employed for training the boats for the College Races, for how were University steerers to be found if they were to have no practice in their College boats. An important principle to keep in view was that coxswains must always be trained up from among gentlemen. Nor do watermen even as watermen supply the place of a gentleman coxswain. They could do no good beyond keeping the men up to their work, they were totally unable to improve individual rowing —a coxswain ought to be a thinking, reasoning being in a higher degree than any watermen have shown themselves to be.'

Thereafter the watermen departed, taking with them professionalism and the art of fouling, and leaving the Boat Race a sadder but a purer affair.

Outriggers, carvel boats, and sliding-seats were introduced in turn. On three occasions they tried racing on the ebb, from Mortlake to Putney. The present course was finally established in 1864. Since then, except during the years of the First and Second World Wars, the University Boat Race has been rowed with religious regularity in the spring on a flood tide from Putney to Chiswick. It has become one of those national institutions, engaging but mysterious to logical foreigners, like cricket or the Church of England. Indeed there are close connexions between the Boat Race and the Church of England. Many clergy have heaved a hearty oar in their prime, and have been immortalized by P. G. Wodehouse in his characterizations of beefy bishops and curates with fat heads and hearts of gold, and muscles rippling beneath their cassocks like mating boa-constrictors.

From Chiswick Bridge, opened in 1933, after a hundred yards the river runs past the stone that marks the finish of the Boat Race. On the right bank stands Mortlake; on the left the handsome outskirts of Chiswick and then Duke's Meadows, a long stretch of open grassland used by Londoners as a park for exercising their dogs, watching the river traffic, and listening to the melodious bumping and trumpeting from the band-stand.

Mortlake is another pretty residential suburb. The perpendicular tower of its church was built in 1543 by order of Henry VIII. Henry's notorious Secretary of State, Thomas Cromwell, known as *Malleus monachorum* because he was the chief author and perpetrator of the suppression of the monasteries, lived in Mortlake until he lost his head. The other famous and unsavoury sixteenth-century resident was John Dee, the alchemist and confidence trickster. Dee claimed to be able to transmute base metals into gold, and proposed a reasonable reform of the calendar, as well as writing books on mathematical subjects. Queen Elizabeth had confidence in his astrological predictions and visited him at Mortlake.

The village was the seat of the English tapestry workshops, which were founded there in 1619 and flourished until the Civil War under the enthusiastic patronage of royalty and the imitators of royalty. None of these Tudor and Stuart buildings survives, apart from the church tower. But there are some good Georgian houses left, especially in the elegant row called Thames Bank facing the river. The most conspicuous building in Mortlake today is Watney's brewery, which has developed from a small, independent eighteenth-century brewery to become a giant source of 'Red Barrel' and a landmark for the finish of the Boat Race.

Barnes Bridge could be left in well-merited obscurity as a piece of architecture, except that once a year it achieves national prominence as the mark of the last stretch of the Boat Race. The 'village' suburb of Barnes occupies the promontory enclosed by the long loop of the river. It is largely taken up with the reservoirs of the Thames Water Authority, successor to the Metropolitan Water Board since 1974, which extracts water from the Thames, purifies it, and distributes it on its circuitous journey to rejoin the river and make its way down to the sea. It has been calculated that Thames water passes through at least five human bodies before it reaches the sea, though it is hard to see how such a calculation could be made with exactitude. But London water is, even so, some of the purest in the world.

Like its neighbours, Barnes is an agreeable and expensive dormitory suburb. Like them, its best houses face the river with pretty verandas and balconies. Its most eminent resident was Sir Francis Walsingham, Elizabeth I's sinister Secretary of State, who was one of the fathers of the English secret service and whose cloak-and-dagger activities secured the execution of the last Queen of the Scots before the kingdoms were united. Walsingham's manor house of Barn Elms has almost completely disappeared. All that is left is his ornamental pond and his ice-house, standing on an artificial mound into which its pit extended. Local schools use the grounds as playing fields.

On the left bank after Duke's Meadows stand the Griffin brewery and Chiswick parish church of St Nicholas, with the chaste, neo-classical lines of Chiswick House rising behind them. The church is Victorian, built on a palimpsest of rebuildings and foundations stretching back to the thirteenth century. Its most sensational claim to historical notice is the doubtful one that the remains of Oliver Cromwell are secretly buried in the crypt. Cromwell's daughter, Mary, Countess of Fauconberg, is buried there in the Fauconberg vault. There are records of an extra, unidentified coffin having been seen in her vault during restoration. On the strength of this, romantics have constructed an ingenious theory that Cromwell's remains were piously and furtively smuggled to Chiswick, and a surrogate corpse left in Westminster Abbey for the necrophobic insults of the restored royalists.

At Chiswick Eyot, Chiswick ends and the Borough of Hammersmith begins. The sixteenth-century maps by John Norden and others show Hammersmith as a straggling village beside the Thames. Its name, compounded from Old English 'hamor' (hammer) and 'smiththe' (smithy), suggests that it was inhabited before the Norman Conquest. On the other hand, different early place names in the borough like Wormwood Scrubbs and 'Wormeholte' suggest that it was an inhospitable place for primitive man, being part of the impenetrable and snake-infested Middlesex Forest that once covered the Thames valley.

Modern Hammersmith was formed in 1965 by the amalgamation of the old boroughs of Hammersmith and Fulham, and has a mixed population of 200,000 and a rich mixture of industrial, commercial, and residential life.

Sir Alan Herbert (1890–1971), better known by his initials A.P.H., lived beside the Thames at Hammersmith for more than fifty years. A.P.H. was one of the most eloquent lovers and celebrators of the Thames, in addition to being a brilliant light author, maker of APHorisms, playwright, and witty crusader for minority causes, a Don Quixote whose targets were usually more substantial than windmills. His boat was moored at the end of his garden and he used to take it on cruises all over the Thames, parking his floating caravan by night beside Cleopatra's Needle or by the massed lighters in the public roads of the river. He returned to the Thames time and again in his books and musical revues, saying that the only way to know and love it truly is 'to ride it in your own boat from Oxford to the sea, till every island and lock, every bridge and buoy is a familiar friend, and every trick of tide and eddy a familiar foe'.

As Thames pleasure boats chugged up-stream past Sir Alan's house, the magnified voice of the guide could be heard pointing out The Doves public house on the right, Chiswick Eyot on the left, and 'there, between them, him without his shirt, is the famous writer, A. P. Herbert'. Sir Alan pretended that they embarrassed him and persuaded them to stop. His books about the river ranged from the charming novel, *The Water Gypsies*, dealing with the lives of ordinary people who live by the Thames, to *The Thames*, one of his last books about one of the great loves of his life. He said: 'There are almost as many books about the Thames as there are about love. There will always be more; for the river is always changing its clothes.'

Besides living by the Thames, writing incessantly about the Thames, and campaigning for better use of the Thames, Sir Alan was seized with the extravagant ambition to become the first writer to swim from Waterloo Bridge to Westminster Bridge. This was an audacious project. For one thing, Sir Alan was a poor swimmer. For another, those who were less enthusiastic about the Thames than he was, suspected that he would poison himself.

On the day of the great swim Sir Alan was making his way up-stream by his majestic breast-stroke when an old story and a paddle steamer caught up with him. He heard an urgently didactic voice through the loud-hailer inform the passengers: 'Right ahead is the Hungerford Bridge; beyond is Rennie's Waterloo Bridge, about to be pulled down and rebuilt by Mr Herbert Morrison. On the left is the Savoy Hotel and Cleopatra's Needle. The gentleman swimming in the water is Mr A. P. Herbert, the well-known novelist.' Sir Alan said that when he laughed, he sank. So he laughed and sank his way triumphantly to Westminster Bridge.

He had his own boat, *The Water Gypsy*, and used it to commute to the House when he was a very independent Member of Parliament for fifteen years. An argument against ending the extra University Members of Parliament after the Second World War was that the chance of individualists like Sir Alan penetrating Parliament was diminished. When the Second World War started, Sir Alan immediately joined the River Emergency Service on the Thames and later the Naval Auxiliary Patrol. He served as a Petty Officer, gained two conduct badges, and left some characteristically vivid descriptions of the Port of London at war seen from the fragile cockpit of *The Water Gypsy*. At first, during the blackout and the Phoney War the darkness was so intensely impenetrable that anxious care was necessary to hit the bridge-holes. Later, in 1940, when the Blitz broke over the Thames, *The Water Gypsy* was in the thick of it. From his front seat Sir Alan saw and recorded the terrible raids, for instance the night when half a mile of the Surrey shore was burning, and the Pool was a lake of light.

Inside the comedian Herbert, a serious propagandist and campaigner for minority causes, was always struggling to get out. When the campaigner did contrive to get out, as he usually did, he bore a remarkable resemblance to Albert Haddock, the litigious hero of Sir Alan's *Misleading Cases*, who was a *doppelgänger* of his author. Sir Alan's cases ranged from the reform of the betting laws to the demand that authors of books, like the authors of songs, should receive a fee for the repeated enjoyment of their work. He helped to civilize th law on divorce and fought valiantly against Entertainment Tax, Whitehall ,argon, D.O.R.A. (the absurdly restrictive Defence of the Realm Act), and dozens of other excesses of Bumbledom and sanctimonious illiberality. Much of his propaganda warfare was conducted in the correspondence columns of *The Times*. He calculated that he had written more than a thousand letters to that paper on every subject under the sun from summertime and the desirability of a Thames barrage to the rights and wrongs of authors. Sir Alan once said that if he had been paid for all the letters he wrote, he would have been able to buy the yacht of his old friend, the proprietor of the paper, the late Lord Astor of Hever, in which he had often sailed as a guest on holiday cruises.

The Times, in those days subscribing to the maxim that England is a foggy country that demands gravity in her statesmen, was not always amused by Sir Alan. In the old days, before he became a national institution, the paper occasionally discharged a magisterial thunderbolt on his head from the peaks of Printing House Square: 'Questionable levity . . . DID MR A. P. HERBERT GO TOO FAR?' Going too far was the element in which A.P.H. was most at home.

One of Sir Alan's dearest causes was to persuade London once more to make proper use of the Thames instead of turning its back on its greatest piece of open space. He saw the river as a people's playground, from which the people are almost shut out by sluggish, stubborn, or witless authority. He pointed out that careless comparisons were sometimes made between the London Thames and the Paris Seine: 'Why, they say, has London not got the same little passenger boats running about? Why have we no water-taxis, swimming-baths, and floating restaurants? Why can the ordinary Londoner make so little use of the river for transport or pleasure?'

One answer is that London, unlike Paris, is still primarily a great port, and her river must accordingly be regulated for the traffic of the big ships. Another is that the Thames, unlike the Seine at Paris, is tidal. Sir Alan made a persuasive case for Bunje's imaginative scheme of constructing a Thames barrage with ship locks at Woolwich. This would turn the Thames above the barrage into a tideless river always flowing serenely in one direction. Ships of all sizes could always lie afloat in her and the stinking banks of mud would no longer be exposed at low tide twice a day. The river would be cleaner. There would no longer be an intermittent danger of flooding. The fish would come back. Small boats could safely use the river again; more safely than in the great days of Pepys and Evelyn, when the river was as full of private boats as of great flocks of swans. Sir Alan died just too soon to commend the barrier that was started at Woolwich in the 1970s as a prophylactic against flooding, and which could, if legislation were passed, be used as a barrage. There are so many obvious advantages to using the barrier as a barrage that naturally there is official resistance to the notion. Sir Alan is sadly missed from his post of prodding authority in the rational direction with pin-pricks of wit and common sense. The barrage will eventually come, but not until the docks and the commercial centre of gravity of London have moved downstream from Woolwich.

A.P.H. argued convincingly that the old Thames stairs and piers should be restored and maintained and new piers built, if the river was to become London's main road again. The Greater London Council is beginning to follow his advice. He campaigned for water-buses and water-taxis to carry Londoners across their city. They are starting to operate. He once said, explaining his terrier spirit for reform: 'It was better, I thought, for those of us who have neither the power of supermen nor the position of dictators to try to get a few small things done than to vapour vainly about the woes of mankind.'

In the case of his water-buses as well as his barrier Sir Alan has succeeded posthumously in getting a few small things started. In the summer of 1973 a pioneer commuter service by hovercraft was opened between Greenwich and Westminster with a stop at Tower Pier. It was only a modest service to start with. Two hovercraft of sixty seats each making the journey every half hour will not solve London's traffic problems overnight and, indeed, had difficulty in paying their way in the beginning. But they could be significant forerunners and fugelmen of the days when the Thames will be full of traffic again.

Sir Alan, who also campaigned to liberalize the British licensing laws to Continental standards, would have been gratified that the hovercraft contain bars from which, according to the manager of the hovercraft service, 'specially chosen stewardesses offer beverages and souvenirs to the passengers'. However, being a punctilious stylist and a scourge of pretentiousness, he would not have cared for the word 'beverages'.

The Thames at Hammersmith still runs softly and gaily with memories of the witty waterman who said: 'London has a great river. It could be greater still.'

Sir Alan's favourite Hammersmith haunt on dry land was The Black Lion, on the river next door to his house and the only known pub in England that still runs a full-size, operational skittle-alley. A hundred yards farther downstream stands The Doves, formerly The Dove, that important landmark and gallery of the Boat Race.

It was first opened as The Dove coffee-house in the 1740s, and became one of the favourite resting-places of James Thomson in his long walks between London and his cottage at Richmond. Local tradition records that in The Dove Thomson caught the inspiration for and composed some of *The Seasons*, his four books of blank verse instinct with sentiment for nature. The young man from the Borders, with an eye for the beauties of the countryside, whose verse first challenged the precious artificiality of eighteenth-century poetry, wrote *Winter* under stress of poverty when he first came to London in 1725. It is agreeable and convincing to imagine him writing in The Dove the lines from *Spring*:

> The stately-sailing swan
> Gives out his snowy plumage to the gale,
> And, arching proud his neck, with oary feet
> Bears forward fierce, and guards his osier-isle,
> Protective of his young.

Chiswick Eyot, in full view of the windows of The Doves, is still a nesting-place for philoprogenitive swans, and still yields an annual crop of osiers for making baskets. Thomson also wrote the better-known but arguably less poetical words of *Rule Britannia* in his masque, *Alfred*.

Next to The Doves, by Hammersmith creek, are Furnivall Gardens, a scrupulously laundered stretch of lawns and flower borders open to the public beside the Thames. They are named in memory of Frederick Furnivall, another eminent Hammersmith literary personage. Furnivall (1825–1910) was a distinguished scholar of English literature and a critic of Chaucer and Shakespeare. He was editor of the Philological Society's proposed English dictionary, which was gradually evolved into the peerless *Oxford English Dictionary*.

While Furnivall was researching at the British Museum, he used to lunch at an A.B.C. cafeteria opposite, and there became platonically interested in the welfare of the waitresses. He had been an enthusiastic oarsman at Cambridge, and so, to provide recreation for his waitresses and other working girls, he founded the Hammersmith Sculling Club for Girls. It was later expanded to admit men, and Furnivall regularly spent Sundays with his girls on the reach opposite the gardens named after him. In 1891 he founded the National Amateur Rowing Association.

Hammersmith has an old, proud, rowdy reputation as a centre of radical thought and action, stretching back to before Feargus O'Connor, who lived in the Borough. In 1842 in Hammersmith there was a Chartist branch that advocated direct action. Frederick Furnivall added to this local tradition by supporting the Chartists and the early Co-operative and Labour movements. He was one of the founding fathers of the Working Men's College in London in 1854.

William Morris, another more famous pioneer of Socialism, lived on the river front at Hammersmith from 1878 until his death in 1896. His plain, five-bay, three-storeyed house still faces the river in the Upper Mall, a memorial to a man of fiery reforming energy, love of craftsmanship, and a sympathetic understanding of men and materials. Morris named it after Kelmscott Manor, his earlier, Tudor home higher up the Thames in Oxfordshire. From Kelmscott House he founded the Socialist League, a secessionist splinter group split from the Social Democratic Federation; and in it he edited and published the League's paper, *The Commonweal*. In the adjacent cottage he also founded the Kelmscott Press, for which he designed founts of type and ornamental letters and borders. From it he published fifty-three books comprising his own works, reprints of English classics, and various smaller books.

Morris used the stables of Kelmscott House for meetings of the socialist, literary, and artistic worlds. He had a tapestry loom installed in his bedroom on which he worked the designs that brought about a complete and necessary revolution in public taste. Kelmscott House became the base from which he and his friends made devastating guerilla raids on contemporary philistinism and the unpleasant and unacceptable face of Victorian capitalism. The radical reputation of Hammersmith subsists to this day. There was a strong Communist group in the Borough in the 1920s, and Communist candidates still stand regularly at local and general elections.

Opinions vary about Hammersmith Bridge at the end of the Malls. The original bridge, opened in 1827, was the first suspension bridge over the Thames. Thomas Faulkner, an impressionable Victorian local historian, wrote:

'From Kew Bridge the river flows majestically on in sweeping courses between shores skirted with villages and fine seats, passing Mortlake, Barnes, Chiswick and Hammersmith, where it is enlivened and embellished with one of the most magnificent works of art that modern skill and ingenuity have produced—the Suspension Bridge.'

Its replacement, designed by Sir Joseph Bazalgette, was opened in 1887. Some find it pretty, but Sir Nikolaus Pevsner, a more fastidious critic of bridges than Faulkner, stigmatizes it sternly as: 'Suspension bridge with atrocious, partly gilt iron pylons crowned by little Frenchy pavilion tops, and with elephantine ornament at the approaches.'

The Bridge is the lowest over the tideway, and can be an obstruction to navigation. When it is high water at spring-tides, the Bridge only affords fourteen feet three inches of headroom, and flotillas of pleasure steamers are sometimes kept waiting for the tide to go down. Whatever is thought of the elaborate ornamentation of Hammersmith Bridge, it has been persuasively argued that the stretch of river between it and Chiswick Bridge is the most civilized two miles of scenery in Britain.

Hammersmith has grown in this century into a large industrial and dormitory suburb with a population of about 200,000. Vast organizations like the Television Centre of the BBC, the British Oxygen Company, Jo Lyons (the catering and food-manufacturing tea-room giant) and George Wimpey, the building contractors, have their headquarters and employ thousands in Hammersmith. Two great roads pass across and above the Borough, the famous, or infamous, depending on your point of view of the traffic jam, Hammersmith fly-over and the Western Avenue extension, running from White City to Paddington, which cost £30 million and is the longest section of elevated road in Europe.

This immense industrialization and urbanization has transformed Hammersmith within the past century. Before that, like its neighbours, Chiswick, Brentford and Isleworth, it was a pastoral and agricultural district, which supplied London's markets with fruit and vegetables. Daniel Defoe, in his pioneer guide-book, *Tour through the Whole Island of Great Britain*, published in three volumes between 1724 and 1727, described Hammersmith as a well-to-do village:

'Formerly a long scattering place, full of gardeners' grounds with here and there a house of some bulk: I say in this village we see not only a wood of Great Houses and Palaces, but a noble square [Broadway] built as it were in the middle of several handsome streets, as if the village seemed inclined to grow up into a city. Here we are told they design to obtain the grant of a market tho' it be so near to London, and some talk also of building a fine stone bridge over the Thames; but these things are yet in embryo, tho' it is not unlikely but they may be accomplished in time.'

An even earlier record of Hammersmith's reputation as a market-garden is given in *The Portledge Papers*. In mid-September, 1696, a certain Richard Lapthorne was seized with a violent craving for strawberries, and found that they were unobtainable in the City gardens and markets. He therefore had to send to Hammersmith for them, because he could find 'none neerer'.

Thomas Faulkner, the London local historian, gives a vivid picture of Hammersmith as one huge garden as late as 1839. He describes Hammersmith and Fulham as 'the great fruit and kitchen garden north of the Thames', which had supplied the London market regularly since the time of Charles II. Having explained how the farming gardeners of Hammersmith keep their land as clean and nearly as rich as a good kitchen garden by various rotations of crops, Faulkner writes that it was the business of the gardener to gather his produce one day and sell it the next: 'Hence the intervening night is the period of conveyance: every gardener has his market cart, which he loads at sun set.'

He also describes a pastoral scene, incredibly only just more than a century removed from the urban and industrial giant that Hammersmith has become: the hundreds of women, mainly from Shropshire and Wales, who would make two journeys a night from Hammersmith to Covent Garden, carrying on their heads forty- to fifty-pound baskets of strawberries. After the strawberry season was over, they picked and carried to market the vegetables, before returning home in the autumn.

In 1801 the first systematic British census recorded that the population of Hammersmith was about 6,000. By 1841, at the time of Faulkner's itinerant strawberry-pickers, the number had increased to about 13,000. The number continued to increase up a steeply rising graph, indicating statistically the growth of a straggling riverside village full of strawberries and vegetables to a great metropolitan suburb full of industry and commuters: 1861: c. 25,000; 1881: 72,000; 1901: 112,000; 1931: 136,000; 1975: 200,000.

As the vegetables receded, the factories moved into Hammersmith. The first modern industry in the district of which there is record arrived in Fulham in 1674, when John Dwight of Wigan was granted a patent for the manufacture of 'transparent earthenware' and stoneware there. He manufactured pottery in Fulham for the rest of the century, and, according to the industrial historians, very nearly succeeded in manufacturing hard paste porcelain. A Fulham pottery survives on his site, though it has ceased manufacturing.

However, the principal if not the oldest industry of Hammersmith in the eighteenth century was brick-making. The bricks for the elegant Georgian developments of the rich West End and north London came from poor Hammersmith. At one time a hundred and fifty acres of the village were occupied by large and unornamental lakes from which the earth for the bricks had been dug.

The industrial revolution brought gas-manufacturing and other factories to the village. But the event that finally transformed Hammersmith from a country village to a metropolitan suburb was the extension of the tentacles of the underground railway system, which had the same effect on hundreds of other villages north of the Thames. The Metropolitan Line was extended to Hammersmith Broadway in 1864, followed ten years later by the District Line. From that date it became possible to commute to work in the City and the West End from the cleaner and quieter atmosphere of Hammersmith. Consequently there was a prodigious boom of cheap speculative building. The market gardens and brick-making lakes were built over. And Hammersmith swelled to a dormitory suburb.

The rapid increase of population brought a vigorous cultural life. At one time Hammersmith had four flourishing theatres, including the famous Lyric. They are all now closed, redeveloped or converted into bingo halls. The Lyric was opened in 1888, but reached the zenith of its brilliance after 1918, when it was acquired by Nigel Playfair with the help of Arnold Bennett. It opened under its new management on Christmas Eve, 1918, with A. A. Milne's first play, a Christmas play called *Make Believe*. Hermione and Angela Baddeley, Herbert Marshall and Leslie Banks all played their first London parts in it, and the play was said to have been written, cast, dressed and rehearsed and the music for it composed in only three weeks. A series of successes followed, including *The Way of the World*, in which Edith Evans made her name. Several of A. P. Herbert's light operas and revues such as *Derby Day*, *Tantivy Towers* and *Riverside Nights* were appropriately performed at the Lyric. The old Shepherd's Bush Empire, the variety theatre where Marie Lloyd, George Robey and Harry Lauder performed, has been degraded to a BBC television theatre. But the Hammersmith Palais, opened in 1919, survives as London's most popular dance hall. Dixieland jazz was introduced to Britain at the Palais and at one time those who arrived unaccompanied could hire partners for sixpence.

In spite of Defoe's hyperbolic description, Hammersmith was never a place for grand mansions and palaces like Richmond or Kew. The grandest was Brandenburgh House, just downstream from the suspension bridge, built in the early seventeenth century and bought by Prince Rupert for his mistress, Mrs Margaret Hughes. Appropriately, in all the circumstances, it was chosen as her residence by Queen Caroline, when her husband succeeded as George IV in 1820 and she made the mistake of coming back to England to claim her rights. Unfortunate Caroline was cynically used as a weapon against George by Henry Brougham and the other extreme Whigs who called themselves *The Mountain* after the French democrats led by Danton and then Robespierre. It killed her. At first she lived in Mayfair in the home of her noisiest supporter, Alderman Matthew Wood, M.P., a rabid radical who had made a gratifyingly large fortune out of his chemist's shop and his politics. He had been twice Lord Mayor of London and had a swollen sense of his own importance and a love of the lurid limelight that played upon Caroline. Crowds rioting in her support compelled the Queen presumptive to move farther out and she chose Hammersmith, so becoming the first and last royal resident in the Borough. It was a suitable place, with its radical tradition, to increase her support among 'the lower and middling classes'.

A Bill of Pains and Penalties was introduced in the House of Lords to deprive her of her rights and title of Queen and to dissolve her marriage with the King. Its preamble asserted that she had carried on 'a licentious, disgraceful and adulterous intercourse' with Bartolomeo Pergami, her Chamberlain and raffish travelling companion; and it stigmatized her conduct as 'scandalous, disgraceful and vicious'.

As soon as she arrived at Brandenburgh House a public meeting voted a dutiful and loyal address to 'Her Gracious Majesty, Queen Caroline', promising the support of all classes of people in Hammersmith against her 'relentless and vindictive enemies'. Caroline's grateful reply included a marvellous peroration, which bears traces of Brougham's rhetoric:

'All Europe has its eyes fixed on the present procedure in the House of Lords. I shall have to appear at the Bar of that House, but that House itself will have to appear at the Bar of Public Opinion throughout the World. I shall have to Defend myself against their accusations but they will have to Defend themselves against the reproaches of Individual Conscience as well as the impartial condemnation of the Age which now is and of that which is to come. To have been one of the Peers who after accusing and condemning affected to sit in judgement on Queen Caroline will be a sure Passport to the Splendid Notoriety of Everlasting Shame.'

Frequent processions and deputations bearing such watchwords as 'The Queen's Guards are the People' besieged the gates of Brandenburgh House, and the mob swarmed cheering through its gardens. Thomas Creevey, that cheerful gossip and friend of Brougham, sitting in the window of Brooks Club, saw 'the Navy of England marching to Brandenburgh House . . . nothing like this before, thousands of seamen, all sober, each man with a white cockade in his hat'.

On another day Creevey saw the Brass Founders: 'I never saw such a beautiful sight, I had no notion there had been so many brass ornaments in all the world. Their men in armour, both horse and foot, were capital; the procession closed with a very handsome crown borne in state, preceded by a flag with the words "The Queen's Guard are Men of Metal".'

The watermen and lightermen of the Thames came up river in their decorated barges, and moored off Brandenburgh House to present their addresses to the accompaniment of music and firing of cannon.

Caroline kept open house for all who cared to call on her. This hospitality inspired Theodore Hook to write his verses, full of the crude fun and snobbery of the period:

> Have you been to Brandenburgh—heigh, ma'am; ho, ma'am?
>   Have you been to Brandenburgh, ho?
> —Oh, yes; I have been, ma'am,
>   To visit the Queen, ma'am,
> With the rest of the gallanty show—show,
>   With the rest of the gallanty show.

And who were your company—heigh, ma'am; ho, ma'am?
    And who were your company, ho?
—We happened to drop in
    With *gemmen* from Wapping,
And *ladies* from Blowbladder—row—row,
    And ladies from Blowbladder—row.

The Bill was abandoned in November, after the Government majority in the House of Lords had fallen to nine when the Bill was read the third time. Caroline's friends claimed this as a triumphant acquittal and vindication of her 'immaculate innocence', which it was not. Lord Ellenborough, who was a Whig and voted against the Bill, said: 'The Queen of England was the last woman in the country which a man of honour would wish his wife to resemble, or the father of a family would recommend as an example to his daughters.' (Loud cheers.)

Brougham had made his name by his brilliant advocacy on behalf of the Queen. The effect of his opening speech was so intense that one Peer was seen to rise from his place and rush sobbing from the House. If the Government had persevered and forced the Bill through, finding the Queen guilty and divorcing her, it is likely that George IV's position as King would have been imperilled. As it was, the feverish popular support for Caroline found a safety-valve in the presentation of addresses of sympathy, which poured in to Brandenburgh House from all parts of the country.

A fresh wave of deputations descended on Hammersmith after the Bill was dropped. It included one composed of the Lord Mayor, Recorder, Sheriffs, Common Sergeant, and all the other officers of the City of London in dress robes, with a hundred members of the Common Council, accompanied by twenty-five carriages. The mob was not as interested as the politicians in the delicate question of the Queen's chastity. When the crowds round Brandenburgh House saw William Austin, her young protégé, about whose relationship with her there was talk, they called, 'God bless your mother.' But they considered, justly, that she had been badly treated by George, whose own private life would have stood no manner of investigation, however delicate or indelicate.

The hot popular support for Caroline cooled as quickly as immoderate emotions tend to cool. In July 1821, she demanded admittance to Westminster Abbey for George's magnificently pompous coronation, and was peremptorily turned away from the door. This characteristically embarrassing and spectacular scene aroused much less excitement than the events of the previous year.

Caroline was suddenly taken ill at Drury Lane Theatre, and died at Brandenburgh House in August. She may have died of inflammation of the bowels and bitter disappointment, but her doctors accelerated the process.

Brougham told his friend Creevey that she was bled sixty-four ounces, given fifteen grains of calomel and a quantity of castor oil that would have turned the stomach of a horse.

The news of her death reached her husband at Holyhead, where he was waiting for the stormy weather to abate to let him begin his state visit to Ireland. George did not consider it sufficient cause to cancel his travels and it was reported that 'he partook most abundantly of goose pie and whiskey'.

Caroline's death revived her support. Her funeral from Brandenburgh House was as tumultuous and degrading as anything in her unhappy and disorderly life. The Government ordered that the route of the funeral procession should pass outside the City, which was, traditionally and contrary to what it has become, a hotbed of Whiggery and hostility to the King. When the cortège reached Hyde Park, the mob hustled it in triumph off the official route and through the City, as if it was the procession of a popular election candidate. The Life Guards opened fire, killing Richard Honey, a carpenter, and George Francis, a bricklayer, both from Hammersmith.

After this final disgraceful scene Caroline's coffin reached Harwich and then Brunswick, where she had asked to be buried beside her father. Even the Duke of Wellington, who was no friend of the Whigs, or Caroline, or the mob, criticized the Government's handling of her funeral. He wrote to Mrs Arbuthnot: 'I would have embarked her in her own Garden. I would have filled it with Troops and would have sent her in one tide from Hammersmith to Long Reach. This would have settled the matter.'

Brandenburgh House was pulled down after Caroline's death. Other large and fine houses used to occupy the agreeable sites beside the river in the long reach running almost due south from Hammersmith to Fulham. They included Craven Cottage, a famous and picturesque *cottage orné* with Egyptian interiors that gave a delightfully inappropriate Nilotic atmosphere on the grey-green, greasy banks of the chilly Thames. It was burnt down in 1888. And, with the single important exception of Fulham Palace, the other big houses have vanished and been replaced by streets of ordinary homes, industrial buildings and Fulham football ground. The Crab Tree public house, first landmark in the Boat Race, preserved in its name the memory of the days not much more than a century ago, when Fulham like Hammersmith was in the country and famous for its gardens.

By far the oldest and most historically important building in Fulham is the former Palace of the Bishop of London. The estate of Fulham is said to have belonged to the Bishops of London since about A.D. 691, when it was transferred by the Bishop of Hereford to Erkenwald, Bishop of London. The accuracy of the names, dates, and other facts of the history of the Dark Ages is inevitably doubtful. But the accurate commissioners who compiled what is popularly known as *Domesday Book* for William the Conqueror in 1086 described the estate as having 1560 acres, and wrote: 'Hoc manerium fuit et est de episcopatu.'

The *Anglo-Saxon Chronicle* describes how a force of Danes invaded London in A.D. 879 and wintered on the river bank at Fulham. Tradition records that the Danes dug the huge moat nearly a mile long, the longest moat in the country, that used to surround Fulham Palace. Regrettably this ancient piece of civil engineering was drained and filled in in 1921, because, as in the case of the moat of the Tower of London, it had always been difficult to keep the water in it clean.

The early Bishops of London probably had a country house on their estate of Fulham and held their manorial courts there. But the main courtyard and the present palace were constructed by Bishop Fitzjames and date from early in the reign of Henry VIII. It is built of the usual Tudor red brick with black diaper patterns and looks too unpretentious and domestic to be described as a palace. The embankment of the river, constructed in the eighteenth century, has removed its chief external attraction, its river frontage, a hundred yards and a main road away.

The gardens of Fulham Palace have long been famous for their magnificent, exotic trees. Many of the Bishops have become keen gardeners and contributed to the gardens. Bishop Grindal introduced the tamarisk into England here in the reign of Elizabeth I. John Evelyn described in his *Diary* a visit to the Bishop of London at Fulham, when he saw *sedum arborescens* in flower, which was exceedingly beautiful. The manorial rights of Fulham Palace and its estate were taken from the Bishops of London and vested in the Church Commissioners in 1868. The outer gardens have been opened to the public as the Bishop's Park.

In 1972 the Bishop of London, Dr Stopford, removed from the ancient Palace of his predecessors into a more modest and convenient residence in Westminster. The Church Commissioners decided that it had become impractical and socially incongruous for the Bishop to live so far out on the outskirts of his diocese, with the result that he was spending more time in traffic jams than at the meetings he was travelling towards. In any case the ostentatiously large Palace had been built for the vanished days when the Church had a more grandiose style of living, and her Bishops had to be seen to be keeping up with secular princes by living in palaces. Fulham Palace is still used to house the Ecclesiastical Insurance Office and other Church offices. In 1974 Hammersmith Borough Council took it over on a long lease to use it as a centre for civic community uses, particularly for such cultural uses as exhibitions and art galleries.

Next to Bishop's Park Putney Bridge crosses the Thames and marks the start of the Boat Race. Fulham parish church of All Saints stands at the north-west end of the bridge facing Putney parish church of St Mary the Virgin at the south-east end. The symmetry of their positions and the similarity of their towers make them look like one church reflected in a mirror. Next to Fulham church the Hurlingham Club provides spacious lawns beside the Thames for lawn tennis and croquet, bowls, cricket, and miniature golf, and a club-house for dining, dancing, and associated activities. The club was originally started for pigeon-shooting, and when Charles Dickens compiled his *London Guide* in 1879, it was used for polo and pigeon-shooting. The rules then stated that 'no person is eligible for admission who is not received in general society'; and each member was entitled to admit two ladies without payment to all the privileges of the club except shooting and polo-playing. Since then the rules have become less exclusive, but not much less.

The first Putney Bridge was built of timber in 1729 by the King's Carpenter, to replace an ancient ferry. It was at first a privately owned toll-bridge. Turner immortalized the old bridge in a romantic riverscape. However a contemporary looking at it through less imaginative eyes saw only 'an ugly black structure with no redeeming feature to recommend it in point of taste'. The new bridge, designed by Sir Joseph Bazalgette, was opened in 1886. It was widened in 1933 and has become one of the busiest of all the crossings of the Thames.

At the end of the bridge Putney parish church of St Mary was gutted in the summer of 1973 by a fire evidently started by burglars, who stole plate and valuable paintings from the vestry. The fire burnt out the roof and body of the nave, which was rebuilt in 1836, but the fine fifteenth-century arcading was spared. And the notable architectural gem of the church, the Tudor chantry chapel built by Nicholas West, Bishop of Ely and one of Henry VIII's ministers until they fell out over the divorce of Katherine of Aragon, also escaped.

St Mary's became briefly a national cockpit in 1647, when Cromwell's army was stationed at Putney and held 'the Putney debates' in the church. In a session lasting three weeks and interspersed with fervent prayer-meetings Cromwell debated with the army the revolutionary new political philosophy of the Levellers. Some of the phrases and philosophy of the Putney debates were later incorporated as a basis in drafting the first constitution of the United States after the Declaration of Independence.

Samuel Pepys, naturally, attended service at St Mary's, and, equally naturally, noted: 'I saw the girls of the schools, few of which pretty ... Here was a good sermon and much company, but I sleepy, and a little out of order, at my hat falling down through a hole beneath the pulpit, which, however, after sermon, by a stick, and the help of the clerk, I got up again.'

Putney is another riverside village that has swollen into a large dormitory suburb in the past hundred and fifty years. In 1792 its population was only 2,294. Putney Embankment beside the river is a wide and agreeable thoroughfare lined with boat-houses and little factories making boats and oars. Steps lead down to the river. In addition to the Boat Race, rowing and sailing take place off this bank all the year round. It is in many respects the headquarters of British rowing. Beyond the embankment Barn Elms Park, where polo is played, lies beside the river.

There were once a few great houses in Putney, but even the memory of them has now faded. The Palace was built for John Lacy and visited by Elizabeth I and James I. Putney House, a fine seventeenth-century mansion that used to stand on the river front, was visited several times by George II. It later became Putney College, and was demolished when the College was closed in 1857.

The golden age of building in Putney was the middle of the nineteenth century, when successful City businessmen constructed their expensive, Italianate villas along Putney Hill and Putney Heath. Today Putney is a name of national significance on only one day in the year, because of a ritual sporting occasion. For the other 364 days it gets on in peace with the more serious business of being a busy residential suburb. A similar annual metamorphosis for a sporting event overtakes Putney's neighbouring suburb to the south, Wimbledon.

1a.   The Fair on the frozen Thames, December 1683 to February 1684.
Printed by M. Haly and J. Millet, 1684

1b.   Cardinal Wolsey, by an
unknown artist

2. Hampton Court from the air, the Tudor Palace to the left, Wren's Renaissance reconstruction to the right

3a. Richmond Bridge

3b. Strawberry Hill, from Sandby's select views

4a. Horace Walpole, 4th Earl of
Orford, in 1754, by J. G. Eccardt

4b. Alexander Pope, c. 1737,
attributed to J. Richardson

4c. A view in Pope's garden, by William Kent

5. The Thames at Isleworth, photographed in 1895

6a.
Sir A. P. Herbert,
by Ruskin Spear

6b.
John Rennie, 1803,
by George Dance

7a. The Royal Hospital, Chelsea, and the Rotunda in Ranelagh Gardens in 1744, engraved by Vivarez from a drawing by J. Maurer

7b.
Sir Thomas More,
attributed to Holbein

8.
Battersea Power
Station by night

CHAPTER FIVE

Chelsea to Lambeth

BELOW the unofficial headquarters of British rowing along Putney Embankment and beyond Bazalgette's fine bridge, the river next runs beneath railway and foot bridges supported by plump cylindrical legs, as inelegant as the back view of fat girls in mini-skirts. It then runs between two of the expanses of green lungs of London that survive in surprisingly large numbers beside the Thames, even into the heart of London.

On the left are the crew-cut and exclusive lawns of Hurlingham Club, that bastion of the bourgeoisie, where they no longer shoot pigeons or play polo. Hurlingham House, the club house, is a large building of the 1760s not highly regarded by *cognoscenti* of Georgian architecture. But, grandiose with giant Corinthian pilasters and a giant four-column loggia, it presents an appropriately imposing stuccoed front to the river.

On the right is Wandsworth Park, public lawns and paths beside the river, which supply a very necessary patch of green civility for the crowded suburb of Wandsworth.

The river now plunges between a mile of heavy industry on either bank. Monstrous gas-holders, reeking smokestacks and warehouses hedge in the Thames in a way that confirms William Morris's gloomiest predictions about the direction of the industrial revolution. The view has a dark, satanic majesty on an overcast day, when the air is sharp with the smells of smoke, gas, and hops from the breweries. But, in retrospect, it seems a strange order of priorities that put so much industry rather than people in the best sites beside the river.

Wandsworth, an abbreviated form of 'Wandlesworth', takes its name from the Wandle, a small tributary that runs into the Thames unnoticed beside the huge power station and gas-works. Izaak Walton noted 'the fishful qualities' of the Wandle, which rises near Croydon and formerly supplied the water for the moat of Lambeth Palace. He described it as 'the blue, transparent Vandalis'. In 1776 Harrison, the topographer, wrote of 'the many handsome seats in this village belonging to the gentry and to those who have retired from the fatigues of business'. But times and the river have changed since Wandlesworth was a little village.

The first public railway, the Surrey Iron Railway, used to run parallel to the Wandle. It was opened in 1802 and closed in 1848. The wagons were drawn by horses and proceeded on iron rails with a gauge of five feet. Some of the sleepers can still be seen beside the public library.

Wandsworth Bridge, designed by E. P. Wheeler, was built in 1938 to replace its predecessor of 1873. It does not excite admiration or even attention from arbiters of elegance in bridges.

For a mile the left bank also is occupied by the erections of heavy and, in some cases, antiquated industry. The British Gas Corporation headquarters has strikingly modernistic mosaics on its walls, but they are closed to all except pass-holders, on the surprising grounds that top secret scientific research is conducted behind them. Presumably the gas-men live in fear of spites from the National Coal Board and the Electricity Council.

There is a petroleum station, a gas-works with fat gas-holders and a tangle of girders and steaming pipes like a giant's construction of 'Meccano', and acres of dumps for wrecked cars, seedy garages, and derelict industrial wasteland. Fulham electricity power station, built in Townmead Road beside the river in 1936, with four tall cream chimney-stacks with black tips standing in a row, dominates this reach of the river like a huge and impressive ocean liner.

Chelsea Creek opens into Chelsea Docks and the freight depot of British Railways. After working hours this whole bank of the river is largely deserted and wholly sinister, suitably creepy terrain for the culminating pursuit scene in a bloody and thunderous film. The floodlights of Stamford Bridge, the home ground of lost causes and Chelsea Football Club, protrude skeletally from the shadows of the gas-holders. On the waterfront the Chelsea Wharf Refuse Transfer Station carries out its necessary business surrounded by clouds of scavenger sea-gulls, who know where to find the best garbage along the river.

Here is the beginning of an embankment that runs continuously along the north bank for three miles from Chelsea to Blackfriars Bridge, interrupted only by the Houses of Parliament. It was built by that great engineer and cleanser of London and the Thames, Sir Joseph Bazalgette, one of the most important drainers in history. Bazalgette, born in 1819, was appointed engineer to the London drainage commissioners and their successors, the Metropolitan Board of Works. He designed and constructed the majestic pipes, confluences, and cathedralic chambers of the main drainage system of London, which runs into the Thames and was completed in 1865. At the same time he embanked the north bank of the Thames in three sections, first from Westminster to Vauxhall, second from Westminster to Blackfriars, and third the Chelsea Embankment, built between 1871 and 1874. Bazalgette also had the original conceptions of the Blackwall Tunnel and Tower Bridge. So he has left his mark along and under the London river more conspicuously than any other builder.

After London Transport's electricity generating station in Lots Road, a vast and ceaselessly bombinating brick box with four chimneys that supplies the power for London's underground railway system, the north bank is finally free from industry and slum. Frequent blue commemorative plaques of famous men on the fine houses are a sign that the river is entering one of the most agreeable and exclusive inner suburbs of London. Whistler, Turner, Wilson Steer, and many other eminent artists lived in and around Cheyne Walk. Lindsey House, a grandiose pedimented and pavilioned block built in the seventeenth century, was the home of, among other eminent Victorians, Marc Isambard and Isambard Kingdom Brunel, those patriarchs with patriarchal names of the nineteenth-century engineering revolution. Sir Marc designed the Thames Tunnel at Rotherhithe and his son Isambard designed the s.s. *Great Eastern*, the *Great Britain*, and many other revolutionary ships and machines.

Crosby Hall, an international hostel of the British Federation of University Women, is built in the collegiate Tudor style. Its central room was transferred bodily to Chelsea from Bishopsgate, where it was the sumptuous hall of Sir John Crosby, a fifteenth-century wool merchant. Its magnificent timber roof with oriel and ornate arches and pendants is impressive evidence of the high standard of building and living among the merchants of medieval London. Shakespeare knew the house when it stood in Bishopsgate, and introduced it aptly into *Richard III*. Richard occupied Crosby Hall when he was Duke of Gloucester. Shakespeare makes Richard tell his hired murderers to repair to Crosby-place when they have disposed of his brother George, Duke of Clarence, in a butt of malmsey.

George Eliot died at Number Four Cheyne Walk, next door to the home of John Camden Nield, the eccentric miser who left about £250,000 to Queen Victoria. At first Victoria thought that it was a practical joke, but later she wrote that she supposed that her benefactor had done it because he knew she would not waste it. Number Ten was the home of David Lloyd George and later of Randall Davidson, Archbishop of Canterbury for twenty-five years.

Dante Gabriel Rossetti and Algernon Charles Swinburne lived at Number Sixteen. Elizabeth Cleghorn Stevenson, alias Mrs Gaskell, was born at Number Ninety-Three. Joseph Turner died as a recluse at Number 119 beside the Thames and the bridges whose moods he translated brilliantly into oil paint. Dominicetti, an Italian doctor who became a society craze in the eighteenth century, spent £37,000 in making Number Six into a fashionable establishment for medicated baths. Number Fifty-Nine: William Holman Hunt, the Pre-Raphaelite; Number Sixty: Thomas Shadwell, the seventeenth-century Poet Laureate, dramatist and unfortunate 'hero' of Dryden's *Mac Flecknoe*:

> The rest to some faint meaning make pretence,
> But Shadwell never deviates into sense.
> Some beams of wit on other souls may fall,
> Strike through and make a lucid interval;
> But Shadwell's genuine night admits no ray,
> His rising fogs prevail upon the day.

There is hardly a house along the three-quarters of a mile of riverside of Cheyne Walk that has not been the home at one time of somebody notable, notorious, or simply rich.

At the western, slummy end of Cheyne Walk the Chelsea Yacht and Boat Company has a kind of harbour, with dry docks for repair and moorings on the mud for many old vessels of all sorts. Long lines of house-boats linked by a labyrinth of gangplanks and decorated with geraniums and bright paints rise and fall twenty feet to the muddy bottom rhythmically twice a day on the tides. At the place misleadingly known as World's End, Kensington and Chelsea Council are building a big estate of 2,500 houses and flats.

The entire river front here is still haunted with memories and memorials of Chelsea's most distinguished resident, Sir Thomas More. A bronze statue of the statesman, scholar, and saint is seated on Chelsea Embankment a hundred yards from the site of his old home. His head is turned downstream in the direction of his last journey to the Tower and martyrdom. The sculptor, Mr L. Cubitt Bevis, has gilded More's face and hands and the Lord Chancellor's chain of 'S's that lies across his lap.

In fact More considered his official gold chain a badge of servitude and took a commendably contemptuous attitude to worldly wealth. In a letter to his close friend and ideological ally, Erasmus, he wrote that in comparison with the Utopians of his ideal, revolutionary republic, other men of the real world seemed 'poor creatures in comparison with us, inasmuch as they pride themselves on coming out laden with puerile ornaments and womanish finery, bound with chains of that hateful gold, and ridiculous with gems and other bubbly trifles'. Yet, oddly, when he was being taken away to the Tower, he refused to take off his golden chain, although an officer advised him to send it to his wife, since it would only be confiscated.

The sixteenth century, the bridge that links the medieval to the modern world, has an abnormal share of outsize personalities, either attractive or repulsive, but generally full of vigour and appeal. Thomas More may not be the most historically important of them, but he is one of the most engaging. With Erasmus he was a herald of humanism and the new learning of the Renaissance in the north. His *Utopia* was a remarkable anticipation of modern thought and a devastating criticism of contemporary social and political conditions, under which England was run for the wealth and pride of a few rich men, who conspired to heap up money exorbitantly at the expense of the labourers and the poor. More was an exceedingly rare creature in that or any period: a notoriously incorruptible politician and Lord Chancellor. He was a devout and strict Catholic, who practised his religion in his daily life. He chose imprisonment and the axe rather than trim his conscience and his religion to the demands of the tyrant King. He died for the unfashionable beliefs that conscience mattered more than expediency, that the Christian church was a divine society wider than states and nations, and that duty to King yielded place to duty to God. There was clearly no room in England for both such a man and the absolutism of the Tudor state.

But they are the private elements in his idiosyncrasy that make More peculiarly attractive to modern values. He was one of the first biographically recorded owners of qualities on which the modern English pride themselves but in fact seldom possess: their sense of humour, their love of family, friends, and even pet animals, and their ability to be tolerant of difficult wives. More was a confirmed and incorrigible joker all his life. His favourite adjective of commendation in his talk and writings was 'merry' and he made witticisms even on the steps to the scaffold; not bad ones, considering the awesome circumstances. His life style in his 'Great House' in Chelsea, surrounded by his family, dependants, and menagerie of stray animals was an archetype of happy family life, in which all members, irrespective of age and sex, were devoted to each other, to learning, to religion and to merriment.

More is particularly associated with Chelsea, although he only removed there for the last ten years of his life, having lived in the City before that. The reason for this traditional association is that the two unforgettably vivid and attractive contemporary descriptions of More were made at Chelsea by two great artists. It has always been assumed that Erasmus's famous account of More and his family circle was written about Chelsea. Ulrich von Hutten wrote to Erasmus asking for a description of More. Erasmus's reply, in the lucid, fluent Latin that was still the international language of the learned, is a masterpiece of early biography, dealing in lively detail with More's appearance, character, and way of life.

Of More's English sense of humour and love of life Erasmus wrote that More seemed sent into the world for the sole purpose of making witty jests: 'In human affairs there is nothing from which he does not extract enjoyment, even from things that are most serious. If he converses with the learned and judicious, he delights in their talent; if with the ignorant and foolish, he enjoys their stupidity. He is not even offended by professional jesters. With a wonderful dexterity he accommodates himself to every disposition. As a rule, in talking with women, even with his own wife, he is full of jokes and banter.'

Summing up, Erasmus wrote in a well-known passage:

'Ad amicitiam natus factusque videtur, cuius et syncerissimus est cultor et longe tenacissimus est . . . Si quis absolutum verae amicitiae requirat exemplar, a nemine rectius petierit quam a Moro.' (He seems born and made for friendship and is a most faithful and enduring friend . . . If you want the perfect model of friendship, you will find it in nobody better than in More.)

In a letter to the French scholar, Budée, Erasmus gave a fuller description of More's crowded household in Chelsea: 'This amiable circle, with the two husbands [More's sons-in-law], all live in his house. In that house you will find no one idle, no one busied in feminine trifles. Titus Livius is ever in their hands. They have advanced so far that they can read such authors and understand them without a translation, unless there occurs some such word as would perhaps perplex myself. His wife, who excels in good sense and experience rather than in learning, governs the little company with wonderful tact, assigning to each a task and requiring its performance, allowing no one to be idle or to be occupied in trifles.'

In another passage about More's remarkable house in Chelsea, Erasmus wrote: 'Such is the excellence of his temper that whatsoever happeneth that cannot be avoided, he accepteth it as if it could not have fallen out more happily. You would say there was in that place Plato's Academy—but I do his house an injury in comparing it to Plato's Academy . . . I should rather call his house a school or university of Christian religion; for though there is none therein but readeth or studieth the liberal sciences, their special care is piety and virtue; there is no quarrelling, no intemperate words are heard; none appear idle: that worthy gentleman doth not govern with proud and lofty words, but with well-timed and courteous benevolence; everybody performing his duty, yet is there always alacrity, neither is sober mirth anything wanting.'

Erasmus's descriptions of More are complemented by Hans Holbein's sketch of the More family in the dining-room of their Chelsea home. Holbein, already known to More as the illustrator of *Utopia*, came to England in 1527 furnished with a letter of introduction from Erasmus to More. He became intimate with the Chelsea house and painted at least two portraits of its master. The final version of Holbein's famous portrait of the More family has perished, but his preliminary sketch for it survives in the Basel museum. In it More and his father are shown seated in the handsomely panelled room, surrounded by the rest of the family. Erasmus's observation that the Mores were always reading books, especially Livy, is supported by the fact that six of the ten people in the picture are either reading or about to read and that other books lie around, ready to hand for the end of the sitting. Lady More, Sir Thomas's second wife and the kindly stepmother of his children, is shown kneeling at a prie-dieu in the right-hand corner of the picture, while, typically in that animal-loving household, a monkey is climbing up her legs. Holbein evidently felt that this was an improbable posture for prayer even in the More house, and scribbled above Lady More: 'Diese soll sitzen' (This one shall sit). The picture is dominated by the dignified, calm, scholarly, gentle face of More.

Critics have always admired the intimacy of this window into the sixteenth century and the private life of a great Englishman. In a characteristically flowery period Ruskin wrote of Holbein's painting: 'A grave man, knowing what steps of men keep truest time to the chaunting of Death; having grave friends also—the same singing heard far off, it seems to me, or perhaps even low in the room, by that family of Sir Thomas More; or mingling with the hum of bees in the meadows outside the towered walls of Basel; or making the words of the book more tuneable at which meditative Erasmus looks.'

More bought land on the banks of the Thames in the pleasant little country village of 'Chelsey', commonly called 'Chels-hithe', in 1520 and again in 1524. There he built a large and comfortable house, surrounded by garden, fields, and farm buildings running down to the Thames, with green meadows and wooded hills on every side. His gardens were famous. It is said that the rosemary that still flowers in many of the little gardens cabined in urban Chelsea today was introduced by More, who liked to 'let it run alle over his garden walks, not onlie because his bees loved it, but because 'tis the herb sacred to Remembrance and therefore to Friendship'.

The house stood where Beaufort Row, the street that leads to Battersea Bridge, runs today. But it was all pulled down by Sir Hans Sloane in the middle of the eighteenth century. No trace of it survives, though Faulkner, the London topographer, reported finding traces of the foundations and parts of the walls, doors, and windows in 1829.

Many of the familiar incidents in More's life, recounted by hagiographers or other cooler admirers, took place in Chelsea. For example, William Roper in his engaging biography of his father-in-law, Sir Thomas, describes the scene when Henry VIII called unexpectedly at the Chelsea House and walked in the garden after dinner with his arm around More's neck. At that period Henry took an embarrassingly eager and characteristically selfish delight in the society and conversation of More.

Roper writes: 'For the pleasure he took in his company, would his grace suddenly sometimes come home to his house at Chelsey to be merry with him. Whither, on a time, unlooked for he came to dinner, and after dinner, in a fair garden of his, walked with him by the space of an hour, holding his arm about his neck. As soon as his grace was gone, I rejoicing thereat, told Sir Thomas how happy he was whom the King had so familiarly entertained, as I never had seen him do to any before except Cardinal Wolsey, whom I saw his grace walk once with arm in arm. "I thank our Lord, son," quoth he "I find his grace my very good lord indeed; and I believe he doth as singularly favour me as any subject in this realm. Howbeit, son Roper, I may tell thee I have no cause to be proud thereof, for if my head could win him a castle in France (for then was there war between us), it should not fail to go."'

More's forebodings about Henry's unreliability were as clear-sighted as his predictions of the consequences of the dangerous social condition of England in *Utopia*. Henry, that pathological egotist, having persuaded himself of the righteousness of his case for getting rid of Katherine of Aragon and marrying Anne Boleyn, insisted that all his subjects should agree with him. Most Englishmen, being realists and trimmers, agreed to humour their rogue tyrant rather than face the terrible penalties for refusing to take the oath of loyalty to the King's revolution. More, being an incurably honest man and a saint, refused. He was eventually willing to be sworn to the part of that Act that vested the succession to the throne in the heirs of Henry and Anne. But his tiresomely and magnificently scrupulous conscience would not allow him to assent to the sections that asserted the invalidity of Henry's marriage to Katherine and repudiated the Pope's authority in England. Such a refusal to accept the political manifesto of Henry's revolution could have only one result in the horribly efficient reign of terror that was being organized by Thomas Cromwell, Henry's secretary.

William Roper gives a marvellous eye-witness account of More's last departure from his Chelsea garden to face the Commissioners appointed to administer the oath to him at the Archbishop of Canterbury's Palace at Lambeth:

'And whereas he evermore used before at his departure from his wife and children whom he tenderly loved, to have them bring him to his boat, and there to kiss them all and bid them farewell, then would he suffer none of them forth of the gate to follow him, but pulled the wicket after him and shut them all from him; and with a heavy heart, as by his countenance it appeared, with me and our four servants there took boat towards Lambeth. Wherein sitting still sadly awhile, at the last he rounded me in the ear [whispered to me], and said, "Son Roper, I thank our Lord the field is won." What he meant thereby I then wist not, yet loath to seem ignorant I answered, "Sir, I am thereof very glad." But as I conjectured afterwards, it was, for that the love he had to God wrought in him so effectually, that it conquered all his carnal affections utterly.'

Sir Thomas More's house, the most important house in the riverside village that Chelsea remained until the late eighteenth century was demolished in 1740. But traces of its owner still persist. His orchard, known as Roper's Garden, is now a public garden by the river. It contains sculptures, including a striking one of a wind-blown woman by Jacob Epstein to commemorate the years 1909–14, when the most influential sculptor of the twentieth century lived, worked, and made his reputation in a studio in Sir Thomas More's orchard, now Cheyne Walk.

Beside the orchard stands Chelsea Old Church of All Saints, where Sir Thomas, when he was Lord Chancellor of England, shocked the conventional Duke of Norfolk by being caught wearing a surplice and singing in the choir like an ordinary citizen. The church was badly damaged by a German bomb in 1941. But the More chapel in the south chancel suffered less damage. Sir Thomas is said to have rebuilt this chapel in 1528. The timber roof and two lovely Renaissance capitals showing a French influence are intact.

There is a tradition, repeated by that avid collector of traditions, John Aubrey, that More's headless trunk was smuggled out of the Chapel of St Peter ad Vincula in the Tower after his execution and 'interred in Chelsey Church, near the middle of the south wall'. A less nebulous tradition records that his favourite daughter Margaret, the wife of William Roper, secured his head after it had been exposed on London Bridge as an example of the justice of Henry VIII's policy. It is said to have been secretly buried in the Roper family vault at St Dunstan's, Canterbury.

Sir Thomas More did more than anybody to make Chelsea famous and to popularize it as a place to live in. He influenced even Henry VIII, who might have been supposed to have a guilty conscience or at any rate uneasy memories of walking in a Chelsea garden with Sir Thomas. No such sensitivities disturbed Henry's sublime selfishness.

In the year after More's execution he acquired the manor of Chelsea and built himself a manor house about a quarter of a mile from More's old home, on the site that has today been translated into 19–26 Cheyne Place. On his death Henry's house in Chelsea became part of the jointure of his sixth wife, Catherine Parr. After Catherine Parr's death, Chelsea manor passed to the other Queen Dowager who had been clever enough to survive Henry, Anne of Cleves. From her it passed to a succession of royal favourites, and eventually to Charles Cheyne, the Lord Cheyne who has left his name broadcast frequently in street-names around the Borough.

Chelsea remained a small riverside village until London spilled over into it in the nineteenth century and made it contiguous with Belgravia and Mayfair. In those days it was by no means the smart and exclusive suburb that it has become. Dickens described it in 1879: 'Chelsea contains a great population of the working class. Chelsea is Radical, while Kensington may be looked upon as Conservative.' He would not be able to describe Chelsea so today.

In the midst of life, we are in the King's Road, Chelsea, which for a few gaudy years in the 1960s became the navel of swinging London. It is named the King's Road because Charles II had it built as a private and more direct route for carriages from his Palace at Whitehall via Brentford to Hampton

Court. Metal pass tickets admitting privileged people to use the royal road have survived from the seventeenth century; and the King's Road remained an exclusive and semi-private road until 1830.

In the early 1960s a combination of brilliantly original young British dress designers, extremely professional, and unscrupulous publicity, and the national cult of youth with money to spend transformed the King's Road briefly into the Mecca of liberated fashion and thought. Dark little boutiques with trendy names like 'The Quick Nicker' and 'Kleptomania' proliferated, throbbing with the continual beat of the Beatles's latest record. Dark little bistros became the most popular manufacturers of indigestion and hang-over in London. The mini-skirt became the symbol of the King's Road, Carnaby Street, and the rest of the profitable fantasy of swinging London.

In the King's Road brevity became the soul of kit. Girls, not so much skirted as pelmeted, wistfully fingered the latest gear, while tourists from all over the world came on Saturday mornings to ogle one of the spectacles of London. The heady excitement of those swinging years has been partially dissipated in the same way that the mini-skirt has ceased to be compulsory uniform for the youthfully-inclined, whether their thighs and buttocks are as graceful as those of gazelles or of hippopotamuses. But some of the magic of the temple of eternal youth and iconoclasm lingers along the King's Road, although the boutiques have generally been taken over by professional, hard-headed, and middle-aged businessmen.

Back on the Embankment stands a statue of Thomas Carlyle, after Thomas More the most notable of Chelsea's many literary and artistic residents. The bronze statue by Sir Joseph Boehm shows the sage of Chelsea and Ecclefechan seated in an arm-chair, with legs crossed and hands folded in his lap, and face suitably crevassed with thought and domestic troubles. Carlyle, having made a controversial reputation with *Sartor Resartus*, removed from Dumfriesshire to Twenty-Four Cheyne Row in 1834 and lived there until his death in 1881.

James Froude, his disciple, memorably described the move by the Scot on the old trail of Scots on the make to London, fame and fortune:

'He had some 200l. in money for immediate necessities; of distinct prospects he had none at all . . . He was impracticable, unpersuadable, unmalleable, as independent and wilful as if he were an eldest son and the heir of a peerage. He had created no "public" of his own; the public which existed could not understand his writings, and would not buy them, nor could he be induced so much as to attempt to please it; and thus it was that in Cheyne Row he was more neglected than he had been in Scotland . . . He went into society and was stared at as if he were a strange wild animal. His conversational powers were extraordinary. His unsparing veracity, his singular insight, struck everyone who came in contact with him, but were more startling than agreeable. He was unobtrusive, but when asked for his opinion he gave it in his metaphoric manner, and when contradicted was contemptuous and overbearing, "too sarcastic for so young a man", too sarcastic by far for the vanity of those whom he mortified . . . His money flowed away and with the end of it would end also the prospect of making a livelihood in London.'

In this house in Cheyne Row he courageously rewrote the first volume of *The French Revolution*, after the manuscript had been accidentally burnt while in the careless keeping of his friend, John Stuart Mill, who was revising it. And here he wrote his other books, his magnificently poetic but partisan histories like *The French Revolution* and *The History of Frederick the Great*; and his cloudy political works that campaigned against the social maladies of his time, but contained the anti-democratic view that they would be solved by a return to medieval conditions with the rule of a strong, just hero, who could not emerge by popular election.

In his prolific writing Carlyle found time to write about Chelsea. On August 23, 1840, he finished writing his lectures on *Heroes*, and, as he wrote to his brother, John, went out to recover:

'It was towards sunset when I first got into the air, with the feeling of a *finished* man—finished in more than one sense. Avoiding crowds and highways, I went along Battersea Bridge, and thence by a wondrous path across cow fields, mud ditches, river embankments, over a waste expanse of what attempted to pass for country, wondrous enough in the darkening dusk, especially as I had never been there before, and the very road was uncertain. I had left my watch and my purse. I had a good stick in my hand. Boat people sate drinking about the Red House; steamers snorting about the river, each with a lantern at its nose. Old women sate in strange old cottages trimming their evening fire. Bewildered looking mysterious coke furnaces (with a very bad smell) glowed at one place, I know not why. Windmills stood silent. Blackguards, improper females, and miscellanii sauntered, harmless all. Chelsea lights burnt many-hued, bright over the water in the distance—under the great sky of silver, under the great still twilight. So I wandered full of thought, or of things I could not think.'

Carlyle is the most richly idiosyncratic and vulnerable to parody of British writers. Fitfully fuliginous and atrabiliar, tripudiating over syntax, grandiloquent, his prose sometimes seems to impatient readers in moments of irritation to consist of one long and sustained purple patch. Mark, mark, O reader, how his history is occasionally wayward. For instance his unforgettable epithet of Robespierre, the sea-green, incorruptible monster, is based upon a misreading of a single phrase in Madame de Staël's *Considérations sur la Révolution française*. What Madame de Staël actually said was that the prominent veins on Robespierre's forehead showed greenish-blue against his fair, pale skin. But, according to her, his complexion was healthy and his expression engaging. Nevertheless, even if Carlyle's phrase is not strictly accurate, it has become an honoured part of English literature, and that is true of much of his writing. The sage of Chelsea has a style and a high moral perspective that modern historians and journalists, perhaps fortunately, do not aspire to.

The cow fields of Battersea have been built over; but Carlyle's house, erected in the early seventeenth century, is opened as a museum and maintained as it was when he lived and worked there. It contains many mementoes and memories of Carlyle, including the sound-proof, double-walled room with a big skylight on the top floor, where he wrote, in order to escape from the distracting noises of Chelsea.

After Carlyle's statue on the Embankment, the Albert Bridge, opened in 1873 and named in memory of the Prince Consort, hangs across the Thames. It is an appropriately ornate suspension bridge in the fussy Victorian grand manner, with intricate cat's cradles of cables and curious little pagodas that crown the supports. An interesting comparison can be made between the Victorian convolutions of the Albert Bridge and the clean simplicity of Chelsea Bridge, opened in 1934, half a mile down-stream at the end of the Chelsea reach.

After the Second World War it became apparent that the Albert Bridge was inadequate to carry the increasingly heavy traffic, unimaginable when it was built a hundred years before. The London County Council first proposed to pull it down in 1959, and from then on a running battle has been fought on the bridge between traffic and town planners on the one hand and, on the other, Chelsea conservationists led by that doughty and nostalgic defender of Victorian architecture, John Betjeman, the Poet Laureate.

The underside of the bridge has now been strengthened with an extra pier. Ultimately the conservationists would like the bridge to be restricted to pedestrians and turned into a market and pleasure-ground. Fortunately the conservationist mood has grown so strong that it is unlikely that this impractical but delightful piece of Victoriana will be destroyed in the name of efficiency.

Next along the Embankment three and a half acres of exotic green show that everything is still lovely in the Chelsea Physic Garden, one of the oldest and most influential botanical gardens in the world. The Worshipful Society of Apothecaries of London acquired the lease of the land from Mr Charles Cheyne in 1673, and started to cultivate their garden here. In those days its purposes were pharmaceutical and medical: frequent barges used to tie up at the stairs down to the Thames to load cargoes of medicinal plants.

Dr Hans Sloane, that other Chelsea worthy, eminent physician and President of the Royal Society, acquired the manor of Chelsea in 1712, and with it the freehold of the garden. As a medical student he had studied in the garden and grown to love it. Accordingly he granted the Apothecaries a favourable lease in perpetuity, subject to certain conditions, such as that fifty specimens of plants grown in the garden were to be delivered every year to the Royal Society. The garden was to be 'continued at all times as a physic garden, for the manifestation of the power and wisdom and goodness of God in creation; and that the apprentices might learn to distinguish good and useful plants from hurtful ones'. The statue of Sir Hans Sloane, 'arch healer and most eminent benefactor of botany', robed and wigged like a cauliflower, still presides benignly over his great walled garden in the red-brick heart of Chelsea.

Over the centuries the purposes of the garden have gradually changed from medical to botanical. The Physic in its name has no connexion with quacks, but retains the original Greek meaning of pertaining to nature. Out of these three and a half acres beside the Thames germinal and seminal discoveries have come that have changed the face of the world.

Cotton seeds, probably originating from the South Sea Islands, were exported from the Chelsea Physic Garden to Georgia on the instructions of Sloane, and so started the cotton plantations of the deep Southern States, with historical consequences that are still potent today. Dr Nathaniel Ward, who lectured to medical students at the Garden, developed his 'Wardian Cases' there. These glass-sided boxes were originally invented to protect house plants from the ravages of London fog. They were subsequently developed to enable living plants to be transported around the world. As a direct result tea was introduced into India from China in 'Wardian Cases'; *cinchona* (quinine) into India from South America; and rubber into Malaya from South America.

Choice and master gardeners have always been curators of the Garden. There have only been ten of them in the past three hundred years, so healthy is the life and so attractive the curator's house in the most beautiful private garden in London. The most famous Chelsea gardener was Philip Miller, one of the greatest of all gardeners. His superb *Dictionary of Gardening*, first published in 1724, remained authoritative for many years and is still one of the classics of green-fingered literature. Miller was the first gardener to effect the germination of exotic seeds by growing them in the heat of a tan pit. He devoted himself to the introduction and acclimatization of rare plants from abroad, and had correspondents all over the world with whom he exchanged rare seeds and plants. Linnaeus (Carl von Linné), the great Swedish naturalist and founder of modern botany, visited the Garden in 1733 and wrote in his diary: 'Miller of Chelsea permitted me to collect many plants in the garden.'

William Forsyth was another notable Chelsea gardener. He was appointed to the post in 1770 and gave his name to *Forsythia*, the winsome genus of shrubs from eastern Asia that colours London gardens as bright yellow as the daffodil in the spring.

Bazalgette's Embankment cut the Garden off from the river and altered the soil and the conditions for gardening for the worse.

In 1899 the maintenance of the Garden became too great a financial burden for the Apothecaries' Society, which no longer derived any great material advantage from it. So the London Parochial Charities were appointed trustees, and the Garden is now run as a charity, maintaining statutory educational links with the Royal College of Science and other students of botany.

The most significant pioneering work that has originated in the Garden recently was done by the late Professor F. G. Gregory and his associates, who discovered the control of flowering by day-length (photoperiodism) and winter chilling (vernalization) there between 1932 and 1955. Their experiments demonstrated that the slow-developing winter rye could be made to behave like quick-developing spring rye by means of the appropriate treatments. Since the experiments involved using outdoor illuminations by night, they had to be discontinued during the blackout of the Second World War.

Arcane but important research is still being done in the Chelsea Physic Garden. For example, botanists are at present working in such fields as new methods of producing *ergot alkaloids*, which are used extensively during childbirth and for the treatment of certain types of migraine; on new techniques of detecting and measuring metal contaminants in the atmosphere; and on the mystery of the variable resistance of tomatoes to *verticillium wilt* disease.

Beside the Physic Garden spacious lawns and the long red-brick ranges of one of Sir Christopher Wren's most handsome secular buildings extend along the Embankment to Chelsea Bridge. The Royal Hospital, Chelsea, was founded by King Charles II in 1682 as a retreat for old soldiers of the regular army who had become unfit for duty, either after twenty years' service or as the result of wounds. Popular legend, for which there is no jot of evidence, asserts that the King's unaristocratic mistress, Nell Gwynne, influenced him to found the hospital for his common soldiers. It is based on nothing more than the romantic belief that she had a warm heart and an eye for a smart uniform.

In fact such a foundation had become an urgent practical necessity, even without the influence of tender-hearted Nell Gwynne. England had no standing army before the Commonwealth. Its re-establishment by Charles revived the problem of how to provide for invalided soldiers and veterans. Private alms-houses and poor relief were no longer adequate to look after the numbers of those broken in their King's wars.

Louis XIV had solved the problem for France by founding the Hôtel des Invalides in Paris in 1670. Charles's illegitimate son, the Duke of Monmouth, visited Les Invalides twice and wrote commendatory accounts of it for his father. There was an element of keeping up with the Bourbons in the foundation of the Royal Hospital, as there was in much Stuart policy.

The site chosen as the sanctuary where England's old soldiers could fade away in comfort was a triangle of thirty acres, with the Thames as hypotenuse, beside the Physic Garden. James I, that pedantic but narrow-minded theologian, had founded Chelsea College on the site as a theological college. However his theology had been interrupted by the English Revolution and his buildings had fallen into ruins.

Charles II was, as usual, imbued with good intentions but chronically short of money. He could raise only £7,000 to contribute to the Hospital. But Sir Stephen Fox, who had served as Paymaster-General for many years and still controlled the Pay Office through one of his sons, bought the property out of his own pocket and undertook complete financial responsibility for the management of the future Hospital. He surrendered to the Hospital his huge commission of fourpence in the pound deducted from Army pay, which had been granted to him in return for his services in raising money for the Army. The name of this public-spirited private citizen has more right to be engraved on the stones of the Royal Hospital than the names of the various monarchs who supported his sacrifices from the touch-lines.

Since its beginning the management of the Hospital has been vested in a Board of Commissioners appointed directly by the Crown. Since Stephen Fox took on the job, the Paymaster-General has always been chairman.

Sir Christopher Wren, the King's Surveyor-General of Works, was responsible for designing and building the infirmary. He began in 1682 by building the great four-storey quadrangle known as Figure Court facing the Thames and open to the gardens and the river. The plan followed the lines of Christ Church, Oxford, and was originally intended to be large enough to house all Army pensioners. But James II expanded the Army while Figure Court was still being built, and Wren accordingly designed Light Horse Court and College (originally Infirmary) Court on either side of it. The building was completed in the reign of William and Mary with some subsidiary buildings, most of which have since been pulled down. The first Chelsea Pensioners, four hundred and seventy-six non-commissioned officers and men, then moved in. John Evelyn noted in his *Diary* that they would live 'as in a college or monastery'.

The colonnade in Figure Court is surmounted by a cornice with the Latin inscription:

'In subsidium et levamen, emeritorum senio, belloque fractorum, condidit Carolus Secundus, auxit Jacobus Secundus, perfecere Guliemus et Maria, rex et regina—MDCXCII.' (This hospital for the support and relief of old soldiers retired because of age or broken in war was founded by Charles II,

expanded by James II, and completed by King William and Queen Mary
—1692).

The northern range of Figure Court contains the great hall and the chapel,
characteristic and spectacular examples of Wren's finest interiors. In the side
ranges the In-Pensioners live in the Long Wards, with small but ship-shape
cubicles six feet by nine feet in size arranged in long rows back to back.

A magnificent statue of Charles II, improbably dressed as a Roman
emperor, stands in the centre of Figure Court. It is the work of Grinling
Gibbons and was presented to Charles by his devoted personal servant,
Tobias Rustat, an under-keeper of the royal palace of Hampton Court. The
statue was originally and grandiosely gilded, but it was bronzed in 1787.
Each year on Founder's Day, May 29, Charles's statue is dressed with oak
branches and leaves in memory of the old hollow oak near Boscobel, and the
Chelsea Pensioners parade to cheer their royal founder.

About four hundred and fifty 'In-Pensioners' live in the Hospital at
present. On entering the Hospital an old soldier surrenders his army pension,
and receives in return board and lodging, uniform, a pint of beer a day or
tobacco in lieu, and a small allowance of money. Nearly a hundred thousand
Army 'Out-Pensioners' survive on their pensions in the harsh world outside
the Royal Hospital.

The Chelsea Pensioners are still organized on military lines in six companies under their Governor, Lieutenant-Governor, and other retired
officers. Their uniform of scarlet coat and ceremonial tricorn hat is a modernized version of the service dress worn by Marlborough's armies.

Originally the Royal Hospital was renowned for its magnificent formal
gardens sweeping down to the river. These were dug up and encroached on
when the Embankment was built. The Chelsea Flower Show, that annual
apotheosis of the delphinium, the strawberry, and all other plants, is held in
what remains of the grounds.

Ranelagh Gardens, now incorporated in the Hospital grounds, were once
a popular place of public amusement. They were laid out in the grounds of
the Earl of Ranelagh and encompassed the Great Rotunda, a stately pleasure
dome one hundred and fifty feet in diameter. An orchestra played in the
centre, while the public sat in boxes around the orchestra or promenaded
around the perimeter, listening to the music and inspecting each other for
the famous and the fashionable.

The old pleasure garden was closed in 1804. The modern Ranelagh is a
club at Barn Elms on the south bank of the river where polo and other outdoor games are played.

The National Army Museum was opened in 1971 in the grounds of the
Royal Hospital. It exhibits with all the attractive modern tricks and techniques of museum display uniforms, weapons, and other military objects

illustrating the history of the regular Army from its beginning in the six-teenth century to the early twentieth century. The history shown in the museum breaks off abruptly and illogically at 1914, handing over from that point to the Imperial War Museum in Lambeth. This gives the not entirely erroneous impression that in 1914 something terrible happened to the British Army, which thereafter was changed utterly and ceased to exist except in another building.

The National Army Museum is the place where collectors of the curious can inspect the skeleton of Napoleon's favourite charger, Marengo, looking remarkably fit considering that he has shed all his flesh and had a silver plate fastened to his scapula asserting: 'Wilmott fecit London Hospital.' Other engaging curiosities among the mass of military exhibits include: Welling-ton's travelling shaving-mirror; Florence Nightingale's lamp; the blood-stained saw used to amputate the Earl of Uxbridge's leg on the field of Waterloo; and some of the cartridges, impregnated not, as it happens, with cows' or pigs' fat but with sheep tallow, that sparked the fuse of the Indian Mutiny.

On the Embankment, on the boundary of the Royal Hospital grounds beside Chelsea Bridge, there is a fine bronze war memorial by Adrian Jones to those Carabiniers (Sixth Dragoon Guards) who were killed in the South African War of 1899–1902. The central panel portrays in bas-relief dis-mounted Carabiniers scouting over a kopje.

Opposite Chelsea on the south bank lies Battersea, which since 1965 has been incorporated into the London Borough of Wandsworth. It is generally the case in central London that the districts on the south bank of the Thames are meaner, architecturally poorer, and more heavily industrialized than those on the north bank. An historical explanation of this development is that until the first Westminster Bridge was opened in 1749, the only crossings of the Thames were by London Bridge and the ferries. The south bank was a less convenient place to live. London and Westminster therefore expanded along the north bank, particularly during the seventeenth and eighteenth centuries. The south bank was less developed until the new bridges, tunnels, and railways were built across the river in the nineteenth century. Then the industrial revolution and the Victorian terraced houses for those who worked in its factories spilled across and proliferated over the comparatively empty south bank.

Battersea is no exception to this theory. Hardly a shadow of the original village on the marshy bank of the Thames survives. Battersea Park and Festival Gardens and Fun Fair extend for two hundred acres of the river bank along Chelsea reach, forming one of the largest open spaces in south London. Like most of the south bank, this was originally swamp, flooded at each high tide. Battersea marsh was drained in the sixteenth century and became a common in the Manor of Battersea, noted for its variety of birds and wild flowers. On its southern fringe market-gardens were started, and in them the first cultivated asparagus in England is supposed to have been grown. In the summer gypsies camped on the common, which became known as Battersea Fields; and Captain Thomas Blood hid in the reeds by the river, hoping to put a bullet in Charles II as he bathed in the Thames off Battersea Fields. The celebrated duel between the Duke of Wellington and the Earl of Winchester took place there in 1829.

There was a weekly fair on Sundays in Battersea Fields, which, according to a demure local historian, was notorious for 'horse-racing, donkey riding, boxing, and all the paraphernalia of a pleasure-fair with its concomitant evils'.

The central attraction was the Red House, which used to stand near the present Chelsea Bridge with a jetty for river passengers. This inn was a popular resort of London gentry, who came up river to Battersea for the pigeon-shooting and the local whores. In its heyday the inn was also famous for its breakfasts of flounders caught in the Thames and its sucking-pig dinners.

Sportsmen could buy pigeons at fifteen shillings a dozen and starlings at four shillings a dozen as targets on the large private shooting ground. Henry Mayhew, in his pioneering sociological study *London Labour and the London Poor*, describes how costermongers from the East End used to wait outside the shooting ground with dogs trained to retrieve birds that fell outside the hoarding and guns to shoot whatever escaped the customers inside. The Red House acquired such a notable reputation for gambling, fortune-telling, and amatory activities that the kill-joy government closed it.

In 1846 an Act was passed authorizing Her Majesty's Commissioners of Woods to form a royal park in three hundred and twenty acres of Battersea Fields at a cost not to exceed £200,000. The fields were drained between 1853 and 1858, and their level raised by piling on them a million cubic yards of soil from the Victoria Dock in Canning Town, which was being excavated at the time. The cost of embanking and laying out the park was met by the sale of part of the ground for building.

In 1951, as part of the celebrations connected with the Festival of Britain and the supposed end of wartime austerity, the Fun Fair and Pleasure Gardens were laid out in Battersea Park. There was considerable and sanctimonious opposition to the scheme at the time, mainly from people who lived north of the river. They argued that a pleasant asylum in the heart of London, where people could take exercise, fresh air, and glimpses of the changing seasons, would be violated by the din and crowds of a fun fair. The need for grass walks, fresh air, and relief from the dust and noise of the street was at least as great now as it was in Victorian times, when the park was made. All would be wrecked by the invasion of a fun fair and its customers.

Supporters of the scheme replied that their critics were speaking for class interest, and were seeking to ban the simple, noisy pleasures of the people. The critics replied in Parliament and on that tribal notice-board of the ruling classes, the correspondence columns of *The Times*, that by turnstile standards dirt-tracks or greyhound racing would be 'popular', if they were permitted in Hyde Park or Kensington Gardens.

Nevertheless Herbert Morrison persisted with his pet project, which has now become as much of a landmark as the old Red House among the vulgar and innocent pleasures of Londoners. More than a million people visit the Fun Fair annually to enjoy the dodgems and the hurly-burly of the round-abouts, the sad tricks of the performing dolphins, and the nausea of the Big Dipper.

Since 1948 the park has been the site for an annual exhibition of outdoor sculpture. It contains a group of *Three Women* by Henry Moore, 1947–8, one of the most important recent pieces of open air statuary in London.

Beside Battersea Park rise the four stately chimneys of one of the cathedrals of modern industrial architecture and one of the landmarks of the river, Battersea Power Station. White smoke seethes continuously from the smoke-stacks, which are only fifteen feet short of the cross on top of St Paul's Cathedral. After a few yards the smoke changes colour to dun and creates a phenomenon known to euphemizers on the Central Electricity Generating Board as 'plume droop'. This is another name for the infamous Battersea fog, which irritates the throats and soils the washing of neighbours of the power station. It is one of the few power stations in the world in which flue gases are washed to remove their sulphur dioxide content. After the gases have done their work in the boilers, they are passed through Thames water and then sent along wooden scrubber boards, over which alkali salts are passed, to take out the final traces of sulphur oxides. By-products of this process are plume droop and a district heating scheme that supplies hot water to thousands of homes in Pimlico.

The most famous power station in the world was easily the largest in Europe when it was built between 1929 and 1935. Sir Giles Gilbert Scott designed the exterior of this finest of power stations; its vast turbine hall and other intestine engineering were the work of Sir Leonard Pearce, the engineer-in-chief of the old London Power Company.

The oldest half of Battersea Power Station, the 'A' generating station, is obsolescent and will shortly be closed. The brickwork of the two-hundred-foot-high towers on which the two west chimneys stand is deteriorating. But the 'A' station has a small capacity by modern standards. The 'B' station, which was finally completed in 1956, will continue to belch smoke majestic-ally into the Battersea sky and to dominate the south bank of this reach of the river.

Only a shadow of the old village of Battersea beside the river remains. The parish church of St Mary was mentioned in *Domesday Book*, and the present classical brick building with a spire on the site overlooking a quiet reach of the river was begun in 1775. It is not a particularly memorable building, but like most old churches in London it owns peculiar felicities; for instance, the monument of Edward Wynter, died 1686, which records in relief and rhyme two of Mr Wynter's dashing adventures:

> Alone unarmed a Tigre he opprest
> And crushed to death ye Monster of a Beast.
> Thrice-twenty mounted Moors he overthrew
> Singly on foot, some wounded, some he slew,
> Dispers'd ye rest; what more could Samson do?

The finest historic building in Battersea, indeed, arguably, the only historic building in Battersea besides the power station is Old Battersea House, formerly known as 'The Terrace House'. Battersea's outstanding ancient monument was built in 1699 in the style of Wren upon the foundations of a Tudor house. The big house, now blocked from the river by Dickensian warehouses, has a history of genteel dereliction and decay. It became a girls' school in the nineteenth century, and then the principal's house of a teacher training college. In 1930 it was threatened with demolition, but saved by being scheduled as a building of architectural and historic interest. It was then let to Colonel and Mrs Charles Stirling, who filled it with one of the largest collections of Pre-Raphaelite ceramics and paintings ever accumulated: chiefly pottery by William De Morgan and paintings in the late and highly symbolic Pre-Raphaelite style by his wife, Evelyn De Morgan, who understandably refused to exhibit any of her work for some twenty years before her death.

When they died, Colonel and Mrs Stirling left their amazing collection, much admired by *cognoscenti* of the late Pre-Raphaelites, on trust to the nation. In 1969 Wandsworth Council decided to restore the house, which was gravely threatened by dry rot, dilapidation, and vandals. However, examination showed that its condition was worse than had been feared and would cost more than the Council was prepared to spend. Once again the future of the best surviving house of its period in south London looked short and gloomy. But at the last minute Malcolm Forbes, a philanthropic, Anglophile, cultured, and rich American magazine publisher came to the rescue. He has spent more than £100,000 reinstating Old Battersea House and has taken a ninety-nine-year lease of it for a peppercorn rent from Wandsworth Council. Mr Forbes and his family and friends use the first and second floors as their home when they visit London. The ground floor is opened to the public as the museum and gallery of the prolific De Morgan collections.

After the power station, the best known institution in the overgrown village of Battersea is the Battersea Dogs' Home. This phenomenon has become a national institution, and as stock a signal for laughter as that infallible incantation, mother-in-law, on music hall stages and then television screens. Something like 18,000 lost and distressed dogs are taken into the home every year. Something like 10,000 of them have to be exterminated in Battersea's 'Electrothanator Unit', either because they are not claimed by their owners, or because they cannot be sold, or because they are diseased. The Dogs' Home is in fact more of a final solution than a home for most of its inmates, and makes a curiously ambivalent stigma to beat the traditional dogma that Britain is a nation of hardened and shameless dog-lovers.

The Home was founded in 1860 by Mary Tealby, the caniphilist wife of a timber merchant from Hull. Walking one day by Charing Cross Mrs Tealby was filled with pity and terror by the numbers of sick, stray, and diseased dogs collected there. She at once picked up four of them and took them to her home in Holloway. This piece of Victorian maternalism led her to found 'The Temporary Home for Lost and Starving Dogs'. Within three years she was rescuing 10,000 dogs a year. Her small mews in Holloway was becoming overcrowded and the neighbours began to complain. Accordingly in 1871 she acquired the present site of the Dogs' Home and removed, dog and doggage, to Battersea. Since then more than 2,250,000 dogs have passed through Mrs Tealby's doors on the way to a better life or decent death. There are usually about three hundred dogs in residence at the home and more at Christmas. The worst year for strays was 1896, when local councils introduced muzzling as a protection against rabies and 46,614 stray dogs were taken into care by the home. The largest class of stray dogs at Battersea consists of mongrels, followed closely by Alsatians (a hundred a month) and Labradors (fifty a month). The Dogs' Home has no animal prejudice and, in addition to the dogs, houses a thousand cats a year and the sporadic rabbit.

Much of the industrial waterfront of Battersea is old or derelict. Within the next few years large areas on either side of Battersea Bridge will need to be rehabilitated and redeveloped. If the planners have the courage of their convictions, many of the factories and warehouses looking over the Thames, which do not have to be there for the water, will be replaced by houses, flats, and offices, and Battersea will be able to face Chelsea as an equal and no longer as a poor, ugly sister.

Across Chelsea Bridge on the left bank is another surviving small dock and, beside it, a romantic edifice with a tower, arches, and circular windows rather like a Loire château. It is in fact the Western Pumping Station of London's sewage system. Sir Nikolaus Pevsner, the great and judicious purist, condemns it for its Frenchy windows and its Frenchy roof. However it is an engaging and frivolous quality in an important building in London's sewage system to have such architectural pretensions.

Beyond Chelsea Bridge the north bank becomes the tight little enclave of

Pimlico, and the road beside the river becomes Grosvenor Road. Pimlico is said to derive its name from a Tudor inn-keeper called Ben Pimlico, who kept an inn in the old village of Hoxton, since submerged in north-east London, and whose beer was evidently famous. The favourite source of this derivation is found in a tract of 1598 called *Newes from Hogsdon*: 'Have at ye then, my merrie boyes, and hey for old Ben Pimlico's nut browne.' The name somehow transmigrated across London to the locality lying between Belgravia and the Thames.

The riverside here is occupied by the most famous and influential municipal housing estate in London. When Westminster City Council started to build Churchill Gardens in 1946 it was the first development in England of blocks of flats grouped into tall slabs and terraces. The London County Council and other local authorities followed Westminster's example with enthusiasm. Consequently they have altered the sky-lines of London and most other large towns in Britain more in the past twenty-five years than they had been altered in the previous two thousand. About five thousand slab-dwellers now live in the handsome blocks and towers of Churchill Gardens, which had such a seminal and deplorable effect on the landscape and quality of life of Britain.

Next along the embankment rises the lumpish and vast fortress of Dolphin Square, the largest self-contained block of flats in Europe. It contains one thousand, two hundred luxury flats and covers seven and a half acres. The flats are comfortable and expensive, being served with restaurants, swimming pools, and hot and cold running chamber maids. But it is difficult to see the exterior of Dolphin Square as anything but a grandiose blot on the riverside.

Pimlico Gardens are another patch of green beside the river. The marble statue of a man dressed in a Roman toga and holding a scroll is of William Huskisson, the Tory statesman, Free Trader, and disciple of Canning. He is now best remembered by schoolchildren for the spectacular accident of his death: he was run over by the *Rocket* at the opening of the Liverpool and Manchester Railway in 1830. *The Dictionary of National Biography* remarks, unsympathetically: 'Huskisson, by nature uncouth and hesitating in his motions, had a peculiar aptitude for accident.' There was more to Huskisson, however, than his sensational death. William Lamb, later Lord Melbourne, told Greville that in his opinion Huskisson was the greatest practical statesman he had known, the one who best united theory with practice. Greville as usual scribbled it down that night in his little red book.

The original Vauxhall Bridge was made of iron and erected between 1811 and 1816. It was superseded in 1906 by the present bridge, which is unique among London bridges by being decorated with statuary. A bronze figure, representing some beneficent human occupation, presides over the pier of every arch. The traveller down-stream can recognize, if he has a lively imagination, starting from the north bank: Agriculture, holding a scythe;

Architecture, a woman holding a model of St Paul's; Engineering, holding a steam engine; and Pottery, holding an urn. The traveller up-stream sees, starting from the north bank: a woman variously designated as Learning or Local Government; Education; the Fine Arts; and Astronomy. They were sculptured by F. W. Pomeroy and Alfred Drury working as a team.

Beyond Vauxhall Bridge the road along the north bank is called Millbank, after the old Westminster Abbey mill. This was mentioned in the rate-books from 1565 and used for water supply in the seventeenth century.

The Tate Gallery is an appropriately saccharine piece of architecture in the late Victorian grand manner for the gift of a great Victorian sugar merchant. Sir Henry Tate gave it to the nation in 1897, and Britannia with trident and tin hat sits regally and fatuously above the giant Corinthian portico, facing the Thames, like Impatience on a monument. The Tate houses magnificent collections both of modern art and of the work of British artists. It is being enlarged and extended, but it is arguable that it would be an even greater and certainly a more coherent gallery if it were allowed to concentrate on one or other of its two vast roles.

The Tate stands on the site of the old Millbank Penitentiary, which was opened in 1816 and closed in 1890. This great and grim prison covered eighteen acres, and comprised one thousand, one hundred single cells built around a honeycomb of courts. A contemporary compared it to a Continental fortified château. A bollard from the head of the prison's river steps has been kept on Millbank as a melancholy memento of the thousands of convicts sentenced to transportation, who left England for ever down those steps on the way to Australia.

Vickers's office block on Millbank is one of the largest and most spectacular erections of modern architecture on the river. The headquarters and monument of one of Britain's greatest industrial corporations was finished in 1963, culminating in a shining black tower thirty-two storeys and 387 feet high. This catches the light and reflects different geometric patterns at different times of day and from different aspects of the river. The old-fashioned consider it a disfiguring excrescence on one of the finest reaches of the river and a deplorable memorial to the brutal architecture of the century of machine-made man. A. P. Herbert complained bitterly that what he described as this monstrous glass giraffe was allowed to stick its shimmering neck out of the modest jungle of Westminster between the Tate and Barry's neo-Gothic Victoria Tower. However modernists find it exciting and infinitely preferable to the range of plain, rectangular office blocks on the opposite bank and the inhuman gigantism of the Shell buildings in the next reach downstream.

There was for centuries a ferry at Lambeth. This was replaced in 1862 by what was generally agreed to be the cheapest bridge ever built across the Thames, and what Dickens described as 'perhaps, on the whole, the ugliest ever built'. This was replaced in 1932 by the present Lambeth Bridge, which is guarded at either end by enigmatic twin sentinels of obelisks supporting objects like pineapples in large egg-cups.

On the south embankment once stood Vauxhall or Fox Hall Gardens, which were one of London's chief open air entertainment places in the eighteenth century. They are said to have derived their name from Falkes de Breauté, the notorious captain of King John's mercenaries and lord of the manor in the early thirteenth century. Falkes was described by an impartial and judicious historian as 'a greedy, cruel, and overbearing man of mean and illegitimate birth; able, unscrupulous, and godless'. He gained the favour of John by laying waste the eastern counties and burning the suburbs of London in 1215, when war broke out with the Barons.

The gardens were laid out on the south bank in the middle of the seventeenth century and were originally called the New Spring Gardens, because they replaced the old Spring Gardens adjacent to St James's Park, now covered by Buckingham Palace and its grounds. The gardens became famous for their entertainments and visitors: there were some of questionable character, and others about whom there could be no question at all. Writers and dramatists from Evelyn and Pepys onwards referred to them *passim*. Sir Roger de Coverley visited them with Mr Spectator, on one of their jaunts to enliven morality with wit, and to temper wit with morality, and commented on the scarcity of nightingales in the gardens as compared with less desirable visitors. Horace Walpole wrote to his cousin: 'If you had never seen it [Vauxhall], I would make you a most pompous description of it, and tell you how the floor is all of beaten princes—that you can't set your foot without treading on a Prince of Wales or Duke of Cumberland.'

A poetaster, masquerading under the ambitious Spenserian pseudonym of Colin Clout, wrote in 1741:

> Oh Mary! soft in feature,
> I've been at dear Vauxhall;
> No paradise is sweeter—
> Not that they Eden call.
> At night, such new vagaries,
> Such gay and harmless sport;
> All looked like giant fairies,
> And this the monarch's court.

He carries on for many panegyrical and fatuous stanzas, which nevertheless make it clear that the Spring Gardens, Vauxhall, were a grand place for giant fairies or anyone else on a night out.

The gardens were closed in the middle of the nineteenth century and they and their neighbouring district of Nine Elms were heavily submerged beneath the great Victorian industrial and railway building boom. Nine Elms was once the terminus of the Southern Region railway lines out of London. The main lines out of Victoria and Waterloo now cross this small industrialized pocket of south London. Derelict railway land here is being developed as the new site for Covent Garden market, the largest wholesale market in the country. The move has taken the old sweet smell of flowers, fruit and rotten vegetables from the present Covent Garden in the heart of London to a new and efficient market complex at Nine Elms. It has a new railhead and spacious roads for the lorries that entangled the old market in the most convoluted traffic jams in London. The new Covent Garden is far more efficient, but the curious old vegetable chaos with its ancient flavours is sadly missed from central London, except by those who have to do business in the market.

The Borough of Lambeth was for centuries the colony of Cockneys south of the river. Cockney is derived from *coken-ey*, 'cock's-egg' in Middle English, presumably signifying a puny and misshapen egg. It came to mean 'a cockered child': somebody small, effeminate, and a milksop. It was used derisively by strapping countrymen to describe stunted and undernourished townees. The Londoners adopted it with pride.

The backbone of the old Cockney kingdom of Lambeth used to be Lambeth Walk, the famous old street market that runs parallel to the river behind Lambeth Bridge and Lambeth Palace. On Bank Holidays and Sundays fifty years ago the medical students used to parade down Lambeth Walk dressed as clowns, collecting pennies for St Thomas's Hospital. It was so crowded that they had to force their way through like ice-breakers. Today orange papers and onion skins are blown along the empty pavement and one of the most famous thoroughfares in London has sunk under redevelopment. A vast congeries of construction has cut Lambeth Walk in half and is spreading slowly over the rest of the area.

Seas of concrete and mountains of bricks are as alien as a lunar landscape in the middle of the old street market, which many who have never set foot south of the river still think of, erroneously, as the heart of Cockney London. Strictly and originally a Cockney was born within hearing of Bow Bells, that is in the City or its immediate eastern suburbs. John Stow nowhere mentions this picturesque notion, which is exactly the kind of useless information that appealed to his antiquarian bent. Accordingly it is likely that the tradition originated after his death in 1605.

In the eighteenth century Lambeth Walk was the site of Lambeth Wells, source of mineral waters, musical entertainment, and, no doubt, traditional Cockney wit. After the Walk was made in the nineteenth century it became a general street market, with hundreds of stalls lining both sides all the way from Black Prince Road past Old Paradise Street to the equally sweet-sounding terraces of China Walk.

A medical student at St Thomas's named William Maugham brought the life of Lambeth Walk to the attention of the outside world in *Lisa of Lambeth*, published in 1897. Maugham went on to become the most successful middle-brow author of modern literature. That unbending highbrow, Edmund Wilson, summed him up coldly as 'a half-trashy novelist, who writes badly but is patronized by half-serious readers, who do not care much about writing'. Maugham moved east from Lambeth to Somersetland, that peculiar archipelago where a Pacific sun is always setting purple beyond the atoll, and on the veranda sweating men in double-brimmed terai hats sip gin slings and lust gloomily after mysterious and sophisticated women with guilty secrets. There is a case to be made that his best and most honest work was about Lambeth.

Lupino Lane in *Me and My Girl* at the Victoria Palace in 1939 gave the final touch to the legend of Lambeth Walk and had the whole town singing and dancing:

> Any time you're Lambeth way,
> Any evening, any day,
> You'll find us all doin' the Lambeth Walk—hoy.

The manor of Lambeth belonged to the Archbishops of Canterbury since the end of the twelfth century. Some of Lambeth Palace was built by Archbishop Boniface in 1262, and the whole of it is an attractive and irregular complex of medieval domestic buildings. The great hall with its magnificent hammerbeam roof was rebuilt by Archbishop Juxon after it had been destroyed during the Commonwealth. It has been converted into one of the finest libraries in London, stocked with the rare books, tracts, and manuscripts of the Church of England. Evelyn, Pepys and other hardened sight-seers often visited Lambeth Palace, the home even after the Reformation of one of the great princes of the realm. But it is not on the modern tourist track, perhaps because it is situated on the *terra incognita* of the south bank.

Next door the Italianate blocks and arcades of old St Thomas's Hospital have been replaced by new buildings. Florence Nightingale advised on the construction of the nineteenth-century hospital, which was segregated into separate blocks for reasons of hygiene.

The river has now emerged from its foiled, circuitous wanderings through the suburbs into the heart of Westminster. Ahead lies the first sight of the domes and towers of the City. Opposite to St Thomas's, on the left bank, stands the best-known building in Britain, a cliché of calendars and post-cards, and the pictorial symbol of London instantly recognized from China to Peru.

CHAPTER SIX

Westminster to Blackfriars, and South Bank

WESTMINSTER means 'the monastic church to the west', a description clearly given to it by Londoners living in the Saxon city a mile to the east. Like other districts of Greater London, Westminster has developed in the way that it has because of its location on the Thames. For example, the rich alluvial soil and the convenience of the river for transport made the Middlesex bank higher up suitable for market gardens, fragments of which still subsist among the monstrous overgrowth of brick and concrete.

In an analogous way the district now called Westminster evolved over the centuries from a low-lying, marshy area that was flooded at high tide, making the Thames more than a mile wide. At low tide the water was shallow, and archaeologists have found evidence that there was a ford here from a very early date. Rows of stakes that guided travellers across the shallows have been discovered preserved in Thames mud. This was one of the first crossings of the Thames when the Romans arrived, and before they built their bridge a mile down-stream at London. Westminster was of strategic and commercial importance because of this crossing. It was inaccessible and unfertile because of the marshes. It was close to London. In the middle a sandy island called Thorneye, 'the eyot or isle of thorn', protruded above the Thames at all tides. It was a good place for a monastery, secluded from settlements and farms but at an important crossroads for traffic.

On this prime site a church and monastery were founded, probably early in the seventh century. The marvellous legend tells how Mellitus, a noble Anglo-Roman, was consecrated the first Bishop of London, and persuaded Sebert, King of the East Saxons, to build a church on Thorneye. The church was built and due to be consecrated to St Peter on a Sunday morning in A.D. 616. On the eve of the dedication a fisherman ferried over from Lambeth to Thorneye a mysterious stranger, who, it transpired, must have been none other than another fisherman from the Lake of Galilee, St Peter himself. His ferryman saw the new church brilliantly illuminated in the middle of the night and heard choirs singing with sweeter than human voices. On the return journey St Peter told the fisherman to inform Mellitus that the church had already been consecrated by its patron in person. And he rewarded him with a record catch of salmon, promising him that he and his successors would always have good fishing, if they abstained from Sunday fishing and paid tithe of all they caught to St Peter's Church on Thorneye.

The legend, naturally, has no historical foundation. But it is significant for the message that those who spread it wished to establish: that St Peter's at Westminster was as old as St Paul's in London; that it was independent of episcopal authority other than that of the first Bishop of Rome, St Peter himself; and that the monks of Westminster were entitled to a tithe of fish caught in the Thames.

Edward the Confessor, the Saint and the last of the Saxon Kings, and a key figure in the development of the English monarchy, built a great new church and his palace at Westminster near the site of the original church, which had been destroyed by the Danes. It was consecrated to St Peter in 1065, and a few days later Edward was buried in front of the altar. From that event Westminster derived its importance as the chief stage and Holy of Holies of the monarchy. William the Conqueror, who based his claim to the English crown on an alleged gift by Edward when he was living in exile in Normandy, legitimated his conquest by having himself crowned at Westminster. He had to surround the Abbey with armed troops to protect himself from his reluctant new subjects. Every King and Queen since William has been legitimated by being crowned in Westminster Abbey, except for Edward V, who was presumed murdered before his coronation, and Edward VIII, who preferred Mrs Wallis Simpson before his.

Most of the early Kings and Queens, and their families and chief magnates were buried in the Abbey. It was also the stage for royal marriages and great national celebrations. For three centuries Parliaments met in its Chapter House, which is therefore the cradle of Parliamentary government in Britain and the Commonwealth. For example, Simon de Montfort's seminal Parliament of 1265, which drastically limited the power of the monarchy and thus sowed the seeds of Parliamentary democracy, though the seeds were a long time germinating, sat in the Chapter House.

Edward IV wrote a letter to the Pope in 1478 that conspicuously expressed the view of the monastery church of Westminster as the national shrine of the monarchy. He wrote of the Church as 'placed before the eyes of the whole world of Englishmen', and told the Pope that any favour that he granted to Westminster would be 'welcome to all of English blood'.

Edward the Confessor's palace at Westminster beside his Abbey has been twice burnt down and twice rebuilt. But the Houses of Parliament are still formally a royal palace. In the early centuries Westminster was just one of a large number of palaces in regular use as the King and his court travelled continually around the kingdom to keep the peace, show the flag, keep an eye on the marches and the Barons, dispense justice, and collect rents and taxes. It was an important palace because of its proximity to London; but in

London itself such palaces as the Tower and Baynard Castle were also in regular use.

It is possible to derive a tantalizingly imprecise impression of what the ancient settlement of Westminster was like from the medieval account Rolls, and from contemporary descriptions in prose and verse. A jumble of buildings stood between Westminster Hall and the river, surrounded on the landward side by a wall and connected to the Abbey by an underground passage. The King slept in St Edward's Painted Chamber. Geoffrey Chaucer, who was Clerk of the King's Works at various palaces including Westminster, described in the *Book of the Duchesse* the surprisingly luxurious sleeping quarters of a courtier:

> and sooth to seyn my chambre was
> Full well depeynted and with glas
> Were all the windows well y glased.
> and alle the walles with colour fyne
> were peynted bothe text and glose
> of al the Romaunce of the Rose.

The bed was equally sumptuous:

> I will yive him a fether bed
> Rayed with golde and right wel cled
> In fyn blak satin doutremere
> and many a pilow.

The perpetual motion of the court came to an end with the strong centralized monarchy based on London introduced by the Tudors. The medieval palace of Westminster was partly burnt down and largely dilapidated by the sixteenth century. It was neither luxurious nor magnificent enough to satisfy the megalomania of Henry VIII, who removed his residence at Westminster to Cardinal Wolsey's grand new London palace next door, which he renamed Whitehall. However, those two ancient functions of the monarchy, Parliament and the Law Courts, remained behind in Westminster Palace. Parliament is still there, on the site of the oldest extant palace of the English monarchy.

The residential parts of the palace soon disappeared from the north bank of the Thames and men's memory. By Elizabeth's reign John Norden, the antiquary, could write that Westminster had once been the chief residence of the king, 'though now brought to the ground, and green grass grows where it stood. The place which now carrieth the name of the Old Palace showeth itself to have been in times past full of buildings.'

Only three significant parts of the medieval palace have survived until today. They are: the crypt of St Stephen's Chapel, known as St Mary's Undercroft, where tradition asserts that Cromwell stabled his horses; the fourteenth-century Jewel Tower with its moat filled with trout, built to house the king's personal treasure but now restored and converted into a fine little museum; and Westminster Hall, one of the greatest buildings in England. The Hall, once the home of Parliaments, Law Courts, coronation feasts, and other great national assemblies, is so large, draughty, and un-furnishable that unfortunately it is seldom used today, except as an imposing thoroughfare for Members of Parliament and their visitors. It is sometimes still filled for some great secular gathering. But the assembled modern dignitaries look out-of-place and ill-at-ease in such a tremendous arena, haunted by the ghosts of England's past.

The whole Palace of Westminster resonates with echoes of the great men of politics, the law, the church, and the palace. In the resonance the memory of the extraordinary men who made no speeches but worked behind the scenes of Westminster is blotted out. Men, for example, like Henry Yevele, the architect and master mason, and Hugh Herland, the master carpenter, are relegated to footnotes in the majestic history of Westminster. But in the late fourteenth century they rebuilt Westminster Hall with a mighty hammer-beam roof that makes it one of the marvels of English Gothic architecture.

The Hall was originally begun in 1097 by order of William Rufus, the disagreeable son of William the Conqueror, as part of the work undertaken to enable the royal capital to be transferred from Winchester to London. Its size, about two hundred and forty feet long by seventy feet wide, made it a huge building for its time, as much of a wonder to contemporaries as the Empire State Building was nine centuries later. Originally it was divided into a central nave and parallel aisles supporting a more modest roof.

Richard II, that patron of arts and continental fashion, whose extravagance so outraged the avarice and philistinism of his nobles that they eventually deprived him of his throne, embarked on extensive and expensive rebuilding at Westminster, as at his other palaces. Henry Yevele, director of the king's works at Westminster, rebuilt and reinforced Rufus's masonry, in particular introducing the corbels and flying buttresses of Caen stone to support the great roof. This reconstruction removed the double row of wooden pillars down the centre of the Norman Hall, so making it for many centuries the largest and most spacious room in Europe.

Hugh Herland designed the revolutionary carpentry and built the great roof that spans more than sixty-seven feet in a single, soaring leap. Oak beams two and a quarter feet wide and twenty-three feet long were felled, denuding parks and forests for miles around London. They were shaped and fitted together at a place called 'the Frame' near Farnham in Surrey, then taken apart again, and carted and shipped by the Thames to West-minster. An artist called Robert Grassington carved the mighty angels at the ends of the hammer-beams, and, according to the chronicler, 'he set the cherubim within the inner house and the wings of the cherubim were stretched forth'.

Vertical timber supports begin near the top of the original eleventh-century walls. The horizontal hammer-beams, more than three feet by two feet thick, protrude about twenty feet to roughly where the old side aisle arcading must have been, and are supported by finely moulded curving braces and the tops of the walls. From the hammer-beams spring the vertical posts that carry the main weight of the roof, and at their ends fly Grassington's carved cherubim with shields.

The Royal Commission on historical monuments, consistently careful in its judgements, rates the Hall as 'probably the finest timber roofed building in Europe'. In addition, it is an overwhelmingly strong candidate for the title of the most historic building in England, and the richest in symbolism. After old London Bridge it is the most famous building in London's long history. As the main surviving part of the ancient Palace of Westminster, it is the cradle of the monarchy. It is the nursery of Parliament and the Law, the ceremonial stage for early meetings of the Great Council and state trials like those of Charles I and Warren Hastings.

All this makes the hall a prime target for symbolic acts of sabotage. In the summer of 1974 somebody, presumably somebody with Irish connexions, exploded a bomb against the north wall, slightly damaging the mighty roof. On the night of May 10–11, 1941, the *Luftwaffe* launched the culminating attack of the Blitz upon London, in which, according to Churchill, 'the enemy lit more than two thousand fires in London'. One of the fires was the House of Commons, and, when he heard of it, Churchill sent a message to the firemen: 'Save Westminster Hall at all costs.' They did, at the cost of letting the Chamber of the House of Commons burn. Before that a bomb, presumed to have been placed in the Hall by Fenians, caused severe damage in 1885.

When the great fire burnt almost all of the old Palace of Westminster in 1834, Dean Arthur Stanley wrote that 'one prayer seemed to go up from every upturned countenance of the vast multitude, lighted up in the broad glare with more than the light of day: "Oh, save the Hall."'

The Hall, built by Yevele, Herland, and other craftsmen and artists who have left no name behind them, is the one that still stands there, largely unchanged from the lines on which they designed it, the masterpiece of English Gothic architecture. It may be tempting fate and madmen to say so, but Westminster Hall seems to be a lucky building, less troubled by the periodic violence of psychotic philistines than by the mating habits of *Xestobium tesselatum*, commonly called the death-watch beetle. The Department of the Environment fights a continual and increasingly successful campaign by smoke-bomb and timber injection against the beetles, which over the centuries have burrowed hollows in the hammer-beams large enough to hold a man. It must be a lucky building to have survived nearly nine hundred years as the chief symbolic monument in masonry and timber of that unsubstantial entity, the English constitution.

The Clerks of the House are a group of distinguished ghosts who have done more to develop Parliamentary democracy while preserving its precedents than most politicians. But they avoid the limelight. The Clerk, whose letters patent describe him as 'Under-Clerk of the Parliaments, to attend upon the Commons', is the professional administrator and expert in legislative procedure who keeps the machinery of Parliament turning. It is not only the British who consider that it turns more smoothly and satisfactorily than that of any other legislature in the world. The Clerk has to be, among other things, an expert in Parliamentary procedure of impeccable accuracy, erudition, and authority. Whenever the House slips into difficulty, as it has a tendency to do, it turns to its learned Clerk for rescue.

The most pervasive and potent spectre among the Clerks is that of the eminent Victorian, Sir Thomas Erskine May. He is still the nominal authority for all Parliamentary rule and practice, since his name appears as the author of the standard work and bible of Westminster, *Treatise on the Law, Privileges, Proceedings and Usage of Parliament*. This makes him the most remarkable of all ghost-writers, since his authoritative treatise was first written a century and a quarter ago. The name on the cover is still Erskine May, but hardly another word of his remains in the text inside. Sir Thomas's name has become a convenient appellation for the contemporary work and corporate memory of the Clerks in both houses of Parliament. From his grave in a country churchyard the old gentleman purports to have been able to describe with a prophetic eye the procedures of the North Atlantic Assembly, the Council of Europe, Western European Union, and other modern parliaments around the world. The fiction of Erskine May's posthumous authority is a polite Parliamentary practice, because it avoids the invidiousness of Members of Parliament having to defer to a living authority greater than their own: that of their erudite but modest Clerks.

The *Modus Tenendi Parliamentum*, an early account of the constitution of Parliament probably written about 1327, makes the first reference to a Clerk specially assigned to the Commons. The first appointment by letters patent of an 'Under-Clerk of the Parliaments' was that of Robert de Melton in 1363 at a salary of a hundred shillings a year. From de Melton to Sir Barnett Cocks, who retired at the end of 1973, Parliament has usually been undeservingly lucky in its Clerks, the learned ghosts in wigs and court dress in the background who have kept the Parliamentary machine working. It was said of Henry Elsyng, who was Clerk in the early years of the Long Parliament, that 'for his abilities and prudence, more reverence was paid to his stool than to the Speaker's Chair'. He was succeeded in 1649 by Henry Scobell, whose *Memorials* are the main authority for seventeenth-century procedure. In

1658 Scobell claimed to be Clerk of the 'Other House' that Cromwell substituted for the Lords, and accordingly carried away the Commons Journals so that they could not be searched. In this tricky situation the Speaker observed: 'The Clerk is gone, and you could not carry on business without one.' This was an honest but rare admission by a politician of the indispensability of Clerks to the long and successful history of what goes on in the Palace of Westminster.

One of the unhappiest and most frustrated ghosts in the phantasmagoria that haunts the Palace of Westminster is that of Sir Charles Barry, who devoted most of his working life to rebuilding the Houses of Parliament as they are today in the teeth of constant controversy, misrepresentation, and niggling interference. He was then outrageously bilked of his fair reward by the Government and their majority in the House.

The Palace of Westminster was almost totally destroyed by a fire beginning in the evening of October 16, 1834. Charles Barry, a rising young architect, saw the red glare illuminating the sky above London from the coach in which he was returning to London. As soon as the Brighton coach arrived, he hurried to Westminster to join the huge crowd of Londoners who watched the blaze all night, rapt in the grandeur of the spectacle and apocalyptic intimations.

The fire that destroyed the ancient palace was started in a trivial and ludicrous manner by workmen burning the 'tallies', the old-fashioned wooden pegs used as receipts for payments made in the Court of Exchequer for centuries after less cumbersome methods of book-keeping had been introduced elsewhere. Charles Dickens, at the time a Parliamentary reporter in the Gallery of the Commons, was also a spectator of the great fire. Later, when he had become a grand old man of literature, his description of how the Houses of Parliament came to be burnt down was a star turn in his theatrical performances.

He used to relate:

'Ages ago a savage mode of keeping accounts on notched sticks was introduced into the Court of the Exchequer, and the accounts were kept much as Robinson Crusoe kept his calendar on the desert island. In the course of considerable revolutions of time, the celebrated Cocker [Edward Cocker, a seventeenth-century mathematician and author of arithmetical textbooks] was born and died. Walkinghame [another author of text-books], of the *Tutor's Assistant*, and well versed in figures, was also born and died. Still official routine inclined to these notched sticks, as if they were pillars of the Constitution, and still the Exchequer accounts continued to be kept on certain splints of elm-wood called *tallies*. In the reign of George III an inquiry was made by some revolutionary spirit whether—pens, ink and paper, slates and pencils, being in existence—this obstinate adherence to an obsolete custom ought to be continued, and whether a change ought not to be effected. All the red-tape in the country grew redder at the bare mention of this bold and original conception, and it took till 1826 to get the sticks abolished.

'In 1834 it was found that there was a considerable accumulation of them; and the question then arose—what was to be done with such worn-out, worm-eaten, rotten old bits of wood? The sticks were housed at Westminster, and it would naturally occur to any intelligent person that nothing could be easier than to allow them to be carried away for firewood by the miserable people who live in that neighbourhood. However, they never had been useful, and official routine required that they never should be, and so the order went forth that they were to be privately and confidentially burnt. It came to pass that they were burnt in a stove in the House of Lords. The stove, overgorged with these preposterous sticks, set fire to the panelling; the panelling set fire to the House of Lords; the House of Lords set fire to the House of Commons; the two houses were reduced to ashes; architects were called in to build others; and we are now in the second million of the cost thereof; the national pig is not nearly over the stile yet; and the little old woman, Britannia, hasn't got home tonight.'

The Government held a competition for designs for a new building to house Parliament, the style to be 'Gothic or Elizabethan'. Barry's design came first of an entry of ninety-seven. His troubles then began. Unsuccessful competitors criticized the honesty of the judges, Barry's private character, the antique and venerable barbarism of the Gothic style, and the 'highly ornamented and meretricious' character of the winning design. The Prime Minister, Sir Robert Peel, said prophetically in a debate on the reconstruction that he pitied Barry as a man already 'hunted and pursued, *cui sua mortifera est victoria*'.

Parliament proceeded to appoint various independent committees with no expert knowledge but concomitantly stiff opinions to superintend certain portions of the work. Albert, the Prince Consort, was president of the Fine Arts Commission, set up to advise on the painting, sculpture, and other interior decoration of the palace. But by a curious and insulting decision, Barry himself, who knew the building better than anybody, was not included as a member of it.

The greatest difficulty was caused by the appointment of the amazing Dr D. B. Reid, who had a novel plan to ventilate and warm the palace 'by alternate blasts of hot and cold air'. This evoked an epigram:

> Peel's patronage of Dr Reid
> Is very natural indeed,
> For no one need be told

The worthy scientific man
Is acting on the Premier's plan
Of blowing hot and cold.

Naturally Barry was not consulted about the appointment of Dr Reid, 'the Ventilator', and naturally no arrangement was made about which of them should have authority over the other in matters of common interest. Apart from never showing the least signs of working, Dr Reid's pyrotechnics necessitated alteration all over the building and the construction of great ventilation shafts and towers to create sufficient upward draughts. They were designed to occupy about one-third of the entire cubic content of the building and were one of the chief reasons that the building took twenty years to finish instead of the estimated six and cost about £2,000,000 instead of the estimated £707,000.

The great bell in the clock-tower, known all over the world as Big Ben after the Commissioner of Works, Sir Benjamin Hall, later Lord Llanover, had an equally controversial and calamitous career. There was the customary protracted wrangling, jealousy, and confusion between Barry, the Commissioner, and fanatical horologists, amateur, professional, and lunatic, about its construction. The first great bell was cast at Stockton-on-Tees and cracked while it was being tested. A replacement, cast in Whitechapel and drawn over Westminster Bridge by a team of sixteen white horses, was hoisted to the top of the bell-tower before it too cracked. The clock was stopped, and controversy raged about the clock and bells that have since become a national totem of Britain. The Earl of Derby, known as the Rupert of Debate to an age with a different taste in rhetoric, declared: 'We all know the circumstances under which we have been deprived of the doubtful advantage of hearing the tones of the great bell; but when a clock ceases to address itself to the sense of hearing, that is no reason it should decline to present itself to the sense of sight. One of the hands has disappeared altogether, and the other stands at twelve; so that it has the merit of being right at least once in the twelve hours.'

When Members finally moved into their new chamber, they found the acoustics unsatisfactory. This was not surprising in an assembly where a speaker from any part of the floor, speaking in the conversational, informal style customary in the Commons, expects to be adequately heard in all other parts of the floor and galleries. They concluded on no good evidence that the ceiling was too high, and ordered Barry to lower it to a level beneath the tops of the windows. After this mutilation of his plan, Barry no longer considered the Commons chamber his own work, and never spoke of it or even went into it again unless it was impossible to avoid doing so.

The chapter of accidents is so long and melancholy that it becomes ludicrous. Perhaps fortunately Barry was prevented from redecorating

Westminster Hall as 'a British Walhalla' with frescoes, trophies, and statues. Barry wrote to the Prince Consort's commission:

'I would propose that Westminster Hall should be made the depository, as in former times, for all trophies obtained in wars with foreign nations. These trophies might be so arranged above the paintings on the walls as to have a very striking and interesting effect. I would further suggest that pedestals, twenty in number, answering to the position of the principal ribs of the roof, should be placed so as to form a central avenue, thirty feet in width, from the north entrance door to St Stephen's porch, for statues of the most celebrated British statesmen, whose public services have been commemorated by monuments erected at the public expense, as well as for present and future statesmen whose services may be considered by Parliament to merit a similar tribute to their memories.'

In addition Barry proposed that statues of famous admirals and generals should be ranged along the walls and that twenty-eight huge wall paintings 'might relate to the most splendid warlike achievements in English history both by sea and land'. Nothing came of his proposal, and now that the lawyers have left Westminster, the great hall is usually empty and underused. It is a splendidly solemn stage for the lying-in-state of great men and the attendant pompous obsequies. But it is too large, too uncomfortable, too difficult to heat, and too hard to hear in for daily use by the living. On rare and special occasions it is used for great assemblies.

The final disaster in the rebuilding of the Palace of Westminster was the way in which the Treasury and Parliament by a mixture of niggardliness and sharp practice cheated Sir Charles Barry of his proper fee. The customary architect's fee was five per cent of the cost. On Barry's estimate of £707,000 this would have worked out at more than £35,000. After Barry had been working on the new building for nineteen months, he received a letter from the Treasury and the Commissioners of the Woods and Forests (which later became the Ministry of Public Building and Works, which later became part of the Department of the Environment) suggesting that £25,000 would be 'a fair and liberal remuneration'. Barry foolishly accepted under protest, and continued protesting for the next twenty years, while the expenditure and the duration of the work increased threefold. The Treasury occasionally vouchsafed a further letter, expressing a doubt 'whether they have not taken too liberal a view of the question'—a doubt that was not widely felt outside official circles.

A few Members supported Barry. In one of the debates one of them said that no increase of expenditure or supposed architectural defects could be an excuse 'for robbing—yes! for robbing—Sir Charles Barry'.

Barry himself calculated that he had been done out of at least £20,000, excluding interest on payments that had been delayed for years. This was certainly an underestimate of the fair payment for a work that spread over twenty years, absorbed almost the whole of his time, and gradually destroyed most of his private practice. Barry died to some extent a disappointed and embittered man. The rancour of his enemies and the malignity of his fortune pursued him beyond the grave. The son of Barry's chief assistant, Augustus Pugin, wrote a book putting forward the extraordinary and quite ill-founded claim that Pugin was the true designer of all that was good in the new palace, and that Barry had usurped his laurels. More than a century later the perturbed spirit of Barry can now rest in the Abbey beside his forest of dreaming spires and the screaming tyres in Parliament Square, consoled that his palace has become the best-known and, architecturally at any rate, the best-loved building in Britain.

The greatest tower in Barry's building is the Victoria Tower at the southern end, balancing and surmounting the more familiar northern tower that holds Big Ben. Barry built it as the repository of historic Parliamentary documents. Most of the papers of the House of Commons, with the exception of the original Journals, were destroyed in the fire of 1834. Documents of the House of Lords survived because they were then kept in the more remote Jewel Tower. Today the record office in the Victoria Tower stores some two million documents dating from the fifteenth century and comprising one of the great Parliamentary archives of the world. Ancient records include the Acts and Petitions that have become the milestones of British constitutional history. Recent records, which accumulate at a rate of about 3,000 documents for an average year's work, include two large gravestones, brought into the Lords as evidence in a peerage claim, and a lengthy petition from East Africa, bearing many hundreds of thumb-marks to attest the names of the petitioners.

Beneath the Victoria Tower on the river front Victoria Tower Gardens are decorated with appropriately democratic statuary, including a bronze replica of Auguste Rodin's *Burghers of Calais* and a statue of Emmeline Pankhurst with a tablet also commemorating her daughter, Christabel, who had the audacity seventy years ago to make the revolutionary proposal that women had as much right to vote as men.

Early on the morning of July 31, 1802, William Wordsworth and his sister and most constant companion, Dorothy, left London on a journey to Calais. As they travelled by coach to Dover, Wordsworth wrote his sonnet about London seen from Westminster Bridge, which was to become one of his most-quoted works and one of the best-known poems about London. It was not published until 1807, by which time Wordsworth gave it the erroneous date: 'Composed upon Westminster Bridge, September 3, 1802.' The only alteration that he made in the text that he wrote on top of the Dover coach was in the second line, where he amended the original 'heart' to 'soul':

Earth has not anything to show more fair:
Dull would he be of soul who could pass by
A sight so touching in its majesty:
This City now doth, like a garment, wear
The beauty of the morning; silent, bare,
Ships, towers, domes, theatres, and temples lie
Open unto the fields, and to the sky;
All bright and glittering in the smokeless air . . .

Dorothy's journal for that day confirms, in only slightly less exalted language, that it was indeed a grand morning:

'Left London between five and six o'clock of the morning outside the Dover coach. A beautiful morning. The city, St Paul's, with the river—a multitude of little boats, made a beautiful sight as we crossed Westminster Bridge; the houses not overhung by their clouds of smoke, and were hung out endlessly; yet the sun shone so brightly, with such a pure light, that there was something like the purity of one of Nature's own grand spectacles.'

The grand spectacle has changed since the Wordsworths drove across the bridge. The nearest fields are now twenty miles away in every direction. The pure light, having been stained by more than a century of smoke and pea-soup fogs of the industrial revolution, has been repurified by recent clean air legislation. The south bank down-river from Westminster Bridge has been occupied by a range of some of the most massive and adventurous buildings of modern architecture. And two bridges have been built and then rebuilt across the great curve of the river from Westminster to the beginning of the City at Blackfriars. The first is old Hungerford Bridge, now replaced by Charing Cross railway bridge, a steel erection on gross cylindrical legs that are as disproportionately swollen as if they suffered from elephantiasis. Only Claude Monet in his great series of paintings of this reach of the river ever managed to make Charing Cross Bridge beautiful. And it is noticeable that his most successful versions are of foggy days or sunsets, with the legs of the bridge and the Houses of Parliament beyond looming hazily out of the murk.

The bridge runs from the site of Old Hungerford Stairs, in the same way that Charing Cross Station stands on the site of Hungerford Market. Warren's Blacking Warehouse, where Charles Dickens worked as a child, adjoined Hungerford Stairs, and references to the district lie thick in *David Copperfield*, the most autobiographical of his novels.

From the Houses of Parliament to Charing Cross railway bridge the north bank of the Thames is the river front of Whitehall. Today Whitehall is a sobriquet for the British governmental machine, but until three centuries ago it was the name of the largest and in many ways the most remarkable royal palace in Europe. In the Middle Ages this bank between the river and the road from London to the west was the site of Scotland Yard, the residence where Scottish ambassadors to London stayed, and York Place, the official London residence of the Archbishops of York. This was originally the house of the Bishops of Lincoln, but it was transferred to the Archbishops of York, and is mentioned as such in documents from 1231. Bishops and Archbishops were important pieces on the feudal chess-board, and needed to be close to the centre of power.

When Thomas Wolsey succeeded to the See of York in 1514, York Place emerged from its medieval twilight. Wolsey bought Scotland Yard to the north and other adjoining land and proceeded to build and refurbish his palace in the latest style, sparing no expense. His admiring biographer, George Cavendish, described his lavish entertainments there. For example, in 1518 he gave 'a most sumptuous supper, the like of which was never given either by Cleopatra or Caligula'.

Cavendish also enthusiastically described the unparalleledly magnificent furniture of York Place: 'And in his gallery there were set divers tables, whereupon a great number of rich stuff of silk, in whole pieces of all colours, as velvet, satin, damask, caffa [a rich silk cloth much used by those who could afford it in the sixteenth century], taffeta, grograine, sarcenet . . . Furthermore there was also all the walls of the gallery hanged with cloths of gold and tissue of divers makings, and cloths of silver likewise on both sides . . . Then had he two chambers adjoining to the gallery, the one called the gilt-chamber, and the other called, most commonly, the council-chamber, wherein were set in each two broad and long tables upon tressels, whereupon was set such a number of plate of all sorts, as were almost incredible. In the gilt-chamber was set out upon the tables nothing but all gilt plate; and a cupboard standing under a window was garnished wholly with plate of clean gold, whereof some was set with pearl and rich stones. And in the council-chamber was set all white plate and parcel-gilt; and under the tables in both the chambers were set baskets of old plate, which was not esteemed but for broken plate and old.'

Such regal magnificence, such quantities of gold and caffa and other loot accumulated by not very fastidious means, attracted attention. Unfortunately for Wolsey they caught the attention of the porcine and psychopathic eyes of the King, who was living next door in the far less luxurious and comfortable Palace of Westminster. When Wolsey fell from favour and office in 1529, Henry confiscated, besides the Great Seal, all his property and palaces, including York Place, disregarding the nice distinction that it belonged in fact not to Wolsey at all but to the See of York. He renamed it Whitehall to eradicate uncomfortable memories, possibly because he added some new buildings in stone at a time when brick and timber were the customary materials; or possibly after the White Hall, the second hall after William Rufus's great hall in his old Palace of Westminster. He may have been claiming for his new palace the distinction of being the White Hall or 'Festival Hall' of the whole kingdom.

Although the Government was increasingly centralized under the Tudor autocracy, it retained something of its peripatetic medieval character. Henry and his daughter Elizabeth spent as much time in Greenwich, Richmond, Hampton Court, and their other great palaces as they did in Whitehall. However, Parliament and the Law Courts had stayed behind Henry in Westminster, and from that separation Whitehall, because of its adjacency to Westminster, became the most convenient royal palace for legal and Parliamentary purposes.

It was during the seventeenth century under the new dynasty of the Stuarts that Whitehall became the official headquarters and main residence of the monarchy. It was the stage for most of the royal and constitutional crises of that century rich in crisis. Charles I was executed in Whitehall, stepping out of a window of his Banqueting House to the scaffold, and behaving with the exemplary firmness of a Stuart sure of his self-righteousness:

> Nor called the gods with vulgar spite
> To vindicate his helpless right;
> But bowed his comely head
> Down, as upon a bed.

Marvell was, as usual, historically accurate: Charles did have to lie down as upon a bed for the terrible operation, since the masked, disguised, and incompetent executioners had mislaid the customary waist-high execution block. Cromwell, when declared Lord Protector, made Whitehall his official residence, and died there in a colossal, melodramatic storm considered by the superstitious to be gratifyingly symbolic. In reaction to the austerity of the Puritans, Restoration Whitehall became the most brilliant and scandalous court in British history, with a gilded army of politicians, Ministers, mistresses and other 'cattle' and parasites glittering around the dark and sardonic figure of Charles II. Charles's brother, James II, abdicated from Whitehall, decamping from the river stairs and drowning the Great Seal in the Thames, because of a typically feather-brained notion that without it the business of government could not be carried on. In the last great constitutional scene on the handsome stage of Whitehall Palace, James's daughter Mary and her Dutch husband, William of Orange, were offered the crown jointly in the Banqueting House.

The genius, in several senses of the word, of seventeenth-century Whitehall was a poor boy born in 1573 and distinctively named after his London-Welsh father, a cloth-maker called Inigo Jones. The son became the man more than any other individual who introduced into Britain the new Renaissance style based on Palladio and Roman antiquities. He built his Palladian masterpiece, the new Banqueting House in Whitehall, for James I as a manifesto of the Renaissance style sponsored by the new regime from Scotland. A visiting Flemish diplomat who was also a prolific painter, the chief north European exponent of the baroque, Peter Paul Rubens, was commissioned to decorate the ceiling. With his assistants in his studios in Antwerp he produced a series of vast canvases, depicting with much pomp and mythological symbolism such unlikely subjects as the benefits of the government of James I and the apotheosis of that most ungodlike monarch. Rubens's great ceiling is still there, having in 1973 had its paintings put back in their correct positions after they had been misplaced during an eighteenth-century cleaning into positions even more likely to crick the neck and strain the eyes.

The paintings are rich, recondite in detail, robust, and justly famous. Their general theme is the glorification of the earthly deeds of a King by Divine Right and his reward at death, shown in the central panel, where James ascends majestically and improbably into the empyrean. James, 'the wisest fool in Christendom', looks incongruous surrounded by such allegorical virtues as Heroic Wisdom, Wise Government, Reason, and Royal Bounty, which cannot be said with precision to have surrounded him during his life-time. However he would certainly have enjoyed the processions of plump, pink, and steatopygous *putti* that run down the long sides of the perfectly proportioned double square of the ceiling.

Inigo Jones, the architect of the Banqueting House and today one of the least recognized of British artists, perhaps because of the diversity of his talents, was a man so various that he seemed to be not one, but the epitome of the Renaissance *uomo universale*. His many-sidedness has made him an intractable subject for biographers and the general public. He was at times from his base of patronage in Whitehall architect, painter, engineer, designer, connoisseur, collector, aesthete, and creator of the Masque, that curiously Arcadian form of amateur dramatics that also served as propaganda machine for the autocratic philosophy of Stuart Whitehall.

The Masque was a glorified form of amateur theatricals acted, often in the Banqueting House, by members of the court for the entertainment of the King and his retinue and in order to spread the message about the divine right of kings. It was derived from the mummeries of the Middle Ages and the costumed revelries of The Twelve Days of Christmas; gained formal recognition by that enthusiastic play-boy, the young Henry VIII; and reached its flourishing heyday under the early Stuarts. The Masque celebrates the power of princes. Its spectacular visions of peace, order, and hierarchical harmony are ideals of how the world should be run under the paternalist and theoretically benevolent guidance of God and his deputy, the King. Shakespeare in his last play, the romantic drama called *The Tempest*, tried to combine elements of the current craze for the Masque with his unfashionable belief that plot, character, and the words mattered almost as much in the theatre as dances, disguises, and spectacular stage and musical effects.

Inigo Jones was the designer, dresser, and scene-setter of the Stuart Masques. His sets and costumes for classical goddesses, nymphs, clowns, and monsters, inspired by his travels in Italy, opened new and magic casements for seventeenth-century England. His stage and auditorium in the Banqueting House were the stepping-stones from Shakespeare's Globe to the modern theatre. They made a feature of extravagantly elaborate machinery that could lower a cloud full of ladies-in-waiting disguised, for instance, as wood nymphs down a slope from the ceiling, and then whisk the cloud away to reveal them on a golden throne. His mechanical effects had never been used before in Britain. Perhaps mercifully for the development of the drama they have rarely been used since, outside Covent Garden and the pantomime.

Inigo Jones's genius predictably excited the envy of Court poets like Ben Jonson, the rude mechanics who did the inferior work of hacking out the words for the amateur actors to speak. Jonson told Prince (later King) Charles that, when he needed a name to express the greatest villain in the world, he would call him an Inigo. In his preface to *Time Vindicated to Himselfe and to his Honors* (a title that conveys something of the awfulness of a Masque) Jonson studiously avoided mentioning Inigo Jones, even though Jones had arranged three spectacular changes of scenery during the performance. He then jealously satirized Jones under the laborious name of In-and-In Medlay in his last play, a comedy called *A Tale of a Tub* (1633). The public squabble was stopped when the King told Jonson that he was 'not well pleased therewith'.

As an architect Jones was the first great autocrat, who believed, like the unfortunate Charles Barry, that there should be a single mind behind a single building. In addition to his masterpiece, the Banqueting House, Inigo Jones, or possibly his pupil, John Webb, drew up several different plans for building a vast Palladian palace to replace the irregular jumble of halls, galleries, and courtyards of the Tudor palace of Whitehall. Most of them included the Banqueting House as an integral central part of the design. There would have been seven courts, including a circular Persian court, so called because it was to be decorated with gigantic statues in the Persian style. The largest of the plans was intended to extend along the Thames for one thousand and fifty feet by nine hundred and twenty-eight. If any of them had been translated into stone, mortar, and Persian statues, London would have had the most magnificent neo-classical palace in the world, and the Thames at Westminster would have had a river front as fine as anything along the Seine or the Hudson. Plans went ahead until, sadly, 'His Majesty's [Charles I's] unfortunate calamity [decapitation] caused him to desist'. The later Stuarts were so continuously embarrassed financially that they could never raise the money for such an extravagant building project.

The greatest palace beside the Thames was almost completely burnt down in January 1698, by a fire started by a Dutch washerwoman, who had doubtless come over in the train of William of Orange. She was careless about hanging her washing by a fire in an upper room to dry. John Evelyn visited the smoking ruin on the next day, and wrote in his diary with Tacitean brevity: 'Whitehall burnt; nothing but walls and ruins left.' William III also visited the scene of the fire on the afternoon following the disaster and vowed that 'if God gave him leave he would rebuild it much finer than before'. But the atmosphere of the riverside palace had always irritated his chronic asthma, and he found his own palace in the drier air of Kensington more congenial. In any case, the need for such a great national palace to accommodate the Court, the Council, and the general public had vanished at the Glorious Revolution, along with the idea of divine right and an unlimited monarchy. Sir Christopher Wren surveyed the ruins and prepared designs for a new palace, but nothing came of the dream.

Little remains of Thomas Wolsey's great palace beside the Thames at Westminster. The Banqueting House survives as a superb memorial to Inigo Jones, Rubens, and the Stuarts. Remains of one of the Tudor tennis courts and galleries in the part of the palace known as the Cockpit are preserved in Treasury Green, between the Old Treasury Building and Downing Street. On the Embankment, when workmen were digging the foundations for that unacceptable face of modern architecture, the Ministry of Defence, they uncovered a corner of a wall of the Tudor palace and a terrace and steps down to the river built by Wren in 1691. These are preserved on the site, back from the river, which has been subsequently embanked. And in the gigantic bowels of the Ministry of Defence there is carefully preserved the Henry VIII wine cellar. After the 1939–45 war, when the colossal and distressingly bleak and utilitarian block of government offices was being built on the site for the Ministry of Defence, Parliament was given an undertaking that Henry's cellar would be preserved. It was later discovered that it interfered with both the plan and the elevation of the new building. Accordingly it was decided that the cellar, which weighs about a thousand tons, should be removed to a new position.

With prodigious engineering skill the whole building was moved sideways on staging, lowered almost twenty feet by screw-jacks, and then rolled back to its present position in the basement of the Ministry, approximately beneath its original site.

Scarlet staff majors and civil servants keep the courts where Henry gloried and drank deep. With its bays and central piers, vaulted roof and platforms for barrels, it is an evocative and beautiful relic of the old palace, buried beneath the monstrous pile of modern masonry. It can be viewed on summer

Saturdays by the public who have managed to obtain security clearance from the Department of the Environment.

The most conspicuous object on the Embankment, where the boats used to tie up at Whitehall Stairs, is the Royal Air Force Memorial. A Golden Eagle weighing two and a half tons perches on a pillar and looks south-east towards the Channel and the direction from which danger to England customarily comes.

The north bank from Whitehall downstream used to be the site of other great mansions outside the City: Durham House of the Bishops of Durham, rebuilt around 1300 with characteristic magnificence by that fanatical builder, Bishop Bec; the Palace of the Savoy, built round the hospital of St John the Baptist; Salisbury House of the Bishops of Salisbury; and the royal castle of Bridewell, which later became a palace and was then given by Edward VI to the City of London as a workhouse for the poor and 'a house of correction'. In this devious way the name of the old castle near St Bridget's Well beside the Thames became a sobriquet for any prison.

The opposite bank to Westminster and Whitehall is famous as 'the South Bank'. It is in fact the east bank. In many of the reaches of a river as mean-drous as the Thames east or west, and even north-east or north-west, would be more pedantically correct than the south bank. When the South Bank was redeveloped for the Festival of Britain, the post-war exhibition and celebra-tion of the end of austerity, there was a national debate about what to rename the renovated South Bank. Suggestions ranged from the undue seriousness of Commonwealth Quay to the undue facetiousness of Dollar Drive. A. P. Herbert proposed Waterloo Bank. Others suggested commemorating eponymously Shakespeare or the Mr Cuper who once had a famous pleasure garden on the site.

Boydell Cuper was a gardener who had been in the service of the famous collector, Thomas, Earl of Arundel. Cuper begged from his master any old, mutilated statues that he did not want and stuck them around the walks of Cuper's Gardens on the South Bank. In 1736 an orchestra was added to the garden's attractions, and it later became famous for its firework shows. Like most pleasure gardens it eventually became chiefly famous for the rough and predatory society that it harboured, and it was therefore deprived of its licence in 1753. But Cuper lives on, his name having been deliciously and ungrammatically transformed by the folk-singers:

> Twas down in Cupid's garden
> For pleasure I did go,
> All for to see the flowers
> That in that garden grow.
> The first it was the Jessamy,
> The Lily, pink and rose;

They are the fairest flowers
That in that garden grows.

With their instinctive conservatism about nomenclature, Londoners eventually decided to continue calling the south bank South Bank.

From Westminster Bridge down the South Bank extends a range of monumental buildings representing distinctive periods of twentieth-century architecture.

County Hall, headquarters of the Greater London Council, the government of about seven and a half million Londoners, is a splendid example of Edwardian baroque at its most baroque, out-baroquing the Italians. Its river front of more than seven hundred feet, with a concave giant colonnade as its central motif, was designed by Ralph Knott, who won an open competition for the commission, was begun in 1911 and finished in 1922. Sir Nikolaus Pevsner judges: 'Knott must have had a real understanding of Piranesi, and the Edwardian mood was enterprising and melodramatic enough to allow him to do in solid stone what Piranesi had done only on paper.' County Hall has subsequently had new blocks built at either end. Its one thousand two hundred rooms and five and a quarter miles of corridors are the work-place of the ninety-two Councillors, fifteen Aldermen, and seven thousand headquarter's civil servants who run London.

Next down-stream rise the massive slabs and fat tower of the Shell Centre, erected in the 1950s, but designed in the monumental graveyard style of the 1920s. Critics argue that the vast ant-hill of the oil industry, throbbing with ambition, and graded in hierarchies of offices and restaurants, typifies something that is distasteful, paternalist, and élitist about modern industry. This may well be true, but, as modern industrial giants go, Shell is a good employer, in spite of being something of a supranational state with its own foreign and domestic policies.

Next comes the Royal Festival Hall, opened in 1951 for the Festival of Britain, the first major public building in London designed in the modern style of architecture. As such it was widely and ineffectually mocked by the Babbitts and reactionaries of the time. The concert hall holds about three thousand, and is acoustically and architecturally the finest hall in Britain. Saucy critics have said that the tiers of boxes cantilevered out on each side look like drawers pulled out by burglars in a hurry. The main façade towards the river is symmetrical, with much glass and a dignified plainness and functionalism that echoes the austerity of the years just after the war.

Next, beside Waterloo Bridge, comes a cluster of very solid-looking concrete structures comprising the Queen Elizabeth Hall, the Purcell Room, and the Hayward Gallery, homes for smaller concerts, chamber music, the National Film Theatre, and temporary or touring art exhibitions. Professor Reyner Banham, the eminent architectural critic, has suggested that they represent a 'true manifestation of the Archigram vision of cities as giant single buildings of capsules connected by tubes and ducts. Into the Queen Elizabeth capsule and the Purcell capsule—each carefully insulated against external disturbances—flow audiences, conditioned air, performers, electric light, instruments, and scores. Fuelled by the constant flow of air and catalyzed by electric light, certain musical reactions take place within these capsules, and afterwards the products of this fusion process flow out again into small mobile capsules or large underground tubes and go home.' It is one way of describing the business of going to a concert in the second half of the twentieth century. Others describe this style of architecture as Brutalism, and the Hayward Gallery and Purcell and Elizabeth Halls as most brutish examples of the style.

This reach of the river between Westminster and the South Bank has always been an attractive subject for artists, from the itinerant etchers and engravers of the Renaissance and Canaletto to the Impressionists. Monet and Pissarro arrived in London in 1870, on the outbreak of the Franco-Prussian war, refugees, like so many other talented immigrants to Britain. Both carried on with their lives' obsessions of painting landscape and townscape in their new style, and Monet produced a celebrated 'London Series' of riverscapes, showing Westminster Bridge, Waterloo Bridge, and the Houses of Parliament in different lights and atmospheres. An exhibition of the work of the Impressionists in London was organized by the Arts Council in 1973 to celebrate Britain's entry into the European Economic Community. Visitors could see no less than twenty-six of Monet's paintings of the Thames assembled in one place for the first time, and then step out of the Hayward Gallery to the ganglion of pedestrian walks and bridges on the South Bank to examine Monet's subjects in fog and mist, or sunshine; usually fog and mist, since it was January.

Opposite the Festival Hall, on the north bank stretching back to the Strand, once stood the Adelphi, one of the boldest and most elegant property developments in the history of London. The great terrace of houses raised on vaulted warehouses above the Thames was built between 1768 and 1774 by Robert Adam and his brothers: James, also an architect, and William, their business manager. Its name is a transliteration of the Greek word for 'brothers'. The brothers themselves lived in their development, next to the central house, which was taken by their friend and supporter, David Garrick. The scheme was a financial failure, only redeemed from disaster by a Parliamentary lottery. But the architecture of the Adelphi was an ornament to its site by the river. A perceptive critic (Rassmussen) wrote: 'In the case of the Adelphi the *commercial* idea is no less grand and full of imagination than is the *artistic* one. The scheme is a fantasia upon antique motifs: the enormous subterranean vaults, the terrace on to the river, and the simple classical houses with their Pompeian decorated pilasters executed in terra-cotta. But Adelphi was not only a dream of antique architecture; it was just as much a finance-fantasia over risk and profit; the financier was an artist and the artist a financier.'

Subsequent generations defaced its delicate façade with stucco and spoiled the architecture in other ways to bring it into line with current taste. In 1936 the Adelphi was demolished in an act of vandalism that is still conspicuous even in a century that has destroyed and vandalized so many other beautiful and important buildings beside the Thames.

On the Embankment in front of Adelphi Terrace and the perturbed spirits of the Adam brothers rises the exotic erection of Cleopatra's Needle, encompassed by giant bronze and slightly sheepish British sphinxes. The obelisk has nothing to do with Cleopatra, apart from the fact that it was originally transported from Alexandria in a ship called the *Cleopatra*. It was made of pink granite on the banks of the Nile in the Middle Kingdom in the second millennium B.C. It dates from the reign of Thothmes, alias Tutmoses, the Third, the Pharaoh who presided over the greatest period of Egyptian territorial expansion and who left his mark grandiosely across the land, but especially in Karnak. Unlike the Elgin Marbles and other 'national' treasures, Cleopatra's Needle was not purloined or picked up cheap from the unsuspecting natives, but a present. Mohammed Ali presented it to Britain in 1819 'to mark the services of Nelson and Abercrombie'.

En route from Alexandria a storm forced the *Cleopatra* to abandon the obelisk in the Bay of Biscay. A tug named *Anglia* eventually collected it and brought it to its long home beside the Thames in 1878. After a century of absorbing the London atmosphere its granite is no longer pink. A twin of Cleopatra's Needle stands in Central Park, New York.

Down the Embankment from Cleopatra's Needle rises the block of Shell-Mex House, crowned with a large clock that is nicknamed 'Big Benzine'.

Next comes the Savoy, formerly the palace of the Counts of Savoy, today the luxury hotel preferred by rich Americans and stars of show business. The precinct between the Strand and the river was given by Henry III to Peter of Savoy, his wife's uncle, in 1246. Peter built a famous palace there, described by a contemporary as 'the fayrest mannor in Europe'. King John of France was lodged in the Savoy when he was a prisoner in England in 1357. The palace was sacked and burnt down by Wat Tyler's freedom-fighters and tax-resisters, and restored as a hospital of St John the Baptist under the Tudors. The hospital was replaced by a military prison in the eighteenth century, and all the old buildings of the Savoy except the chapel were demolished when Rennie built Waterloo Bridge.

The chapel, once in unpermissive days popular with divorced people who wanted a religious service on remarriage, is a chapel royal of the Sovereign as Duke of Lancaster.

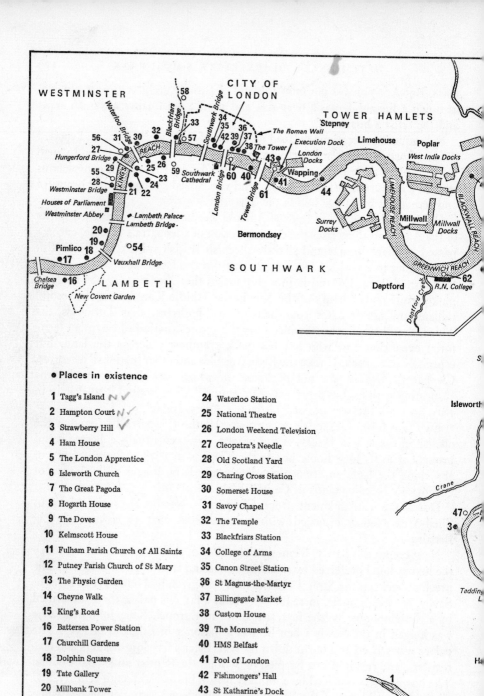

WESTMINSTER   CITY OF LONDON   TOWER HAMLETS

Waterloo Bridge   58   Stepney   Limehouse   Poplar

56 31 30 32   Blackfriars Bridge   33   34   The Roman Wall   Execution Dock   West India Docks
27   57   Southwark Bridge   35   36   London Docks
Hungerford Bridge   REACH   59   42 39 37   The Tower   Wapping
55 29   25 26   Southwark Cathedral   38 The Tower   43
28   23   60 40   London Docks   41   Millwall   Millwall Docks
Westminster Bridge   KING'S   21 22   London Bridge   Tower Bridge   61   44   BLACKWALL REACH
Houses of Parliament   LIMEHOUSE REACH
Westminster Abbey   Lambeth Palace   Surrey Docks
    Lambeth Bridge   Bermondsey
20   GREENWICH REACH
19   SOUTHWARK   62
Pimlico 18   54   Deptford   R.N. College
17   Vauxhall Bridge
Chelsea Bridge 16   LAMBETH   Deptford Creek
New Covent Garden

● Places in existence

1 Tagg's Island	24 Waterloo Station
2 Hampton Court	25 National Theatre
3 Strawberry Hill	26 London Weekend Television
4 Ham House	27 Cleopatra's Needle
5 The London Apprentice	28 Old Scotland Yard
6 Isleworth Church	29 Charing Cross Station
7 The Great Pagoda	30 Somerset House
8 Hogarth House	31 Savoy Chapel
9 The Doves	32 The Temple
10 Kelmscott House	33 Blackfriars Station
11 Fulham Parish Church of All Saints	34 College of Arms
12 Putney Parish Church of St Mary	35 Canon Street Station
13 The Physic Garden	36 St Magnus-the-Martyr
14 Cheyne Walk	37 Billingsgate Market
15 King's Road	38 Custom House
16 Battersea Power Station	39 The Monument
17 Churchill Gardens	40 HMS Belfast
18 Dolphin Square	41 Pool of London
19 Tate Gallery	42 Fishmongers' Hall
20 Millbank Tower	43 St Katharine's Dock
21 County Hall	44 Brunel's Tunnel
22 Shell Centre	45 Blackwall Tunnel
23 Festival Hall	46 Thames Barrier, Silvertown

Isleworth

Crane

47

3

Teddington L

1

2

East Molesey   Hampton

Thames Ditton

Ha

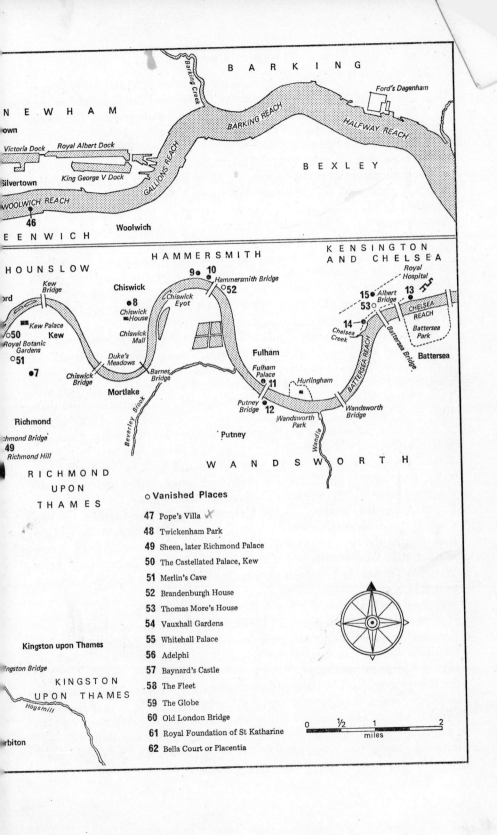

BARKING

NEWHAM

Barking Creek

Ford's Dagenham

BARKING REACH

HALFWAY REACH

Victoria Dock   Royal Albert Dock

BEXLEY

Silvertown   King George V Dock   GALLIONS REACH

WOOLWICH REACH

46

GREENWICH   Woolwich

KENSINGTON AND CHELSEA

HAMMERSMITH

Royal Hospital

HOUNSLOW

Chiswick

9 10

Hammersmith Bridge

○52

Kew Bridge

15 Albert Bridge

13

CHELSEA REACH

ford

○**8**

Chiswick Eyot

Chiswick House

53○

Kew Palace

50

Kew

Chiswick Mall

14

Chelsea Creek

Battersea Park

Battersea Bridge

Royal Botanic Gardens

○**51**

Duke's Meadows

Fulham

Battersea

●**7**

Chiswick Bridge

Barnes Bridge

Fulham Palace

11

Hurlingham

BATTERSEA REACH

Wandsworth Bridge

Mortlake

Richmond

Beverley Brook

Putney Bridge **12**

Wandsworth Park

Richmond Bridge

49

Richmond Hill

Putney

Wandle

WANDSWORTH

RICHMOND
UPON
THAMES

○ **Vanished Places**

47 Pope's Villa

48 Twickenham Park

49 Sheen, later Richmond Palace

50 The Castellated Palace, Kew

51 Merlin's Cave

52 Brandenburgh House

53 Thomas More's House

54 Vauxhall Gardens

55 Whitehall Palace

56 Adelphi

Kingston upon Thames

57 Baynard's Castle

58 The Fleet

Kingston Bridge

KINGSTON
UPON THAMES

59 The Globe

60 Old London Bridge

Hogsmill

61 Royal Foundation of St Katharine

62 Bella Court or Placentia

0   ½   1   2

miles

Surbiton

The luxury hotel was built by Richard D'Oyly Carte, the impresario of that brilliant but neurotic partnership of Gilbert and Sullivan, and opened in 1889. The great César Ritz was the first general manager, and the greater Auguste Escoffier the *maître-chef*. The original brochure offered what were then unimaginable luxuries: 'Shaded electric lights everywhere at all hours of night and day. No gas. Large and luxurious ascending rooms [*scilicet*, lifts] running all night. Top floor rooms equal to the lowest. All the corridors warmed night and day. Seventy bathrooms.' Seventy bathrooms? The builder asked D'Oyly Carte if his guests were going to be amphibians. The Savoy's nearest rival for size and luxury, the Hotel Victoria, had four bathrooms for its five hundred guests. The rest managed as the English had managed since the Roman occupation: with flat tin baths kept under their beds until the infrequent occasions when they were needed. Savoy guests were invited to use the speaking-tubes in their rooms: 'Please command anything from a cup of tea to a cocktail, and it will come up in the twinkling of an Embankment lamp.'

In the Savoy restaurant Johann Strauss conducted Viennese waltzes; Caruso sang and Pavlova danced in cabaret; George Gershwin played the piano solo in *Rhapsody in Blue*; and characters as diverse as Winston Churchill, Noël Coward, and Bob Hope have found a congenial haven. It is still the resort of those who value their comforts and their stomachs more than their bank balances.

There was passionate but ineffective conservationist uproar when old Waterloo Bridge was destroyed in 1939. The old bridge, first called the Strand Bridge, was designed by John Rennie and built between 1811 and 1817. Its nine stately elliptical arches, each fitted with a pair of Doric columns, were widely admired. Dickens described it as 'the handsomest bridge across the Thames'. A. P. Herbert said that the London County Council could destroy Rennie's bridge, if it must. But it should not replace it, so leaving the river empty and restoring the view of London from Westminster that Wordsworth and Canaletto saw. Instead, there should be a Waterloo Tunnel. As happened too often, nobody paid the slightest attention to A.P.H.'s sensible suggestion.

Beyond the bridge on the South Bank the National Theatre has risen to join the majestic fashion parade of the changing face of modern architecture. For nearly a century and a half radicals of the theatre like Bernard Shaw and Granville Barker campaigned for a national theatre building worthy of Britain's place in the drama of the world. The dream was first realized by the remarkable Lilian Bayliss, and for decades the National Theatre was an inquiline domiciled at the Old Vic by Waterloo Station. In 1975 it removed physically to its new complex on the river front, where three theatres, the Lyttelton, the Cottesloe, and the Olivier can seat about two thousand five hundred people. The progressive theatre design by Denys Lasdun provides three theatres of the future under one roof, each intimate, each particular in character, and none with spectators more than sixty-five feet from the stage. In addition the bars, the restaurant, the buffets, the workshops, the rehearsal rooms, and the hundred and thirty-five air-conditioned dressing-rooms compose the official headquarters of British theatre, a far cry from the brave old makeshift days by Waterloo Road. There was the inevitable criticism of appearance and soaring costs that attends the appearance of any new building in London. When the Royal Festival Hall was opened, Sir Thomas Beecham remarked: 'I question whether in three hundred years there has been a more unattractive, more ugly, and more monstrous structure.' Yet the Festival Hall is now accepted as an ornament of the London riverside. Its neighbour, the National Theatre, will no doubt be generally accepted as a worthy successor to the Globe and the other great and seminal playhouses that also stood on the South Bank.

Beside the National Theatre the new square tower of London Weekend Television's studios and offices has added its handsome exclamation mark to the panorama of the South Bank. This half-mile below Waterloo Bridge called King's Reach is gradually being cleared of derelict warehouses and wharves as the port and industry remove from central London. It is to be hoped, though not expected, that they will be replaced by buildings worthy of their site opposite Somerset House and the Inns of Court.

Under Waterloo Bridge attached to the north bank is the only recorded floating police station in the world.

Somerset House was once another of the chain of palaces that occupied the prime site of the north bank of the river between Westminster and London. It was originally built by Edward Seymour, Duke of Somerset and the Lord Protector on behalf of his nephew, Edward VI, until Seymour was executed for treason in 1552. In its day the old palace was an innovatory modern building, introducing to England the wind of change that the Renaissance was blowing through Continental architecture. It was a Tudor mansion with a courtyard, a gatehouse facing the Strand, and a great hall opposite the river front, but it used Italian and French elements of planning and decoration not seen in Britain before. After Somerset had lost his head, his palace reverted to the Crown and became an official residence of queens, including Elizabeth, Anne of Denmark, and Catherine of Braganza. Busy Inigo Jones built a chapel for it, and after the Restoration his assistant, John Webb, added a gallery along the river front, possibly to a design by Jones.

The old palace was demolished at the end of the eighteenth century and replaced by the present grand building designed by Sir William Chambers. The river front eight hundred feet long rests on mighty arches, and was clearly designed to surpass the Adelphi next door. For many years the elegant interiors were occupied by the offices of the Inland Revenue, the principal Probate Registry, and the Registrar-General of births, marriages, and deaths. The rooms were divided with plasterboard partitions and desecrated in other ways, and civil servants slept here, where once the Queens of England slept. In the 1960s there was a long, running argument, led by Simon Jenkins of the London *Evening Standard*, that parts of Somerset House should be opened to the general public, for instance as art galleries. The victory was won in 1973, when the apartments, engagingly known to the Civil Service as the Fine Rooms, were opened to the public for the first time for a hundred and fifty years. The occasion was a grand commemorative exhibition of Churchilliana to celebrate the centenary of Sir Winston's birth and to raise money for the two national memorials to him. The Fine Rooms, handsomely decorated in 1722 by Sir William Chambers, were built as the original home of the Royal Academy. Now that the precedent of opening them to the public has been set, it would be difficult to close them and immure their beauties for so long again. In due course they will be used to house the Arts Council's proposed permanent exhibition of the theatre or, more suitably, the Turner Bequest.

The final stretch of the north bank leading up to the site of the old walls of London is occupied by the Inns of Court known as Middle Temple and Inner Temple. The lawyers of London have lived on this bank of the Thames with their close-shaven lawns, medieval halls, and reactionary habits since the thirteenth century.

The Temple derives its name from having been the headquarters of the Templars, that unfortunate Order of Chivalry whose knights made the mistake of growing so rich and so internationalist that they aroused the rapacity and suspicion of the kings of Europe. The Templars were suppressed with great savagery early in the fourteenth century on bogus charges of blasphemy, sorcery, and sodomy. Their wealth, which was one of the true reasons for their suppression, was confiscated. Their Temple was given to the Order of St John, which leased it to the growing associations of law students, whose descendants have congregated there in sable flocks ever since.

Because of the innate conservatism and adventitious wealth of the Bar the Temple is one of the few surviving enclaves of medieval and Tudor life left in London. The Inns of Court could afford to restore their old buildings damaged by bombs in the Second World War. And men who feel no absurdity in persisting in wearing eighteenth-century wigs and other ludicrous uniforms, more sensibly persist in preserving their contented and congenial style of collegiate life beside the Thames.

Temple Bar, dividing the Strand from Fleet Street, marked the old boundary of the City, and used to be surmounted by a handsome gate of Portland stone made by Sir Christopher Wren and decorated with statues of Queen Elizabeth and James I. The City of London was notoriously republican and jealous of its ancient privileges from the Norman Conquest onwards through the Middle Ages. Consequently, since the Civil War, the monarch has been forbidden to enter the City without an invitation. The tradition persists today, although the City has developed into a barbican of conservatism and the British hierarchy. When the Queen visits the City, for instance for a banquet in Guildhall, the Lord Mayor and other great officers of the City of London wearing medieval costumes meet her at Temple Bar and invite her in.

Dickens evidently disliked this old London landmark. In *Bleak House* he called it 'that leaden-headed old obstruction' and observed that in hot weather it is 'to the adjacent Strand and Fleet Street what a heater is in an urn, and keeps them simmering all night'. In the interest of traffic circulation Temple Bar was removed in 1878 to Sir Henry Bruce Meux's estate of Theobald's Park, near Waltham Cross. In the 1960s and 1970s there were proposals to return it to some suitable site in London, but they came to nothing. The famous old western gateway to the City of London, which was once used to display the severed heads of traitors as a discouragement to others treasonably-inclined, remains in exile in Theobald's Park. It was dilapidated and vandalized until, in 1974, the local authority restored it.

Moored along the Embankment in front of Temple Gardens lie four handsome antique ships: the *Discovery*, which carried Captain Scott's fatal expedition to the South Pole from 1910 to 1912; the *Wellington*, headquarters of the Company of Master Mariners; and H.M.S. *Chrysanthemum* and *President*, former naval vessels now used as training ships for naval cadets. The Thames slides past them under Blackfriars Road Bridge and two contiguous Blackfriars Railway Bridges, and enters the old City of London, with an historic flow that moved Dylan Thomas to write, with lovely extravagance:

'This is the first time I have ever truly seen that London whose sweet Thames runs softly; that minstrel mermaid of a town, the water-streeted eight-million headed village in a blaze. This is London . . . The arches of the bridges leap into light; the moon clocks glow; the river sings; the harmonious pavilions are happy. And this is what London should always be like, till St Paul's falls down and the sea glides over the Strand.'

These lower, dirty reaches of the tideway are still haunted by companies of swans that tourists to the London River have always found remarkable. For instance, Paul Hentzner, that admirably conscientious tutor to a young German nobleman who toured England in the reign of the first Elizabeth, commented in his journal that a great concourse of swans frequented the Thames. They wander up and down, he wrote, 'in great security, nobody daring to molest, much less kill, any of them, under penalty of a considerable fine'. The reason for this immunity was that the Thames swan, *Cygnus olor*, has always been and still is considered a royal bird, in the same way that the sturgeon is considered a royal fish, if caught to be presented to the monarch.

The Elizabethan poet, Michael Drayton, eulogized the 'silver Thames' in *England's Helicon*, grossly flattered his flattery-loving Queen under the name of *Bita*, and, naturally, brought in her swans:

> Range all thy swans, fair Thames, together in a rank
> And place them duly one by one upon the stately bank.

Swans were considered royal partly because of their size and regal appearance, and partly because of the legend that the first swans to come to England were a present to King Richard I from Queen Beatrice of Cyprus. Such reverence for swans is not confined to the Thames: the ancient Greeks made the swan sacred to Apollo and Venus. The legend of Queen Beatrice is probably as baseless as the fable that the swan sings beautifully just before it dies, a superstition as old as Plato and Aristotle. Shakespeare refers to it more than once. In *Othello* Emilia, stabbed and on the point of death, says:

> I will play the swan,
> And die in music.

Coleridge turned the fable into a sharp epigram about a volunteer after-dinner singer:

> Swans sing before they die—'twere no bad thing
> Did certain persons die before they sing.

In fact unromantic ornithologists confidently assert that the *Cygnus olor* has no song at all, even when moribund. The only swan for which song of any kind can be claimed is the Whistling Swan, *Cygnus musicus*, of Iceland. Of this Nicol's *Account of Iceland* reports charmingly: 'During the long dark nights their wild song is often heard resembling the tones of a violin, though somewhat higher and remarkably pleasant.'

The Thames swans were eaten as a delicacy at royal feasts; the survivors were decorative, being plucked annually to repair the upholstery of the royal palaces beside the Thames.

The royal interest in *Cygnus olor* subsists. The Queen still employs a Keeper of the Swans as an official of the Royal Household. His full title descended from the Middle Ages is 'Keeper of the Swans in the Thames from the town of Graveshende to Cicester'. He presides over the remarkable survival of swan-upping. This derives from the practice by early monarchs of allowing a few favoured noblemen also to own a few swans. They marked their particular swans by making special patterns of nicks in the bills of the unfortunate birds. Only two City Livery Companies still retain this ancient right to own swans as well as the monarch: the Vintners and the Dyers. In July the Swanherd of the Vintners and the Swan Master of the Dyers accompany the Royal Keeper of the Swans on a traditional round-up of the new season's cygnets on the Thames from London Bridge to Henley. They 'up' the swans, in the rebarbative jargon of their mystery, and mark their beaks, a single nick for the Dyers, two for the Vintners, and none for the Queen. The function of the Keeper of the Swans is to see fair play and prevent poaching by the greedy liverymen. Only on the Thames in high summer could such a perfectly useless and charming tradition survive.

CHAPTER SEVEN

Blackfriars to London Bridge

'WHEN some traveller from New Zealand shall, in the midst of a vast solitude, take his stand on a broken arch of London Bridge to sketch the ruins of St Paul's.'

Macaulay's New Zealander, from his essay on Von Ranke's *History of the Popes*, is as justly famous as Macaulay's schoolboy, that odious little prig of fourteen who is repeatedly invoked as knowing better than the author of a book under review about some appallingly abstruse historical point that the reader has never heard of. The reader feels put in his place, namely several hundred fathoms beneath that cocksure Niagara of erudition, the reviewer.

In the past decade Macaulay's New Zealander has come nearer to truth than the resounding rhetorical fiction that he started as. The nineteen arches of old London Bridge, by far the most important building in the whole history of the Thames and London, obstructed the flow of the river so that it sometimes froze in winter. This is the point of the old riddle:

> As I was going o'er London Bridge,
>   I heard something crack;
> Not a man in all England
>   Can mend that.

The solution is *Ice*, recalling the frequent phenomenon in hard winters, before the Thames was canalized and the obstruction of old London Bridge was removed. The old bridge was replaced by John Rennie's new bridge in 1831. This new bridge in turn became too narrow and fragile for modern traffic, and was replaced by an even newer London Bridge in 1973.

If Macaulay's New Zealander were to take his stand on newest London Bridge today and look upstream to Blackfriars, he would see a vast desolation of redevelopment occupying either bank. The jungle of wharves and warehouses that was erected on both banks during the industrial revolution, spoiling the grand view of St Paul's from the river, was heavily bombed during the Second World War. From the 1960s onwards, as the port and associated commercial activities have been removed from the centre of London, a chance that will not recur has been given to build something on the banks worthy of a great river running through the heart of a great city. The small, slab-like skyscrapers that increasingly hem in St Paul's and have changed the skyline of London more drastically than the Great Fire, do not give much confidence that the chance will be taken.

During the 1970s the Corporation of the City redeveloped the north bank of the river from Blackfriars to London Bridge. They reclaimed land from the river to carry a new riverside dual carriageway, which vastly improves the east–west traffic flow through the medieval street plan of the City. To save space, which is worth its volume in gold inside the Golden Square Mile, along Upper Thames Street the highway is buried beneath a deck that carries buildings. Above the road stand: the new City of London School (incorporating in its chapel the tower of the ruined church of St Mary Somerset); Mondial House, an international telecommunications centre linking the City to the world; a new centre for the fur trade, which has been based on the Thames since the Hudson Bay Company sailed from London; and an hotel at the old quay of Queenhithe. The paddle steamer, *Princess Elizabeth*, which won a battle honour at the evacuation of Dunkirk, is harboured in Queenhithe as a floating restaurant and pub. The development includes a long riverside walk that gives more access for citizens to their river than has been available since the Great Fire.

When the Roman Londinium was fully developed and covered about three hundred acres, its western wall ran down to the Thames at Blackfriars. Just outside the wall the Fleet River ran into the Thames. It still does so today as one of London's lost rivers, having been encompassed and buried in a pipe in 1765. The black cloud of the Fleet's confluence with the slightly less black Thames can still be seen at low tide at Blackfriars. A Roman ship was excavated here in 1962 during the construction of the Blackfriars underpass.

The Fleet has had an unsavoury reputation for a long time. The records show that in the thirteenth century the stench from the Fleet River or 'ditch' was so offensive that the Black Friars complained to the King about it. The stink was caused not so much by the fishmongers, who had permission to throw their dirty water in it, as by the butchers of the St Nicholas shambles. These were allowed to use a special wharf opposite the Fleet Prison for cleaning their carcasses in after the weekly slaughtering, and they threw their offal into the water at ebb tide. The unhappy prisoners in the Fleet became so poisoned by the stench that the privilege of the butchers had to be withdrawn.

In the *Dunciad* Pope summed up the most conspicuous feature of the filthy Fleet:

> Fleet Ditch, with disemboguing streams
> Rolls the large tribute of dead dogs to Thames,
> The king of dykes! than whom no sluice of mud
> With deeper sable blots the silver flood.

The Black Friars were the Dominicans, the mendicant order of preachers with black habits, who removed from Holborn to the site still named after them in 1274. After the Dissolution of the Monasteries James and Richard Burbage built their theatre on part of the site, so giving a name that subsists to Playhouse Yard. Shakespeare bought a house next door in Ireland Yard, so as to be near his work. However, the Puritan objections of the City fathers to 'the great inconveniences and ill rule that followeth the players' forced the Burbages to move on. They crossed the river to Bankside, where they built the Globe.

Excavation of the Blackfriars development in 1972 exhumed temporarily the remains of one of London's great buildings, Baynard's Castle. This Norman and medieval fortress and palace was the equivalent stronghold on the west wall to the Tower of London on the east wall of the City, both built to dominate and terrorize the Londoners, who did not acquiesce in the Norman Conquest for many years and were never friendly to kings or other masters who interfered with trade.

Ralph Baynard, or Bainardus, was one of Duke William's followers who came to England with him for the good of Normandy and to improve their fortunes. *Domesday Book* describes a Bainard as holding the lands across the Fleet. Baynard's Castle was built facing the river, near the angle of the City wall.

His stronghold was eventually inherited by Robert FitzWalter, one of King John's malcontent Barons, around whom a thick accretion of medieval romance has grown. History rather than legend establishes the fact that FitzWalter was one of the leaders of the Barons who extracted the charter of privileges, especially privileges for Barons, called Magna Carta from King John. He became chief bannerer and castellan of the City, the leader of its armed forces in war, with rights of jurisdiction in his own *soke* (a district under a particular local jurisdiction) independent even of that autocratic feudal dignitary, the Mayor. FitzWalter was also responsible at Baynard's Castle for the execution of traitors, each one being tied to a post in the Thames, 'at a good wharf, where boats are fastened, two ebbings and two flowings of the water'. In an excess of brutality as if to teach the victims savagely not to repeat their treasons, they were fastened to their stakes to watch the tide ebbing away, before it flowed in again to drown them.

The Norman fortress was replaced in 1428 by a new and equally embattled Baynard's Castle, built a little to the east by Humphrey, Duke of Gloucester: the 'Good Duke Humphrey', who earned his approving epithet not from any purity of character, but because his fine collection of books was the seed of the Bodleian Library, and because he was a benefactor of Oxford University in other ways. When Humphrey was attainted of treason, his castle was seized and thereafter held by the Crown. Baynard's Castle became one of the royal palaces of London, and as such was the stage for many notable scenes of English history. The most notable was the assumption of the crown there by Richard III, in a scene vividly described by Shakespeare, who was closely following the *Life of Richard the Third* attributed to Sir Thomas More. Shakespeare sets the scene brilliantly with the court of Baynard's Castle filled with the Lord Mayor, Aldermen, and citizens of London in a panic about the political crisis. Richard appears above in a gallery of the castle, holding a prayer-book and standing between two bishops, as a disingenuous exemplar of piety.

Catesby and Buckingham pretend to act as go-betweens to persuade an apparently unwilling and diffident Richard to take the crown:

> Alas, why would you heap these cares on me?
> I am unfit for state and majesty:
> I do beseech you, take it not amiss,
> I cannot nor I will not yield to you.

Not surprisingly Richard is soon persuaded to yield.

> Buckingham: Then I salute you with this royal title.
> Long live King Richard, England's worthy king.

> All: Amen.

Shakespeare's portrait of Crouchback may have been coloured by official Tudor propaganda, but it is so overwhelmingly powerful that it is by now impossible to discover any other personality for Richard behind Shakespeare's portrait. It is historical fact that Richard assumed the crown at Baynard's Castle.

Queen Jane lost it there. The Council met in Baynard's Castle on June 19, 1553, and resolved to uphold Mary Tudor's claim to the throne, and deny the claim of Lady Jane Grey, lately proclaimed by Northumberland. The Lord Mayor was sent for. He acquiesced in the decision and he and the Council rode into Cheapside and proclaimed Mary with fanfares of trumpets. The decision taken in Baynard's Castle and London's acceptance of it secured the throne for Mary Tudor for good or ill, mostly, in the distant perspective of history, for ill.

Subsequent monarchs used Baynard's Castle as their regular lodging in the west end of the City. For example, the records show Henry VIII staying there for the trial of the cause of Dr Standish, when Wolsey pleaded the case for the clergy.

Elizabeth leased Baynard's Castle to the Earl of Pembroke. There is a charming account of her visiting him there for supper, showing how the Thames was still used as the main road of London: 'And after supper she took a boat and was tossed up and down upon the River Thames, hundreds of boats and barges rowing about her, and thousands of people thronging at the waterside to look upon her Majesty, rejoicing to see her, and sights upon the Thames.'

Such private and public recreation is a proper use for the Thames, and once the port and attendant commerce have finally removed downstream from London, the river will be safe for such use again.

Pepys noted in his diary shortly after the Restoration that 'My Lord [Lord Sandwich] went at night with the King to Baynard's Castle to supper, and I home'.

The Great Fire of 1666 almost completely destroyed the old royal palace to the west of the City. A single turret, built into a private house, survived until 1720. Remains of the Tudor castle, including the waterfront with projecting towers, were uncovered briefly over Easter 1972, while the site of the new City of London School for Boys was being excavated. They have been reburied beneath the school to wait for their resurrection by archaeologists or, perhaps, for Macaulay's New Zealander some centuries into the future.

Just back from the waterfront here stands the College of Arms, that remarkable survival of medieval chivalry and the home of the modern heralds, Garter and Norroy, Richmond and Rouge Croix, Blue Mantle and Portcullis, and the rest in their incongruous modern suits and ancient titles. A century ago Dickens made the unkind judgement of the College: 'This is one of the old-fashioned institutions that still survive, although it is difficult to see of what particular service it is to anyone but its officials. In the days when the herald was really an important functionary, not only in state ceremonials, but also in registering the various grants of arms, superintending and chronicling trials by battle and chivalric exercises, it is possible that the thirteen kings-at-arms, heralds, and pursuivants may have been usefully employed.' It still survives, its inmates profitably if not precisely usefully employed designing arms for new life peers and local authorities, and tracing the pedigrees of ambitious Americans. Their college is a remarkable architectural survival. The Earl of Derby in the sixteenth century gave his mansion, a courtyard house, to the College of Arms, which rebuilt it in the next century as the present house on the same site.

The next notable building on the north bank is a striking contrast to the College, Cannon Street Station, terminus for City commuters from the south-east. The station's two tall cathedral towers are monuments to Victorian attitudes to industry and commerce. Cannon Street railway viaduct is built on the site of the Steelyard of the Hanseatic merchants. The merchants of the Hanse received the prime site on the river from Henry III and retained it even after the League was expelled from England by Elizabeth I. It remained the property of the League and its successors until 1853. The founding fathers of the Hanseatic League, the fraternity of German merchants called the Easterlings, first appeared in the Thames as early as 979 in the reign of Ethelred II. They gradually established a monopoly of all foreign trade in the port, so laying the foundation for the future position of the City as the mart and entrepôt of the world. In its heyday the Hanseatic League included eighty of the richest cities of Germany and Scandinavia and brought the trade of the whole known world up the London River.

There were predecessors to the Easterlings on this part of the palimpsest of the north bank of the Thames in London. Cannon Street station itself is built on the remains of a great official Roman palace, with assembly rooms, offices, and a central courtyard with a large ornamental pool. The palace was built towards the end of the first century A.D., and it is a reasonable supposition that so grand a place was the official residence of the governor of the province himself. No Roman palace of anything like the same size has been found in Britain, with the single exception of Fishbourne, a special case, and probably a reward to Britain's first Quisling: Cogidubnus, king of the Atrebates, who lived in the district that later became Sussex, Hampshire, and Berkshire.

Not only the old Romans, but also Charles Dickens, that great Thames lover and connoisseur, haunts this reach. His characters walk on the water more thickly between Southwark and London Bridges than anywhere else on the congested river. Here Sarah Gamp shook her umbrella at 'them smoking monsters' (all steam machines), wished the 'Antworks package' in 'Jonadge's belly', and pronounced definitively: 'Them Confugion steamers has done more to throw us out of our reg'lar work and bring ewents on at times when nobody counted on 'em than all the other frights that ever was took.'

'Floating on the Thames between Southwark, which is of iron, and London Bridge, which is of stone, as an autumn evening was closing in' marks the limits of Gaffer Hexam's river beat in search of corpses to snatch and the beginning of *Our Mutual Friend*. Here walk or row the spirits of Pip in *Great Expectations*, David Copperfield, a surrogate for the young Dickens himself, who says 'I was wont to sit in one of the stone recesses [of old London Bridge], watching the people go by', and many more.

Cannon Street railway bridge stands on four rows of the graceless fat iron legs favoured by Victorian railway engineers. Next to it upstream the first Southwark Bridge was designed by John Rennie and built between 1815 and 1819. It was replaced a century later by the present inoffensive but un-memorable erection by Sir Ernest George.

Bridging the Thames has been a controversial matter since the Romans arrived. The river was for centuries on the one hand the chief highway of London, but on the other hand a broad obstacle to expansion on the South Bank. New bridges made north–south communications easier. But they harmed the vested interests of such bodies as the City Corporation, the watermen, who ferried travellers across the Thames, and conservatives and conservationists generally. The change from river to road traffic was as significant in the development of London as the introduction of the railways or of the tower blocks of flats and offices. A prominent date in the change is 1564, when Guilliam Boonen, a Dutchman, became the Queen's coachman, and, according to the Continuation of John Stow's *Annals*, 'was the first that brought the use of coaches into England'.

Not surprisingly the London watermen, who had been making their living by ferrying people and goods on the Thames since the early Middle Ages, objected to this innovation that threatened their livelihood. Stow claimed, in what was probably a wild exaggeration, that there were '40,000 watermen and those that lived and were maintained by them'. John Norden gave the same number in 1594, but he included stevedores, porters, boat-builders, and associated trades. Even so his estimate is as suspect as contemporary Greek estimates of the size of Xerxes's army.

The waterman found a remarkable, vociferous, and engaging spokesman in John Taylor, who gloried in his self-appointed sobriquet of 'the Water Poet'. His fastidious literary obituarist in the *Dictionary of National Biography* considered that 'literary bargee' was a more appropriate designation. Even Taylor himself, who was seldom given to understatement or underestimation of himself, was aware that he was not exactly Shakespeare:

> Though I deserve not, I desire
> The laurel wreath, the poet's hire.

But although the Water Poet's doggerel was sometimes as abominable as that of McGonagall, that master of the bathetic anticlimax and the engaging irrelevancy, his knowledge and love of the river were as profound as those of A. P. Herbert. He is a rare and interesting demotic voice of the common but no means ordinary man of the sixteenth and seventeenth centuries. Taylor was born of humble parentage at Gloucester in 1580, and sent to the local grammar school where, he tells us, he became 'mired' in his Latin accidence. He was then apprenticed to a Thames waterman, and subsequently, in a common accident to watermen, pressed into the Navy and present at the siege of Cadiz. On retiring from the Navy he became a waterman, and for fourteen years collector of the perquisite of wine extracted by the Lieutenant of the Tower of London from all ships that brought wine up the Thames.

He increased his earnings by poetastery and by a series of madcap exploits that made him a celebrity and sold his writings. He went on foot from London to Braemar, starting without a penny in his pocket and rhyming as he went. He made a similarly extravagant visit to the Queen of Bohemia at Prague. And he set out to row from London to Queenborough on the Kent coast in a boat made of brown paper, with two stockfish tied to canes as oars. Taylor and his companion took with them eight bladders filled with air to keep them afloat if the paper bottom fell to pieces, which it predictably did within half an hour. Nevertheless they made it to Queenborough, more dead than alive, and presented the skeleton of their boat to the mayor 'for a monument'. Taylor commemorated the adventure in a characteristic mock-epic:

> The tossing billows made our boat to caper,
> Our paper form scarce being form of paper.

Taylor's writings were as various and voluminous as his frolics; they occupy no less than nine columns of the *Dictionary of National Biography*, and comprise what he might have described, in a favourite word, as a gallimaufry. But the central and recurring theme is the Thames, the lives of the watermen, and the menace of the new-fangled coaches, which he abused in a typically bombastic and alliterative epithet as 'hired hackney hell carts'. Whatever one thinks of his poetry, Taylor was an accurate and extremely valuable mirror of his age, reflecting an area of life ignored by upper-class observers. In *An Arrant Thief*, 1623, he returns to his favourite topic, the decline of traffic on the river caused by the hackney hell carts:

> All sorts of men work all the means they can
> To make a *Thief* of every Waterman:
> And as it were in one consent they join
> To trot by land i' th' dirt, and save their coin . . .
> Against the ground we stand and knock our heels
> Whilst all our profit runs away on wheels.

The watermen generally carried their passengers in wherries of six or eight oars. The smallest craft on the river crowded with traffic were the coracles of the fishermen and the hoys or double-scullers used by some watermen for short journeys, known and summoned by the shout of 'oars'. A visiting Frenchman in the eighteenth century, hearing the cry 'oars, oars', was shocked by the blatancy of the English, misapprehending that he was being invited to a brothel rather than a boat ride. Charges were higher for journeys against the tide, and watermen received a bonus for 'a barge beneath the bridge', the hazardous shooting of the rapids between the piles of London Bridge. Prudent passengers disembarked at Swan Stairs and rejoined their wherry at the farther side, after it had shot the rapids. It was for long the cheapest form of transport. A Ben the Boatswain in a play of that name by T. E. Wilkes, first produced in 1839, asserted that it was still possible to persuade 'a jolly young waterman to row folks from Wapping to Rotherhithe for a penny a head'. The watermen were renowned for their insolence and scurrility. One of them rashly provoked Dr Johnson to his judicious reply, which any waterman would have been proud to have thought of: 'Sir, under the pretence of keeping a bawdy house, your wife is a receiver of stolen goods.'

Apart from the proliferation of wheels, another complaint of the watermen was the decline of the theatre on the South Bank, which also deprived the ferries of customers. The theatres had originally transmigrated across the river because of the Puritan and public health laws compelling them to give their performances outside the jurisdiction of the Lord Mayor of London. The laws were relaxed, and, when the first Globe was burned down in 1613, there was a proposal to rebuild it on the north bank; a proposal most offensive to watermen. As their champion, John Taylor had a meeting with the actors in the Cardinal Cap Tavern on Bankside and opposed the proposal with his customary vigour. The players replied sarcastically by asking whether the watermen would not also like the Royal Exchange, Paul's Walk, and Moorfields removed to the South Bank for their benefit.

Ned Ward (1667–1731), the tavern-keeper and writer of Hudibrastic doggerel and humorous prose, recorded in one of his sketches of London low life what purported to be a typical exchange between watermen of rival boats, one from Old Swan Stairs and the other from Lambeth:

'You couple of treacherous sons of Bridewell bawds, who are pimps to your own mothers, stallions to your sisters, and cock-bawds to the rest of your relations; who were begot by hustling, spew'd up and not born; and christened out of a chamber pot; how dare you show your ugly faces upon the river of Thames and to fright the Queen's swans from holding their heads above water?'

The City crew replied in the same style, with improbably high-flown and obscene vegetable metaphors:

'You lousy starved crew of worm-pickers and snail-catchers, you offspring of a dunghill and brothers to a pumpkin, who can't afford butter to your cabbage or bacon to your sprouts; who was he that sent the gardener to cut a hundred of sparigrass, and dug twice in his wife's parsley bed before the good man came back again? Hold your tongues, you knitty radish-mongers, or I'll whet my needle upon my arse and sew your lips together.'

John Taylor may have been a modest poet in one sense of the adjective. But he was a good waterman and Thames-lover and a source of gaiety to his and future generations. His most practical achievement was, with the Company of Watermen, to keep the carriages out of London for thirty-five years, unless their journeys ended at least two miles from the river.

The history of the South Bank, Bankside, and Southwark goes back to the first Roman bridge over the Thames, which is the beginning of British history also. Extensive remains of Roman settlement have been found spreading along the South Bank from the southern end of the first London bridges. For seventeen hundred years London Bridge was the hub of the growth of London. The South Bank, refuge of unlicensed actors who were pursued by the law as vagabonds, was a convenient haven for other activities prohibited within the City Liberties, notably bear-baiting, bull-baiting, and prostitution.

John Stow, the founding father of London topography and patron saint of the London guide-book industry, noticed Bankside in his *Survey of London* of 1598 and 1603 for its bears, bulls, and stews. Until the middle of the sixteenth century it was commonly known as Stew Bank or Stewside. Stow records that Henry II introduced laws regulating the brothels and giving them certain privileges on the South Bank 'for the repaire of incontinent men to the like women'. The regulations included such prudent provisions as: 'No single woman to be kept against her will that would leave her sinne; no single woman to take money to lie with any man, but shee lie with him all night till the morrow; and, no stewholder to keepe any woman that hath the perilous infirmitie of burning, nor to sell bread, ale, flesh, fish, wood, coale, or any victuals.' The distinction between an inn, a brothel, and a yard for the performances of the travelling players was nice, but the authorities were continually anxious to try to enforce it.

Henry VIII tried to close the stews. As might be expected of so close an observer of contemporary scene, John Taylor had a more or less apt rhyme or two for the episode:

> The stews of England bore a beastly sway
> Till the eighth Henry banished them away.
> And since those common whores were quite put downe,
> A damned crew of private whores are grown.

By Stow's time there was a row of twelve permitted stew-houses along the waterfront of Bankside, with their heraldic signs such as The Boar's Head and The Cardinal's Hat not on hanging boards but painted on their walls facing the Thames so as to attract trade from across the river.

The English have had a passion and a reputation for savage blood sports from time immemorial. As early as the twelfth century William FitzStephen wrote in his *Descriptio Londinii*: 'In winter, every holiday before dinner, the boars prepared for brawn are set to fight, or else bulls and bears are baited.' The ludicrous passion still persists in such Lilliputian fields as fox-hunting and syndicate pheasant shoots. Baiting itself was not finally illegalized by Act of Parliament until 1835, and in the angry debates on the subject conservative John Bulls argued that it was all a filthy anti-British plot by the Jacobins and the Methodists, and that the British constitution must stand or fall with the British bear garden. Bankside was the most famous place in England for baiting in various bear gardens and in the adjacent Paris Garden. This pleasure park, gaming-house, and bowling-alley seems to have been a synonym figuratively, as 'bear garden' still persists obsoletely in being, for a scene of strife and uproar. For instance, the porter in Shakespeare's *Henry*

VIII, Act Five, Scene Four, says: 'You'll leave your noise anon, ye rascals. Do you take the court for Paris Garden?'

By the time of Stow's *Survey* there were two bear gardens on Bankside, 'the olde and new places, wherein be kept Beares, Buls and other beastes to be bayted. As also Mastives in severall kenels, nourished to baite them.' The wild animals were baited in enclosed arenas, with the spectators protected by being raised on scaffolding. Generally several dogs at once were set upon a bear. The bear was further handicapped by being chained and having its teeth filed down so that it had to rely entirely on buffets and hugs with its forepaws. In spite of this, the bear often won and survived long enough to become famous. 'Harry Hunks' was the champion bear at Paris Garden in the seventeenth century; and Slender in *The Merry Wives of Windsor* drops the name of another bear called 'Sackerson', which was clearly intended to be familiar to the audience. John Taylor discussed the bears of Bankside in instantly recognizable style:

> No ravenous, savage, cruel bears are these,
> But gentle, milde, delighting still to please,
> And yet they have a trick to bite all such
> As madly use their company too much.

One of the differences between the socially cohesive society of the Tudors and fragmented modern society is that all classes used to go to the bear-baiting as well as the theatre, to a court ceremony as well as a public execution. In the modern world different sections live in their private compartments, and there is little overlap in the audiences for a symphony concert or *Hamlet* on the one hand and a wrestling match or greyhound racing on the other.

Bulls were generally matched with one highly trained and savage dog at a time. The bull was tethered by its horns to a stake with a rope about fifteen feet long. Owners stood around outside the perimeter of the rope holding their dogs by the ears, and releasing them to make their charges one at a time. The dog tried to dodge past the bull's defences and sink its teeth into vulnerable flesh. The bull warded it off with its feet and horns, which were cased in wooden sheaths for the benefit of the dogs. The bull tried to slip its horns beneath the dog and toss it high in the air to break its neck or back, if the spectators did not manage to catch it. A French lawyer called Misson, who travelled in England at the end of the seventeenth century, has left a vivid and bloody description of a bull being baited:

'But unless the dog is totally stunned with the fall, he is sure to crawl again towards the bull, come on't what will. Sometimes a second frisk into the air disables him for ever; but sometimes, too, he fastens upon his enemy, and when once he has seized him with his eye-teeth, he sticks to him like a leech, and would sooner die than leave his hold. Then the bull bellows and bounds and kicks, all to shake off the dog. In the end, either the dog tears out the piece he has laid hold on, and falls, or else remains fixed to him with an obstinacy that would never end, did they not pull him off. While some hold the bull, others thrust staves into the dog's mouth, and open it by main force.'

The German tourist to the court of Queen Elizabeth I, Thomas Platter, describes a fight he saw where a great white bull tossed every dog that was set on him, the attendants catching them on sticks to break their fall, so that they would not be damaged, but could be nursed back to health for more fighting.

On August 14, 1666, Samuel Pepys took his wife to the Bear Garden on Bankside, 'where I had not been, I think, of many years, and saw some good sport of the bull's tossing the dogs—one into the very boxes. But it is a very rude and nasty pleasure. We had a great many hectors [sc. Flash Harrys] in the same box with us, and one very fine went into the pit, and played his dog for a wager; which was a strange sport for a gentleman.'

A few years later John Evelyn recorded a visit to Bankside in his diary:

'I went with some friends to the bear garden, where was cock fighting, dog fighting, beare and bull baiting, it being a famous day for all these butcherly sports, or rather barbarous cruelties. The bulls did exceedingly well, but the Irish wolfe-dog exceeded, which was a tall greyhound, a stately creature indeede, who beate a cruell mastiff. One of the bulls toss'd a dog full into a lady's lap as she sat in one of the boxes at a considerable height from the arena. Two poore dogs were killed, and so all ended with the ape on horse-back, and I most heartily weary of the rude and dirty pastime.'

The Puritans disapproved of baiting and suppressed it, but it was revived at the Restoration. Robert Crowley, a strictly Puritan Archdeacon of Hereford and a versifier of the John Taylor school, wrote:

> What follye is thys to kepe wyth daunger,
> A greate mastyfe dogge and a foule ouglye bear?
> And to thys onelye ende, to se them two fyght
> Wyth terrible teaarynge, a full ouglye syght.

Macaulay, in one of his perceptive flashes, wrote that the Puritan hated bear-baiting not because it gave pain to the bear, but because it gave pleasure to the spectators. A further and more serious Puritan argument against it was that the crowd and the atmosphere and the adjacency of the stews were thought to foster such pleasant vices as drunkenness and, especially, irregular sex. When the gallery of the Paris Garden collapsed in 1583, killing several spectators and injuring several hundred, the Puritans claimed that the accident was 'an extraordinary judgement of God' and the fruit of 'jolity' upon a Sunday.

We know what London by the Thames looked like just before the Great Fire of 1666 destroyed it largely through a Bohemian artist called Wenceslaus Hollar. Hollar was brought to London by his patron, Thomas Howard, Earl of Arundel, the first great private connoisseur of art and antiquities in England. He was lodged at Arundel House, next to Somerset House on the Strand, and employed in making the topographical etchings for which he was famous and copying his patron's collection of paintings and classical sculpture. He became drawing master to the young Prince, later Charles II. It can be demonstrated from internal and external evidence that Hollar's views of London and the Thames were punctiliously faithful in their detail.

At some time about 1642, with all art and aristocratic patronage interrupted by the Civil War, Hollar made a series of drawings of the whole of London from the top of the tower of St Mary Overie's, now Southwark Cathedral. His purpose was to publish a great panorama built up from a series of seven large etching plates, which would form the longest and most comprehensive portrait of a city and its river ever made.

The war interfered with his project, and Hollar found himself helping the Royalists to defend Basing House, near Basingstoke, having as commanding officer the court portrait painter, Sir Robert Peake, and as comrades-in-arms a regiment of aesthetes including the engraver, William Faithorne, the writer, Thomas Fuller, the comic actor, William Robbins, and the aged architect and impresario of the Masque, Inigo Jones. Perhaps not surprisingly the beleaguered ivory tower was sacked by Cromwell's troops. Hollar retreated to Antwerp and finally completed his *Long View of London* there, publishing it in 1647.

Even by then some of the skyline had changed, and in 1666 it was blotted out. Bankside is prominent in the western foreground of the *Long View*, with two of the Bankside theatres protruding from the ribbon of houses, doubtless of ill repute, along the river front. The architecture of the Shakespearean theatre is a subject of awesome intricacy that excites almost theological odium among the differing experts. But it is generally agreed, even by men so averse to agreement, that Hollar, separated by time and distance from his model, confused the two theatres in his *Long View*. The one with the St George's flag that he labelled *The Globe* was actually The Hope, and the other he labelled *Beere bayting house* was actually the Globe, mark two.

The second Globe was built by Burbage in 1613 to replace the original Globe of 1599, the Globe of *Hamlet*, *Macbeth*, and *King Lear*, which was burned to the ground after the over-exuberant discharge of a cannon during a performance of *Henry VIII* had set its thatched roof alight. Sir Henry Wotton described the calamity:

'Now, King Henry making a masque at Cardinal Wolsey's house, and certain cannons being shot off at his entry, some of the paper or other stuff wherewith one of them was stopped did light on the thatch; where, being thought at first but an idle smoke and their eyes more attentive to the show, it kindled inwardly and ran round like a train, consuming within less than an hour the whole house to the very grounds. This was the fatal period of that virtuous fabric, wherein yet nothing did perish but a few forsaken cloaks; only one man had his breeches set on fire that would perhaps have broiled him, if he had not by the benefit of a provident wit put it out with bottle ale.'

Ben Jonson celebrated the event:

> Against the Globe, the glory of the Bank,
> Which though it were the fort of the whole parish,
> Flanked with a ditch and forced out of a marish,
> I saw with two poor chambers taken in
> And razed ere thought could urge this might have been!
> See the World's ruins! Nothing but the piles left.

After the Restoration and the Great Fire, Puritan prejudice and proclivities had less power to regulate the social life of London. Theatres were no longer restricted to their ghetto in the suburbs, and, after a brief but glorious period of not much more than fifty years, Bankside ceased to be the home of the English drama. At intervals ever since persuasive enthusiasts have been suggesting that there should be some memorial on the site to Shakespeare, the Globe, and the greatest flowering of the English theatre.

In theory the most appropriate memorial would be a reconstruction of the Globe on its original site. The idea is simpler in theory than practice. We have only the haziest guesses about the structure of the first Globe, Shakespeare's theatre. The scholars are strongly opposed to each other on many of the crucial questions of the Elizabethan stage. Was the stage structure arranged to provide seven distinct and permanent acting areas having specific functions? Did the actors rise to curtained stage-houses from a tiring-house beneath the stage, or emerge from curtained doorways? It is a subject so poor in hard facts and so rich in romantic possibilities that it breeds speculation and fanaticism.

The latest attempt at a memorial is being made by the American actor and theatrical producer, Sam Wanamaker, who has founded 'the World Centre for Shakespeare Studies, limited', and the Bankside Globe Cinema and temporary playhouse near the site of the original Globe. His eventual aim, if he can raise the money, is to reconstruct the Globe. The antiquarians want as faithful a reconstruction as possible, which would be a picturesque and educational museum, but, with all those curtained stage-houses, an inconvenient and possibly a dangerous stage for presenting living plays on. The actors want a Globe that they can act in.

Wenceslaus Hollar's engraving of the second Globe in his *Long View* is the only detailed contemporary picture we have of an Elizabethan playhouse. The second Globe was not the theatre of Shakespeare's heyday, but it was built for his company. It can be presumed that its design improved upon that of the old Globe and included all the modifications and refinements necessary to present the works of the Globe's most popular playwright to the best advantage. John Taylor considered the new building an improvement on the old:

> As Gold is better that's in fire tried,
> So is the bankside Globe that late was burn'd:
> For where before it had a thatched hide,
> Now to a stately Theator is turn'd.
> Which is an Emblem, that great things are won,
> By those that dare through greatest dangers run.

In 1973 a Mr C. Walter Hodges with infinite pains projected from the *Long View* an accurate ground plan of the Globe, and elaborated detailed ideas on the design and interior organization of the building, solving such notorious cruces as the functions of the lantern and the twin-gabled superstructure known to the Elizabethans as the Heavens: he argues persuasively that it was self-supporting, without obtrusive pillars. If we ever get round to building a third Globe on Bankside as a memorial to Shakespeare, Mr Hodges has provided a convincing and architecturally coherent plan.

The players, prostitutes, bear-wards, and others classed by Puritan laws with vagabonds were attracted to Bankside and the rest of Southwark by an ancient form of sanctuary known as the Liberty of the Clink. This liberty encompassed Winchester House, the town palace of the Bishops of Winchester. Southwark, the gateway of London to the populous and rich southern counties, was always a favourite area for inns for travellers and the town houses of southern English church dignitaries.

Chaucer's Canterbury package-tourists assembled at this southern bridge-head of London, with one of the most softly compelling introductions in English fiction:

> Befelle, that, in that seson on a day,
> In Southwark at the *Tabard* as I lay,
> Redy to wenden on my pilgrimage
> To Canterbury with devoute corage,
> At night was come into that hostelrie
> Wel nine and twenty in a compagnie . . .

Stow catalogues Southwark inns in addition to The Tabard: 'Spurre, Christopher, Bull, Queen's Head, George, Hart, King's Head, etc.' The Hart comes into Shakespeare's *Henry VI* as well as the *Pickwick Papers*.

In addition to the Bishops of Winchester, the Bishops of Rochester and the Abbots of St Augustine at Canterbury, Battle, and Hyde all had their town palaces in Southwark. All have vanished except for a thirteenth-century wall of Winchester Palace, which has become the wall of a fruit and vegetable warehouse in Winchester Square by the river.

It seems likely that Henry of Blois, a great builder-bishop and one of the most notable holders of the see, built himself the first palace here. Some projecting foundation courses excavated in 1971–72 are of the twelfth century. But the upstanding remains of the south wall and west gable wall of the great hall appear to date from the first half of the fourteenth century. The great hall was on the first floor and entered by a door that can be seen in the south wall by those who take the trouble to get the key from the fruit and vegetable warehouse. On the gable wall at the same level can be seen the three service doorways that led into the hall from the kitchens, buttery, and pantry. High up in the gable is a superb rose-window with an inserted hexagon made up of eighteen cusped triangles. It is bricked up and damaged by fire, but still one of the finest examples surviving in Britain.

In the basements beneath Winchester House the Bishops had their own jail, a fine and private place for both ecclesiastical and lay malefactors, called the Clink and in convenient and symbolic propinquity to the stews. The notoriety of this jail gave its name to a slang term for being in prison generally that has only recently started to become old-fashioned: 'in clink'. The 1972 supplement to the *Oxford English Dictionary* recorded *clink* as being a current synonym for prison or cells. A resonant example occurs in Kipling's *Barrack-room Ballads*:

> And I'm here in the Clink
> For a thundering drink
> And blacking the Corporal's eye.

Besides inns, theatres, stews, and ecclesiastical palaces, prisons were another of Southwark's specialities: a less attractive one. There were no less than seven of them, including the Clink, which was burnt down by the Gordon rioters in 1780: the King's Bench and the Marshalsea, both of venerable and unsavoury medieval reputation; the Compter; the White Lion; the new eighteenth-century King's Bench debtors' prison, demolished in 1869, where Dickens's father, to say nothing of Wilkins Micawber, senior, did time; and the Horsemonger Lane Gaol, a model prison where Leigh Hunt had a comfortable stretch for characterizing the Prince of Wales, later George IV, in the *Examiner*, with more truth than charity, as:

'This delightful, blissful, wise, pleasurable, honourable, virtuous, true, and immortal Prince was a violator of his word, a libertine over head and ears in debt and disgrace, a despiser of domestic ties, the companion of gamblers and demireps, a man who has just closed half a century without one single claim on the gratitude of his country or the respect of posterity.'

The waterfront of Bankside, where the stews used to hang out their banners on their outward walls, is a mess of industrial development, and, at present, redevelopment. The colossal brick tower of Bankside power station belches a thick stream of white smoke and steam for the London Electricity Board, and as a side effect supplies domestic hot water and heating to the South Bank. Beside it at Cardinal's Wharf in Cardinal Cap Alley is the modest little house where Christopher Wren lived while he was rebuilding St Paul's from the ashes. Katherine, the Infanta of Castile and Aragon, lodged in the same house when she first landed in London aged sixteen on her unfortunate journey to marry first Arthur Tudor, Prince of Wales, and then, on his death, his brother, later Henry VIII.

In the seventeenth century Wren had a magnificent view across the river of his crowning masterpiece of the great dome of St Paul's 'looming like a bubble o'er the town', and above the astonishingly multifarious spires and towers of the fifty-one churches that he rebuilt in the City after the fire. He would probably not be amused today to see even St Paul's hedged about and dwarfed by the less elegant and monotonously rectangular commercial erections of the 1960s and 1970s. No other great riparian city has allowed its finest view to be so degraded. Macaulay's New Zealander might well ask himself what decadent, philistine race had obscured the rising sun of its greatest building with tall boxes.

Wren would approve of the warehouse converted into the Mermaid Theatre, the culmination of a lifelong ambition of Sir Bernard Miles to reintroduce the English theatre into its birthplace, the City. He might shed a pious tear for the departure of the glory from Printing House Square in 1974. Printing has gone on in this square fronting the Thames since the King's Printing House was established there in 1667, when Wren was starting to rebuild the City. In 1785 a former coal merchant with ambitions named John Walter started to publish a newspaper called the *Daily Universal Register* from Printing House Square. It was intended to be a temporary advertising gimmick to publicize a new form of printing known as logography, in which Walter was interesting himself. Like so many other British institutions, *The Times* thus evolved by accident and unintentionally. 'The Thunderer' was forged from this ludicrous beginning amid the shrill Babel of squalling eighteenth-century news and advertising sheets. The great newspaper is popularly believed on the one hand to have the power to make and break governments, but on the other, in some devious English way, to be a mouthpiece of the Establishment. Foreigners still sometimes take the latter view, erroneously.

What is more true is that the journalists who have written *The Times*, named 'Ye Black Friars' by their former rogue proprietor, Lord Northcliffe, in a phrase as close to contemptuous respect as he ever allowed himself to come about anyone, have traditionally inclined to the opinion that the world would be a better and more rational place if run from Printing House Square. Often they have been right in this opinion. Sometimes, as in Geoffrey Dawson's blinkered and unscrupulous promotion of the policy they named appeasement in the 1930s, they have been mistaken.

The Times has left for the Gray's Inn Road, a mile to the north-west, but Printing House Square is haunted by the shades of dusty, dead journalists on awkward, clerical, scribbler's toe-in-the-door. Lord Lyndhurst, the Lord Chancellor in the 1840s, described Thomas Barnes, the first editor in the modern sense of the word, as the most powerful man in the country. He did not mean it as a compliment. This was the period when *The Times* was emerging as the organ and representative of the middle classes against the entrenched great aristocratic families that still ran the country from their hereditary positions in both parties. It was considered a dangerously revolutionary and treasonable rag by the rulers of England, and Lord Lyndhurst described it more than once with those epithets in the House of Lords.

Barnes's successor, John T. Delane, was said to have seen more sunrises than any man in London, because of his assiduity at his desk. He was, more is the pity, the last Editor of *The Times* to ride on horseback down Fleet Street talking to two peers of the realm, who walked beside him, so showing a proper sense of Delane's position in the magic circle of power. 'Chinese' Morrison of the Boxer Rising; Henry de Blowitz, who scooped the world with the treaty after the Congress of Berlin redrawing the map of eastern Europe (legend says that he picked up the wrong hat with the text inside it on purpose after dinner with Bismarck; history that he had a good contact among the plenipotentiaries, and a wonderfully retentive memory); above all William Howard Russell, the first modern war correspondent, whose dispatches from the Crimea, the American Civil War, and the Franco–Prussian War finally demolished the myth of the generals that war was in some mysterious way fun and a glorious and glamorous business: the shades of the Black Friars dance a ghostly saraband around Henry Moore's strange sundial in Printing House Square with a phantasmagoria of others, who have left no by-lines behind them.

And ghostly dramatic critics, whose roll includes Leigh Hunt, William Hazlitt, A. B. Walkley, Charles Morgan, and other notables, sweep into the square late at night after curtain-fall, like black bats in their evening dress and opera cloaks, to the carefully arranged decanter of Printing House Square port and the pad of hand-made foolscap waiting for them to pen the words that tomorrow will make a play or kill it stone dead. Among the eccentrics likely to be found in so ripe an English institution, *The Times* has the undesirable distinction of having given employment at one time to each of the notorious trio of spies of the cold war: Burgess, Maclean, and Philby. It scandalized Victorian breakfast tables by publishing one of the most emphatic four-letter words in the middle of a Parliamentary report a century before their use became fashionable: a disgruntled compositor under notice to quit insinuated it there surreptitiously. And egregious from the herd of other Black Friars rises Antonio Gallenga, *The Times* man at the front-line with Garibaldi. Gallenga broke the first rule of a cool *Times* man by becoming personally involved in what he was reporting. He was commissioned into the army of the Italian patriots as an *aide-de-camp* to Garibaldi, in spite of thunderous and despairing letters from Delane, reminding him that a *Times* correspondent had more important duties with his pen than with a sword fighting for freedom.

The ghost of another thunderer haunts Bankside opposite to Printing House Square: that of Dr Samuel Johnson, that fulminating and polysyllabic master of classical English prose and after-dinner conversation, whom Tobias Smollett described, in a happily recondite phrase, as the great Cham of literature. In a sense the whole of the City is the haunt of the man who said, not entirely just to vex Boswell, the Scot: 'By seeing London, I have seen as much of life as the world can show.' But Bankside, Southwark, was the London home of the Thrales, and treated by Dr Johnson as his second home. An apartment was always reserved for him both in their country house, Streatham Park, and their town house on Bankside near Mr Thrale's brewery. For many years he was almost domesticated there.

Henry Thrale was a wealthy brewer in a borough famous for its ale since men brewed barley malt and Thames water. Early evidence for this is the Miller's precautionary apology in case he slurs his story in *The Canterbury Tales*:

And therefore if that I misspeak or say,
Wite it [blame] the ale of Southwark, I you pray.

Thrale's wife, Hester Lynch Thrale, was Johnson's particular friend and hostess, as well as being a lively diarist of her encounters with the great man, a literary lion-huntress, and, clearly, a tiresome woman.

Johnson is known to have written his *Life of Congreve* while staying with the Thrales. The exhaustive and exhausting Boswell gives many delightful descriptions of Johnson at the Thrales' in the Borough, another name for Southwark, as does Mrs Thrale herself. The descriptions do not always agree with each other. For example, taken almost at random, in the spring of 1776 Boswell arrived in London from Scotland, and naturally hurried straight to Fleet Street to visit his *guru*. He found that Johnson was, as usual, in the

Borough with the Thrales. Boswell accordingly made his way there, and found Johnson at breakfast with Mrs Thrale and Signor Baretti, the Italian tutor of the Thrale children who lived with the family.

He was kindly welcomed:

'In a moment he [who else?] was in full glow of conversation, and I felt myself elevated as if brought into another state of being. Mrs Thrale and I looked to each other while he talked, and our looks expressed our congenial admiration and affection for him. I shall ever recollect this scene with great pleasure. I exclaimed to her: "I am now, intellectually, *Hermippus redivivus** I am quite restored by him, by transfusion of *mind*."

'"There are many," she replied, "who admire and respect Mr Johnson, but you and I love him."'

The love and the frequent visits to the Borough ended sadly when Mr Thrale died. Johnson, as executor, helped to sell the brewery, and, like the rest of the family, was upset and estranged when Hester decided to remarry. Her second husband was an Italian, Gabriel Piozzi.

By an irony of literary history Boswell's punctilious record of the great man's life and sayings has lived far longer than the writings of the great man himself. His account of their famous tour to the Hebrides is a masterpiece of literature, while Johnson's account of the same tour is a fine work, but less compulsively readable and a bit sententious and ornate for modern tastes. Like other great figures of English literature (Thomas More and Oscar Wilde, the Anglo-Irishman who left one perfect comedy and the echoes of much scintillatingly witty talk) Johnson's chief talent seems to have been for brilliant conversation.

The southern bridgehead of London Bridge, once the only gateway to London from the south, is still a major gate because of the situation there of London Bridge railway station. London is a great sea, whose tide of humanity flows for two hours every morning and ebbs for two hours every evening, punctual and deaf and loud. In this daily ebb and flow one and a quarter million commuters move in and out of central London, forty per cent of them by rail, thirty-five per cent by underground railway, fifteen per cent by bus, and ten per cent by private car, anti-socially occupying more than their fair share of road space. Every week day 328 trains arrive at London Bridge station carrying about 86,500 passengers, and 319 depart with 79,000 passengers. Nobody knows for certain what happens to the missing 7,500, but it is assumed that they find it more convenient to leave from some other station, and not that they are trampled to sand and sink without trace.

* Can Bozzy have had in mind Hermippus the peripatetic philosopher of Smyrna, or Hadrian's freedman who wrote about dreams, or even the Athenian poet Hermippus who accused Aspasia the mistress of Pericles, of impiety and prostitution?

The morning tide at London Bridge reaches full flood shortly after eight a.m., pouring through every creek as fast as a galloping horse at 35,000 bodies an hour. Scurrying feet rattle over London Bridge to the City as ceaselessly as pebbles in the undertow. Eddies of commuters with a few minutes to spare are caught in buffets, drinking tea with one hand, holding a newspaper with the other, propped against the wall with an elbow, backs turned to the stress of the day. Above the thunder of the surf voices as thin as spindrift proclaim sorrow that the eight-o-eight Selhurst train is late because of emergency engineering works between Epsom Downs and Sutton.

Beachcombers are busy on the edges of the tide: tobacco kiosks reek of wrack that smells of seaweed; bookstalls dangle visions of pneumatic bliss; fruit-shops offer pineapples and all the other provisions essential to civilized commuting on the Surbiton train, crushed as close to the anonymous faces of one's fellow-commuters as a short-sighted scribe peering at a manuscript. The hosiery and underwear bar at London Bridge has been fishing successfully for typists in the rush hour since before the last war.

The rising tide washes up flotsam and jetsam of empty cigarette packets, soft drink cartons, sweet papers, fruit peel, newspapers, particularly special supplements of newspapers, bottles with or without messages in them, and occasional rare and enigmatic objects such as old boots and castaway tights. More than a hundred tons of litter are removed every day from London's main railway stations.

In spite of the notices saying, truthfully, that there is more room at the back, the front of every train is packed to sweaty intimacy with inextricably tangled limbs that would be considered indecent assault anywhere but in a commuter train. Before the trains stop moving, doors are open and there is a race to be first through the barriers, half a game and half obsessive fever not to be late to the daily treadmill. From the station the main torrent flows up ramps and over London Bridge. An urban eagle hovering overhead would see a solid stream of heads, not many bowler-hatted these days, surging ten deep across the Thames. By nine-thirty the tide has dwindled to a trickle. It turns just after five p.m., as the London commuter heads home to Penge West and Tulse Hill:

> A man who shaves and takes a train
> And then rides back to shave again.

As the evening commuters hurry homewards over London Bridge they could see, if only they had time to stop and stare, the tower of Southwark Cathedral protruding above the wharves of the waterfront. The Cathedral of the whole huge metropolitan diocese south of the river is a fine example of London's mountain scenery, seldom visited by the tourists, but with ranges of vaulting and a cordillera of arches of English neo-Gothic architecture 'to suggest mystery upon mystery, curtained and veiled in stone'.

It has been Southwark Cathedral since 1905, so recently have the suburbs south of the river sprawled to need a diocese of their own. In the Middle Ages it was the Augustinian Priory of St Mary Overie. As one would expect in a building of such ancient establishment, there is a colourful and incredible legend from the Dark Ages concerning its foundation. It postulates Mary, the daughter of a Scrooge-like waterman called John Overie, who kept 'the traverse ferrie over the Thames'. In fact *Over-ie* means nothing more miraculous than 'over the water', and it is not necessary to imagine a person of that name to explain the name of the church.

Domesday Book, William the Conqueror's great and greedy inquest of his new property called England, records that there was a *Monasterum* in Southwark in the reign of Edward the Confessor. This Minister was probably the college of priests said to have been founded in the ninth century, when St Swithin was Bishop of Winchester. There are, however, no Saxon remains, and the Church of St Mary Overie only emerges into the plain and unvarnished light of history with the building of the Norman church and the foundation in 1106 of the Priory of Augustinian Canons. The Augustinians were bound by their rule to look after the sick and the poor. They did this in Southwark by founding a hospital at the gates of their Priory and dedicating it to St Thomas. St Thomas's Hospital migrated a mile upstream to its present noble site opposite the Houses of Parliament in 1868.

The Priory flourished in advantageous proximity to the town palace of the Bishops of Winchester until, after the Civil War, the predominant status of religion declined and Southwark deteriorated into a commercial slum. The old Priory church dilapidated and was combined with the church of the adjacent parish, changing its name in the process to St Saviour's.

Throughout the early nineteenth century there was controversy between antiquarians and evangelists over whether to pull down 'St Saviour's Folly' and replace it with a smaller and more practical building. The penultimate outcome resulted in the medieval nave being entirely demolished and rebuilt in an atrocious style. Augustus Pugin, the eminent ecclesiastical and lay architect, complained: 'In place of one of the finest specimens of ecclesiastical architecture left in London—with massive walls and pillars, deeply moulded arches, a most interesting south porch, and a splendid western doorway—we have as vile a preaching-place as ever disgraced the nineteenth century.'

Eventually the antiquarians refought and won the Southwark battle, and at the end of the century Sir Arthur Blomfield replaced the huge nave of 1839, imitating the thirteenth-century style of the chancel with Victorian materials and heavy Victorian good taste. It was a misapprehension of the Victorians that neo-Gothic was the only correct 'churchy' style for adding to medieval churches. Before the nineteenth century ecclesiastical architects like Wren were happy to work in the current contemporary styles, so contributing to the rich diversity of old English churches. The nave of Southwark

Cathedral is spectacular, built in a manner as close as possible to its medieval predecessors with all the resources of nineteenth-century ingenuity. But some find it inhuman, because it is a travesty and an anachronism.

The Cathedral Church of St Saviour and St Mary Overie naturally has a memorial to Southwark's most brilliant resident, William Shakespeare. The memorial window, blasted in the Blitz and replaced after the war, shows a stained glass group of Prospero, Titania, and the other obvious characters from the plays. Beneath it an alabaster figure of Shakespeare made in 1912, with his vast bald dome of a head, reclines against a relief of a reconstruction of Bankside. The Cathedral guides confide, with no evidence other than probability, that Shakespeare may often have attended worship within the walls of St Saviour's. Internal evidence from the plays suggests that he may not have been an enthusiastic church-goer in his adult life. But then his plays are so rich and dense that they can supply internal evidence for almost any theory; and often have.

Shakespeare's brother Edmund, another actor, is buried in the church so conveniently close to the Globe; and so are the other dramatists of Bankside, Philip Massinger and John Fletcher, and the theatre-owner, Philip Henslowe. But the finest tomb and memorial are those of John Gower, the early English poet and friend of Chaucer, who called him 'moral Gower'. The head of Gower's effigy rests on representations of his three most important books: the *Vox Clamantis*, an account of the Peasants' Rising of 1381 in Latin elegiacs; the *Speculum Meditantis*, a very moral and religious allegory in French; and the *Confessio Amantis*, a collection of medieval romances in English.

Opposite Southwark Cathedral in a conspicuous position on the north bank stands Fishmongers' Hall, rising in four-square neo-Greek magnificence upon giant attached Ionic columns and pilasters to a crowning balustrade. The home of the Fishmongers' Company is the grandest livery hall, occupying one of the finest sites on the Thames. It was designed by Henry Roberts, in whose office at the time George Gilbert Scott was chief assistant. Their collaboration began and ended with Fishmongers' Hall, and neither man on his own did such grand or good work again. The previous hall, rebuilt after the Great Fire, had to be demolished to make room for the northern approach road for Rennie's new London Bridge, named King William Street in honour of William IV. The new London Bridge, on which work began in 1968, again threatened the current Fishmongers' Hall but did not involve its demolition.

The livery companies emerged as trade guilds with monopolies and jurisdiction of their particular trades in the medieval city, partly as a native answer to the Hanseatic League. They still survive, far less powerful in the daily life of London than the modern unions that have replaced some of their functions, but often immensely rich and occupied in the grotesque ceremonial fancy dressing up and the prodigious bouts of eating, drinking, and oratory in their livery halls dear to City businessmen after working hours. Most of them also finance such charities as the education of the young and care of the old of their historic trades. But not many liverymen would care to be described as tradesmen these days, except as a whimsy. There are few, if any, practising wheelwrights, tallow chandlers, bowyers, or fletchers left in London. Beneath their quaint medieval robes liverymen of such companies are likely to be boring old stockbrokers, insurance brokers, or accountants. Many of the Fishmongers do in fact retain fishy connexions, but these are at a high business and financial level. Under a Charter of James I officials of the Company, known as 'Fishmeters', still examine all fish coming into London and 'survey wither the same be wholesome for Man's Body, and fit to be sold or no'. The Company also has statutory powers under the Salmon and Freshwater Fisheries Act, 1923, and the Sea Fish (Conservation) Act, 1967. But the Fishmongers generally do not, as in the grand old days, come to livery dinners after a day spent gutting herrings or shovelling shrimps.

The Fishmongers' is fourth in order of precedence among the Twelve Great Livery Companies of the City, and one of the most ancient of the City guilds. The fraternity was in existence at least as early as the twelfth century, for there is a record of it being fined by Henry II in 1154 for being one of the *adulterine guilds* that had failed to contribute to the royal purse.

Another City guild, the Company of Watermen and Lightermen of the River Thames, is trustee of Doggett's Coat and Badge, articles of history that are curious even by Thames standards. Thomas Doggett, born in Dublin, was an actor and a joint manager of first the Haymarket, and subsequently Drury Lane theatre. He died in 1721. He was a friend of Congreve and Colley Cibber, who described him as the most original and the strictest observer of nature of all his contemporaries. Doggett was particularly famous as a character actor for his ability to make up and paint himself to resemble all the ages of man up to extreme senility. This caused Sir Godfrey Kneller, the court portrait painter, to say that Doggett excelled him in his own art: the artist could only copy nature from the originals before him, while the actor could vary them as he wanted, and yet always preserve a true resemblance.

In addition to his acting, Doggett was a keen political animal and an enthusiastic partisan of the Hanoverian succession. He must also have been a friend of Thames watermen. For in 1716 he instituted the prize of a coat and badge for a race among Thames watermen in honour of the accession of George I. It is still rowed each year on or about August 1, to commemorate the anniversary that so curiously excited Doggett. He stipulated that the livery coat for the winner should be orange, the colour of the Hanoverian party, and that the badge should be the white horse of Hanover. The race was first rowed in 1715, and has been rowed annually ever since, apart from interruptions during the war years. This record makes Doggett's Coat and Badge the oldest fixture in the British sporting calendar, antedating the next oldest, the St Leger, by no less than sixty years. It was originally rowed in heavy wherries, the boats that supplied London's taxi services in the eighteenth century. In those days the race against the ebb tide could take four hours; there was heavy betting and frequent dirty work. Wherries were replaced by wager boats, and wager boats in 1906 by best boats. These have now been replaced by craft called matched clinker sculling boats.

The race is now against the ebb tide from Swan Steps at London Bridge past the barge-roads and eleven bridges to Cadogan Pier, Chelsea, a tough course of more than four miles. The ancient sculling race is open to six apprentices who have completed their apprenticeship and taken up the Freedom of the Company as watermen within the twelve months preceding the day of the race. The average time taken for the marathon solo row is about thirty minutes. To punters, tow-path walkers, and other *dilettanti* of the river competitive rowing seems as insanely masochistic a method of transport as pushing a pea up Snowdon with one's nose. But for the *cognoscenti*, if winning the University Boat Race is the blue ribbon of amateur rowing on the tideway, then Doggett's Coat and Badge are the orange ribbon of the professionals. Until 1950 it was an exclusively professional race with small money prizes. In that year it became an optional professional race, with amateurs able to retain their amateur status by declaring before the race that they would not accept a money prize if they won one.

The event amply illustrates John Burns's adage that 'the Thames is liquid history'. Burns, a founding father of the Labour movement and the first artisan to reach Cabinet rank in Britain, was also a far-sighted lover of the Thames and London docks. At the turn of the last century he campaigned for the amalgamation of the proliferating and competing dock companies into a single Port of London Authority. A Canadian from the banks of the mighty St Lawrence and an American from the banks of the mighty Missouri asked, derisively, John Burns's comparative view of the St Lawrence, the Missouri, and the Thames. Burns replied: 'The St Lawrence is mere water. The Missouri muddy water. The Thames is liquid history.' Doggett's Coat and Badge demonstrates that, as well as being history, in eddies and backwaters the Thames is also liquid comedy, tradition, and eccentricity.

CHAPTER EIGHT

London Bridge to the Tower

London Bridge is broken down,
  Broken down, broken down,
London Bridge is broken down,
  My fair lady.
Build it up with pre-stressed, post-tensioned, reinforced concrete,
  My fair lady.

London Bridge is one of the oldest and most haunting of nursery rhymes, with its disturbing images of a mysterious bridge that has to be continually rebuilt and of a children's game revolving around the elementary old fear of being captured.

Iona and Peter Opie, those pioneer anthropologists of the lost tribes of childhood, suggest that the rhyme preserves the memory of a dark and terrible rite from the past. All over the world stories of human sacrifice are associated with bridges, to the erection of which rivers were reasonably supposed to have a peculiar antipathy. Sir James Frazer in *The Golden Bough* cites examples of people being immured alive in the foundations of buildings to serve as guardian spirits. Skeletons and skulls have been discovered embedded in the foundations of bridges all over the world. It will be remembered that in *London Bridge*, after all the various proposed materials for building the bridge up again prove ineffectual, there comes the sinister suggestion:

Set a man to watch all night,
Watch all night, watch all night.

Could he be a distant echo of human sacrifice to pacify the Thames for the violation of being bridged?

Another possible source of the nursery rhyme from the Middle Ages can be found in the *Olaf Sagas*. In these Ottar Swarte, the old Norse bard, chronicles the achievements of the Norwegian King Olaf and his Vikings. In 1014 Olaf with a large fleet sailed up the Thames to attack London, and pulled down its chief defensive parapet, London Bridge. The defenders of the bridge rained showers of stones and other missiles down upon the Vikings, who retreated and built protective canopies for their ships from the timber and wattle of the houses by the river. Then 'Olaf the King and his Norsemen, having rowed their ships close up to the bridge, made them fast to the piles with ropes and cables, with which they strained them, and the tide seconding their united efforts, the piles gradually gave way and were drawn from under the bridge'.

The *Olaf Sagas* commemorate this spectacular victory in faintly familiar rhyme:

> London Bridge is broken down,
> Gold is won, and bright renown.
> Shields resounding,
> War-horns sounding,
> Hildur shouting in the din.
> Arrows singing,
> Mailcoats ringing—
> Odin makes our Olaf win.

In the beginning of London was the bridge. Julius Caesar made two forays deep into south-eastern Britain in 55 and 54 B.C., passing very close to the site of London. In 54 B.C. on his march against Cassivellaunus Caesar crossed the Thames at Brentford. But that punctilious commentator on his own military campaigns makes no mention of any Celtic predecessor to Londinium or of a ford across the Thames lower than Brentford. If they had been there, he would have found them.

The history of London begins nearly a century later with the Claudian invasion of A.D. 43. By then there was probably a trading settlement at London, the tidal limit of the Thames in those days, and the lowest point on the river where there were dry gravel eminences on both banks rising above the vast tidal swamp and surrounding forest of the estuary. The crossing of the Thames, where a great river guarded the frontier of the immediate realm of Cunobelinus, the leader of the British tribal confederacy based on Colchester, was a spectacular event in the northward advance of the Roman army.

The Romans under Aulus Plautius defeated the British at the hard-fought battle of the Medway, that rare event of ancient warfare, a two-day battle. Dio Cassius, the Greek slave who made good out of tactful history and flattery at the court of the Roman Emperors, wrote in the third century A.D.:

'The Britons retreating upon the River Thames, where it falls into the sea (it being stagnant there from inundation) easily crossed over, because they knew the firm and readily fordable places. But the Romans pursuing them were in great danger. However, one unit swam back and crossed by a bridge a little higher up. They then caught up with the Britons and killed many of them. But pursuing the rest incautiously, they became bogged in the marshes themselves and suffered more casualties than the British.'

This is the evidence, however fragile, for a pre-Roman, Celtic bridge. Some have suggested that the bridge mentioned by Dio crossed as high up river as Staines, or was over some less formidable tributary river of the Thames such as the Lea.

Whether the Thames was already bridged when they arrived on the scene or not, the Romans, those choice and master bridge-builders, almost certainly built themselves a bridge to secure their life-line of communication to the south. It is likely that in its earliest form it was a bridge of boats, as depicted on Trajan's column. This was probably replaced by a pile bridge at an early date. No direct and positively identifiable archaeological or literary evidence of the Roman bridge has yet been discovered. But its existence is indicated by iron-tipped wooden piles of the right date and thousands of coins covering the whole period of the Roman occupation, which were found on the river bed when it was being deepened after the removal of the medieval bridge in the 1830s. The coins are in chronological sequence and many are newly minted, suggesting that they were votive offerings to the river whenever the bridge was repaired or rebuilt. Sceptics about the existence of a Roman bridge account for such relics as losses from a ferry or fording point, or as ritual offerings to the river made without any need to atone for bridging it. Reverence for rivers is an inveterate superstition. As Eliot wrote in *Dry Salvages*:

> I do not know much about gods; but I think that the river
> Is a strong brown god.

The precise site of the Roman bridge is not yet fixed, but it was probably close to the site of the medieval bridge, that is, about a hundred feet downstream from the present one. It must have been made of wood, since no local stone was available and no trace of a stone structure has been found; and it must have had a drawbridge section that could be raised to let ships through, since the remains of large Roman sailing ships have been found above it at Lambeth and Blackfriars. It is also probable that it was broken down and rebuilt several times during the Roman period, its position being moved a little each time, since it would have been necessary to continue using the old bridge until the new one was complete.

If the hypothesis of a Roman bridge is accepted, it was probably destroyed by Boudicca in A.D. 61, when she led the Iceni in revolt against the occupying power and put London to the sword and flame. Tacitus estimates that the rebels killed seventy thousand in Camulodunum (Colchester), Verulamium (adjoining St Albans), and Londinium, which, he says, though not yet distinguished by the title of *colonia*, was nevertheless a busy centre, chiefly by reason of its crowd of merchants and stores. Such estimates by ancient historians are not necessarily reliable. Tacitus describes this first sack of London with masterly and graphic economy:

'Caedes, patibula, ignes, cruces, tamquam reddituri supplicium at praerepta interim ultione, festinabant'—the Iceni were in a hurry to massacre, hang, burn, and crucify, as though they knew that their day of reckoning must come, but wanted to take their revenge in advance. Men digging in the City still come upon the orange-red layer of ashes, which is all that was left of London when Boudicca was finished with it. It is unlikely that the bridge escaped.

The first written reference to London Bridge yet found, if one discounts Dio Cassius, as one reasonably might, does not come until the Dark Ages after the Romans had left. The *Anglo-Saxon Chronicle* records that when Aethelwold was Bishop of Winchester, between 963 and 984, a widow was found guilty of witchcraft: 'They took that woman and drowned her at London Bridge.' During the period of the Viking raids on London, the bridge appears in the *Chronicle* and the *Sagas* as a formidable obstacle to the raiders, except the enterprising Olaf and Knut, who circumvented it by digging a ditch around the southern end from Bermondsey to Battersea in 1016. The bridge appears in a charter of William the Conqueror in 1067, and from then on the record becomes more continuous and reliable. It was swept away in a flood in 1091, and damaged by another great storm in 1097. As a consequence William Rufus rebuilt it and endowed it with 'revenue from certain lands' for its upkeep. Common Law provided that a bridge had to be maintained by a levy on the lands that benefited from its existence, and no doubt there was special provision for the only bridge in what had become England's capital city. By 1122 the monks of Bermondsey were getting a grant of five shillings a year from lands belonging to the bridge.

From the beginning a certain secrecy shrouded the finances of the bridge. As late as the sixteenth century John Stow tried to examine the records of benefactors of the bridge, but was not allowed to see them.

The bridge continued to suffer from floods, abnormally low tides, and three great fires, the last of which in 1135 destroyed the greater part of London as well as the bridge. The King, the City merchants, and the Church decided to invest in a completely new bridge. This, the last of the wooden bridges, was built of elm in 1163, probably to the east of the Church of St Magnus. Peter of Colechurch was appointed Bridge-Master in charge of the work. Peter derived his surname from the fact that he was chaplain of St Mary Colechurch, the London church in which Thomas à Becket, the original patron saint of the English and particularly Londoners, was baptized.

Perhaps this bridge was intended to be temporary or an experiment. But within a dozen years Peter of Colechurch made the revolutionary suggestion of building a stone bridge, something not attempted since the fall of the Roman Empire. He may have had links with the Pontist Brothers, the French religious order which was building the famous Pont d'Avignon of stone at about this time. His extraordinary proposal was accepted and about 1176 work began on the first stone bridge across the Thames. This was to be the notable Old London Bridge of the nursery rhyme, one of the great achievements of medieval engineering. It was to survive the tides and turmoil of six centuries and to be acclaimed as one of the wonders of the medieval world. For example, James Howell in *Londinopolis*, 1657, imitating Sanna-zari's elegiac eulogy of Venice, had Neptune on a visit to London on a high spring tide exclaim:

> Let the whole Earth now all Her wonders count;
> This Bridge of Wonders is the Paramount.

Peter worked on his bridge for twenty-nine years under three monarchs: Henry II, Richard Coeur de Lion, and John. It was still unfinished when he died in 1205, and the first Englishman to build a major stone bridge was buried beneath the chapel in the middle of the bridge. King John wanted the work finished by Isenbert of Saintes, who had built the stone bridge at La Rochelle. With characteristic independence the City preferred to give the job to three of its own people, merchants called Serle, Almaine, and Bote-write. These three Bridge-Masters finished the work in 1209.

Medieval architects were not much concerned with symmetry, and London Bridge was agreeably eccentric, carried on twenty irregular piers supporting nineteen arches of widths varying from fifteen to thirty-four feet. The original bridge, until it was widened in the middle of the eighteenth century, was twenty feet wide and about nine hundred feet long. Henry II, that magnificent builder-king, helped to finance its construction by contributing the proceeds of a tax on wool. This gave rise to the ludicrous legend that the foundations of the bridge rested on woolpacks. It is curious that the whirligig of time and trade has turned wool, which was London's chief export in the Middle Ages, into one of its largest imports today.

In less romantic fact the bridge was founded on rammed stones secured inside immense oak and elm palisades. These piers were protected from the scour of the tide by curious structures called starlings: boat-shaped outworks of piles in the river bed around the bases of the piers. These starlings may have been designed as cut-waters, or they may have served as primitive coffer-dams while the piles were driven. Whatever their purpose, they gave the bridge its most characteristic idiosyncrasy at low tide, the appearance of wearing gum-boots or snowshoes.

The piers and their encompassing starlings acted as a dam, so that at ebb-tide the pent-up water cataracted through the narrow gaps between the starlings in a line of waterfalls, dropping by as much as six feet, depending on the state of the tide. As time went on, more piles were added and the starlings grew so big that by the eighteenth century they occupied five-sixths of the river's width. Navigation through the bridge was notoriously perilous. The proverb 'London Bridge was made for wise men to go over and fools to go under' was first written down by the Reverend John Ray in his *Book of Proverbs* in 1670. By then it was probably centuries old.

The prudent got out above the bridge and walked round to meet their boat below it. Or they could change boats, as Dr Johnson did on a jaunt to Greenwich in 1763. Boswell records: 'We landed at the Old Swan and walked to Billingsgate where we took oars and moved smoothly along silver Thames.' Samuel Pepys was more daring. On September 15, 1662, he 'was fain to walk over the piles through the bridge', while his watermen navigated the mill-race. It must have been low tide. Pepys was amused by a French visitor who was terrified of going under the bridge, but, having succeeded, announced that it was the greatest pleasure in the world. Pepys noted: 'The most like a French humour in the World.'

George Borrow in *Lavengro* gave a vivid eye-witness description of the scene in his 'wind on the heath' style:

'The tide, which was fast ebbing, obstructed by the immense piers of the old bridge, poured beneath the arches with a fall of several feet, forming in the river below as many whirlpools as there were arches. Truly tremendous was the roar of the descending waters, and the bellow of the tremendous gulfs, which swallowed them for a time, and then cast them forth, foaming and frothing from their horrid wombs. As I stood upon the bridge, gazing into the jaws of the pool, a small boat shot suddenly through the arch beneath my feet. There were three persons in it; an oarsman in the middle, whilst a man and woman sat in the stern. I shall never forget the thrill of horror which went through me at this sudden apparition. What!—a boat—a small boat—passing beneath that arch into yonder roaring gulf! Yes, yes, down through that awful water-way, with more than the swiftness of an arrow, shot the boat, or skiff, right into the jaws of the pool.' And so on. Yes, yes, the true, the blushful but compulsive Borrow.

The most conspicuous feature of Peter of Colechurch's bridge was the chapel of St Thomas, a two-storeyed building on the east side near the centre, projecting about sixty feet downstream. Thomas à Becket had been martyred in 1170 and canonized in 1173, only three years before the bridge was begun. When Old London Bridge was being demolished in 1823, workmen found the bones of Peter of Colechurch in an enclosure in the lower chapel made 'to contain a person of the middle stature'. The newspaper reports of the discovery are silent about what happened to the bones, suggesting that they may have been thrown unceremoniously into the river, so giving the Thames a petty and belated revenge on the remains of its greatest bridge-builder.

Other dominating features of Old London Bridge were its two gates and drawbridge, protecting the entrance to London from the south across its great natural moat. The outer gate, called the Great Stone Gate, embattled and fortified with massive doors and a portcullis, stood on the pier two arches out from the south bank. Beyond this came a drawbridge thirty feet long across the sixth arch, and beyond that a second gate, the Drawbridge Gate. In addition to its defensive function, the drawbridge could be raised to allow the passage of tall-masted ships, which paid a toll, as originally did travellers across the bridge.

These fortifications made the bridge impregnable and an important fortress in the continual power struggle between the Monarch and the city in the early Middle Ages. It was never taken by force, though sometimes by treachery. The Peasants' Revolt of 1381 associated with the names of John Ball and Wat Tyler achieved a notable success when the peasants surged across the bridge from Kent. They then dissipated this initial success.

Jack Cade's rebellion of 1450 was admitted across the bridge by sympathizers in the City, who lowered the drawbridge. Cade's men then plundered and murdered with such wanton savagery that the Londoners turned against them and drove them out in the violent skirmish known as the Battle of London Bridge. Sir Thomas Wyatt's Protestant rebellion against Mary Tudor in 1554 failed partly because he was erratic and partly because he failed to get popular approval, since men still regarded rebellion as the sin of witchcraft. But the immediate cause of his failure was that London Bridge was held firmly against him.

Wyatt paid for his treason with his head, which was struck off, impaled on a long pole, and exhibited on the traditional stage for traitors' heads, above the Drawbridge Gate of London Bridge. The first head so exhibited of which there is record belonged to William Wallace, the Scottish nationalist, who was treacherously handed over to the English and executed in 1305. Margaret Roper, the daughter of Sir Thomas More, bought her father's head after it had been exposed for some months above the Drawbridge Gate, and took it away for burial, 'lest it should be foode for fishes'. The same pole had previously impaled the head of Bishop John Fisher, who like More had lost it during Henry VIII's megalomaniac struggle to enforce his Act of Supremacy over the Church. But Bishop Fisher's parboiled head did not putrefy, but grew miraculously ruddier and more life-like every day. Great crowds coming to see the miracle so damaging to Henry blocked traffic over the bridge, until the offending head was removed and thrown in the river.

The gruesome custom, presumably intended to discourage potential traitors, continued until 1678 when William Stayley, executed for his part in the panic known as the Popish Plot, supplied the last head to be exhibited on London Bridge. The grisly spectacle was, of course, a famous tourist attraction. Many visitors to London record their impressions of the heads in diaries or pictures. Frederick of Württemberg took a head-count in 1592, making it thirty-four; but this did not stop him describing the bridge as beautiful and covered with 'quite splendid and well-built houses occupied by merchants of consequence'. In 1566 Joseph Justus Scaliger, the greatest scholar of the Renaissance and the founder of historical criticism, reported that there were more than heads up there. He described the poles as looking like 'masts of ships and at the top of them quarters of men's corpses'. However, scholars and historical critics do not necessarily make the best eye-witness reporters. The Drawbridge Gate was demolished in 1577, and its grim decorations removed to the Great Stone Gate at the southern end of the bridge.

Notwithstanding this flower arrangement of heads of villains and saints, the most unusual and memorable feature of the bridge was the houses and shops that lined both sides, projecting over the water, linked by bridges in their upper storeys, and reducing the roadway over the bridge in places to a narrow tunnel. William Camden, the sixteenth-century antiquary, emphasized this feature in his *Britannia*: 'It may worthily carry away the prize from all the bridges of Europe, being furnished on both sides with passing faire houses joining one to another in manner of a street.' A Vatican emissary wrote to the Pope: 'In the river there is a stone bridge, certainly a most wonderful work. Upon both sides of the bridge there are erected houses, so that it might not appear to be a bridge, but one substantial and uninterrupted street.'

The shops and houses were there from the beginning. A letter of King John, written eight years before the bridge was finished, grants that 'rents and profits of the several houses which shall be erected upon the bridge be for ever appropriated to repair, maintain, and uphold the same'. These rents, the tolls from the bridge, which were discontinued in 1782, and other proliferating and multifarious revenues were managed by the Bridge House in Barms Street on the south bank, later to become Tooley Street. The Bridge House was the headquarters of the Bridge Wardens, whose duties included, in addition to the obvious ones of maintaining and repairing the bridge and its houses, such apparent irrelevancies as organizing receptions for royal brides, managing the bridges over the River Lea, and investigating suicides. It was also a storehouse for stone, timber, and other repair materials; the City brewhouse; and a granary with ovens in which bread was baked for the poor. The earliest existing accounts indicate that in 1380 the Bridge Warden was paying half a crown to 'the cook and keeper of the dogs'. No indication is given of what the dogs were for.

The coffers of the Bridge House were swollen by profits from other property bought in and around London. Down the centuries patriotic and pious Londoners left legacies 'to God and the Bridge', of which the Bridge generally got more than God. The stone bridge across a tidal river in the middle of a city seemed to the early Middle Ages a work of God, and was treated with superstitious reverence. The Bridge House Estates have become one of the richest landowners in London. They have used their money to build, rebuild, and maintain the four bridges of the City: Blackfriars, Southwark, London (two successors to Old London Bridge), and Tower, without drawing a penny from the rates or taxes.

In the Middle Ages the shopkeepers sold everything, ranging from glovers and goldsmiths to painters and fletchers, or makers of arrows. By the seventeenth century they had come to specialize in clothing. A survey of 1633 shows thirty-two of the thirty-eight shops listed selling some sort of clothes. The bridge was a good place for merchants. It was central; it was crowded; it was clean: the Thames supplied the machinery for one public privy on it, and most houses took the convenient opportunity to build 'void rooms' overhanging the river.

But the bridge became terribly congested for its primary purpose, the passage of traffic across the river. Consequently the City introduced a rule of the road, the first recorded instance of the British proclivity to drive on the left of the road. Traffic from Southwark to the City was to keep to the west side of the bridge, traffic from the City to Southwark to the east, that is the left. Traffic wardens were appointed to enforce the rules.

The Chapel of St Thomas à Becket was desecrated at the Reformation, Henry VIII, like Henry II, having a particular aversion to St Thomas's view of the authority of the Church. It became a shop, a tenement, and then a warehouse. The Drawbridge Gate was replaced in 1577 by Nonesuch House, an extravagantly ornate timber-framed house prefabricated in Holland and reassembled piece by piece upon the bridge. It was so perfectly made that no nails were needed to fasten it, only wooden pegs. With its carved gables, onion cupolas, and brilliantly painted woodwork it became an unmistakable landmark in contemporary paintings and engravings.

Peter Morris, a Dutchman, devised an ingenious scheme of using a waterwheel in one of the arches of London Bridge to pump water from the Thames to the households of London. He was granted a lease on the first arch of the bridge for his waterworks in 1581. The current turned the wheel, which forced water by piston rods and pumps up pipes against gravity. A contemporary engineer, John Bate, explained the subsequent motions of the admirable contrivance:

'These pipes carry the water to the top of a Turret neare adjoining unto the Engine and there being strayned through a close wyer grate it decendeth into the maine wooden pipe which is layd along the street and into it are grafted divers small pipes of led serving each of them to the use and service of particular persons.'

These waterworks gradually replaced the conduits that had carried water into London from the surrounding countryside for centuries past. Other waterwheels were installed, some to grind grain, until seven of the arches were occupied by them. By the beginning of the nineteenth century the waterworks were pumping four million gallons of water a day. But the great wheels were a danger to navigation, which was dangerous enough without them, and there were growing suspicions that Thames water, especially when pumped through lead pipes, might not be fit to drink. An Act empowering the removal of the waterworks was passed in 1822. But because Peter Morris's original lease was for five hundred years, the Thames Water Authority still pays out £3,750 a year to about 1,500 people in compensation for their shares, and will continue to do so until A.D. 2082, when the Tudor leases expire.

One of the bridge's most spectacular fires in 1633 and the Great Fire of 1666 destroyed many houses on the northern end of the bridge. The higgledy-piggledy medieval shops were gradually replaced by disciplined blocks of uniform height with dormer windows and balustrades. The houses were cantilevered out over the bridge's parapets on timber struts and a staging, which masked the pointed arches.

Until 1750 London Bridge was the only bridge across the Thames below Kingston. In that year Westminster Bridge was opened, a wide, modern, uncluttered crossing, which opened the eyes of Londoners to the fact that London Bridge was obsolete, inefficient *qua* bridge, and dangerous. There was a campaign for its removal. A newspaper wrote: 'Had an alderman or a turtle been lost there, the nuisance would have been long removed.' However a survey showed that the foundations that had stood for so long were still sound and it seemed cheaper to repair than to replace. The City therefore decided to modernize the bridge rather than demolish it. The houses were removed by 1763, and the roadway was widened by adding thirteen-foot extensions on either side of the original twenty-foot bridge. In addition one of the central piers was taken out to produce a single great arch in 'Gothick Taste' in the middle. The river poured through this wider arch, eating away the starlings and lowering the bed of the river by three feet. It became apparent that the wider arch must soon collapse, and Londoners grew frightened to go either under or over their bridge, which had once been the ornament of the City.

The great west tower of Wren's church of St Magnus the Martyr obstructed the extended eastern pavement of the bridge, so that pedestrians had to walk around it into the road. A survey was made to see whether a tunnel could be made through the base of the tower, and it was found that Wren had anticipated the problem by leaving archways in the north and south faces of his tower lightly filled in. The filling was removed and a passage made for the footway, which still survives, though the necessity for it has moved upstream with the bridge.

So improved, the old bridge survived into the nineteenth century. But the removal of the houses that had been London Bridge's idiosyncrasy also removed its ancient charm. And the current concentrated through the great central arch continued to undermine the foundations.

This was the Old London Bridge, in its final mutation, that Dickens knew as a boy. When he worked at Warren's Blacking Warehouse, he was fond of spending his spare time on London Bridge, as he records in an autobiographical passage through the mouth of the young David Copperfield: 'I was wont to sit in one of the stone recesses, watching the people go by.'

The bridge recurs *passim* as a back-cloth in his novels. On the bridge David Copperfield meets 'the Orfling', the little servant, and tells her stories mostly proceeding from his own imagination about the riverside area. Or, to take a darker scene, in *Oliver Twist* Nancy has her fatal conversation with Rose Maylie on the steps of the new bridge, on the Surrey bank near St Saviour's Church. Noah Claypole, hidden behind the abutment, overhears Nancy and tells Fagin. The consequence is Nancy's murder by Bill Sikes.

The medieval structure of the Old Bridge was more than six hundred years old, and inadequate for the traffic of the industrial revolution across it and beneath it. The *Quarterly Review* of 1816 put the case against the bridge strongly: 'This pernicious structure has wasted more money on perpetual repairs than would have sufficed to build a dozen safe and commodious bridges; and cost the lives, perhaps, of as many as a thousand people.' After predictable procrastination, numerous committees, and endless argument about the design, the contract for the new bridge was awarded to the Scottish engineer, John Rennie. He died before his design was finally approved, and his new bridge was built between 1824 and 1831 by his second son, another John Rennie, who was knighted when the bridge was built. Rennie's granite bridge had five arches instead of nineteen and was fifty-six feet wide instead of the forty-six feet of Old London Bridge after its widening. It cost more than £2,500,000, provided out of the huge funds of the Bridge House Estates. Nearly three-quarters of the expense was accounted for by new approaches at both ends, which were the greatest comprehensive street improvements ever made in London until the brutal motorway devastations of the second half of the twentieth century. The broad northern approach road, King William Street, cut ruthlessly into the heart of the City, demolishing nine medieval thoroughfares, 318 houses, and the church of St Michael, Crooked Lane.

Old Fishmongers' Hall, which had been rebuilt just after the Great Fire, had to be demolished, the City paying twenty thousand pounds in compensation to the Company.

The new bridge was opened by King William and Queen Adelaide in 1831 with antique river pageantry and a banquet of medieval extravagance on the bridge itself. The Old Bridge a hundred feet downstream was then demolished and its huge, obstructive starlings, like giant's stepping-stones, extracted. Jeremiahs had prophesied with gloomy relish that the improved flow when the barricade of the Old Bridge was removed would sweep away the other bridges of London and inundate large parts of the City. No such disaster happened, but the bridges and banks had to be largely rebuilt because of the increased scour of the river.

The new bridge could never evoke the romance of the old one, that prodigious fossil from the Middle Ages; and it was often compared to its disadvantage with the Rennies' other bridges, Southwark and their master-piece, Waterloo Bridge. But it was a solid, noble, dignified work that came to be held in affection by Londoners.

In addition to severing the great umbilicus to the Middle Ages and the Romans, the new bridge had other important consequences for London. It gave a death-blow to the ancient trade of the Thames watermen as London's taxi-drivers, for the new 'penny steamers', which were unable to shoot the old bridge, could now carry commuters and trippers through Rennie's broad arches in both directions. The Thames now flowed freely through the new bridge, so that it no longer froze over in hard winters above the bridge as it had done in famous freezes in, for example, 1684, 1740, and 1814. This removed from the London scene that most popular and picturesque of winter entertainments once in a lifetime, the great frost fairs held on the Frozen Thames. A contemporary described the picture in the winter of 1683–4: 'A great street from the Temple to Southwark was built with shops and all manner of things sold: here coaches plied as in the streets. There were also shows, bull-baiting, and a great many other shows and tricks to be seen.'

The continuous and unprecedentedly rapid growth of traffic and popula-tion of the industrial revolution made the new bridge inadequate within half a century. London Bridge was accordingly widened by eleven feet six inches in 1903–4 by projecting granite brackets carrying footpaths and balustrades out of the sides. By the 1960s traffic congestion over the bridge had once again become unacceptable. In addition a survey in 1962 revealed alarming cracks in the arches and spandrels, caused by the slow settlement of the foundations. In its final form the bridge weighed about a hundred and thirty thousand tons, too heavy a load even for London clay. It was decided to build a new London Bridge; and to make things more complicated for the bridge-builders, to rebuild it on exactly the same site, without seriously interrupting the flow of road or river traffic. This marvel was performed by building the new bridge in four longitudinal sections. First two sections were built flank-ing Rennie's bridge on either side. Then, when traffic was flowing over the outside sections, the old bridge was demolished and the two central quarters inserted. The machinery to accomplish this operation included a temporary steel gantry weighing more than two thousand tons stretched across the river and supported on the piers of the old bridge, to carry the pre-cast sections of the new bridge into position and the stones of the old bridge as it was demolished.

The new bridge is a post-tensioned, reinforced concrete, double cantilever and suspended span bridge, which gives my fair lady in the nursery rhyme a fair mouthful to sing as she dances over. It is faced with polished Cornish granite from Bodmin Moor and has three spans, the central one being 340 feet wide, and the side spans 260 feet each. Although it is forty feet wider than the 130,000-ton old bridge, it weighs only 55,000 tons. Its width of a hundred and five feet provides for six lanes of traffic, with pedestrian footways of fifteen feet on the upstream side and twenty-one feet on the downstream side. The reason for this disparity is that on the old bridge seven out of ten foot passengers, for reasons best known to themselves but inexplicable by sociologists, used the downstream side. Both roadways and footpaths are electrically heated to keep them free from snow and ice. The bridge, opened in 1973, though it had in fact never closed, was designed as his last bow by Harold Knox King, who worked for the City of London Corporation for twenty-five years, the last ten as City Engineer.

The odder attributes in his bridge's mountain of statistics include the fact that there are three squash-courts and a museum of the long history of London Bridge beneath its northern span. It cost about five million pounds, as usual supplied by the bottomless funds of the Bridge House Estates, in other words the tolls, rents, and benefactions of former Londoners. It is an elegant and worthy successor to Old London Bridge as the main vein of London, if the Thames is the main artery. It is unlikely to stand for as long as its famous predecessor, considering the pace at which the world moves now.

The granite facing stones of Rennie's bridge were bought for more than a million pounds by McCulloch Properties Incorporated, a subsidiary of the McCulloch Oil Corporation of California. The bridge was dismantled stone by stone, and twelve thousand separately numbered pieces of granite were removed across the Atlantic to Lake Havasu City in Arizona. There it was re-erected across an artificial water-channel named, naturally, 'Little Thames'. There is an engaging but mythical tale that the rich, ignorant American oil-men imagined that for their money they were getting Tower Bridge, the best-known outline in the London of the tourist's image.

Below London Bridge lies the Pool of London, the original port of London for many centuries, until the ships grew too large and too congested, and the docks moved down river towards the sea. The Pool extends from London Bridge to Cuckold's Point a mile downstream on the south bank, where the river starts its great loop to the south between Rotherhithe and the Isle of Dogs. It is called Cuckold's Point because it is supposed to have provided facilities for punishing adulterous wives on a ducking-stool. Legend attributes the name of the Isle of Dogs to the fantasy that Charles II used to kennel his hounds there. Etymology suggests that it is a corruption of Isle of Ducks. In fact for a hundred years from the mid-nineteenth century it became the Isle of Docks, being largely covered by the India and Millwall systems.

The Pool was essential to the existence of London, which was a port long before it became a great city. Tacitus knew London as a port and entrepôt. The Venerable Bede, the learned monk of Jarrow, writing *Historia Ecclesiastica Gentis Anglorum* in the seventh and eighth centuries, also finds the Pool the most significant element in the composition of London. He says that London is the capital of the East Saxons: 'Quorum metropolis Lundonia civitas est, super ripam praefati fluminis posita, et ipsa multorum emporium populorum terra marique venientium.' (Their metropolis is London, set on the bank of the said river Thames, and a market of many peoples coming to it by land and sea.)

For centuries the wide street paved with water, the Pool to which merchants brought their wares by ship from every nation under heaven, was the backbone of London, the source of its wealth and power. John Stow has a story that Mary I, displeased with the Protestantism and anti-Spanish attitude of London, proposed to remove with Parliament and the Law Courts to loyal, royalist Oxford. An Alderman asked whether she also proposed to divert the London River as well as her capital. He was told no. '"Then," quoth the alderman, "by God's grace, we shall do well enough at London, whatsoever become of the term and Parliament."'

When Charles I in his power struggle with Parliament and the City threatened to remove the court from London, the City replied in speeches and broadsheets that they were not bothered so long as he did not also remove the Pool. The parable was clearly a popular tradition, however distorted the details of the stories. After the Great Fire there was again talk of removing the capital to York. London replied confidently: 'Not till the Thames flows under Ouse Bridge.'

William Camden in *Britannia* described the congestion of the Pool in the days when the engravings show merchantmen moored four deep against either bank:

'The Thames is a sure and most beautiful Roade for shipping. A man would say that seeth the shipping there that it is, as it were, a very wood of trees disbranched to make glades and let in light; so shaded is it with masts and sailes.'

After the stone bridge was built, in spite of its drawbridge to allow the passage of masted ships, the cataracts between the piers and their starlings made it hazardous for large ships to penetrate upstream above it. For the next six centuries the expanding trade of the Port of London was concentrated in the Pool, which became increasingly congested. At the end of the

Middle Ages the discovery of America and the ocean trade routes to India and the Far East shifted the centre of gravity of Europe's trade and wealth from the Mediterranean to the Atlantic seaboard. Instead of being on the outer, north-western limit of the world, the Port of London suddenly found itself at the centre. In a few decades from the second half of the sixteenth century the merchant venturers of England founded the Muscovy, Africa, Turkey, Hudson's Bay, East India, and Virginia Companies. The ocean trade created by the discovery of the New World and the sea passage to the Far East flowed into the Pool of London.

To make sure that the Crown got its due share of this new wealth and that Custom duties did not leak, Elizabeth I licensed twenty 'Legal Quays' where all dutiable goods entering the country should be landed. The Legal Quays all lay on the north bank of the Pool between London Bridge and the Tower. Their names, Wool Quay, Brewers' Quay, Great and Little Bear Quays, and the others became part of the familiar nomenclature of international trade and seafaring. They enjoyed an official monopoly for landing goods for two and a half centuries. The wealth of Threadneedle Street and London's predominance as an entrepôt and a centre of banking are founded upon these puny, higgledy-piggledy little quays. Impetus to the movement that made London the financial centre of the world was given by the sack of Antwerp by the Spaniards in 1585, which drove the gold and the credit of the Netherlands bankers across the Channel to London. The great London merchant, Sir Thomas Gresham, who built the Royal Exchange at his own expense for his native city, had been the Crown's financial agent in Antwerp before its sack. He was partly responsible for the transfer of trade and financial power to London, but geography and history were on his side.

As the Legal Quays, with their highly profitable monopoly, became increasingly congested and inadequate, twenty-one 'Sufferance Wharves' mainly on the Surrey shore of the Pool were licensed to supplement them. The system was still obsolete and absurd. There was no room at the official quays and wharves for the great fleets of argosies from all over the world. Ships had to be moored in the middle of the Pool four or five abreast, while lighters and wherries ferried their cargoes ashore. There were intolerable delays. The Pool became a den of thieves, pillaged by gangs of armed pirates, 'scuffle-hunters', and associated villains. By the nineteenth century the port was more than ready for its inevitable centrifugal movement away from the City towards the wider waters downstream.

In the 1970s, as the nineteenth-century waterfront was redeveloped, important parts of the original Roman and medieval quays in the Pool were rediscovered on the sites where they had lain, preserved in Thames clay, for up to seventeen centuries. The Roman waterfront beside the Customs House in Lower Thames Street is the finest wooden quay recovered from anywhere in the Roman Empire, with the possible exception of the Roman wharf at Dover excavated by the Victorians. The great Roman harbours at Ostia and Leptis Magna are more spectacular, but they were built of stone. In Londinium the nearest stone for building was many miles away, and so the Romans built with timber. The mud has preserved it almost intact.

The box structure about forty feet long by twelve feet wide where the galleys tied up is of particular interest for the light it sheds on the arcane subject of ancient carpentry. It includes magnificent examples of half-lap joints, splayed bare-face soffit tenons, and other contrivances of the Roman carpenters. Pottery found on the site and dendrochronology suggest a date for the quay at the end of the second century. The same excavation uncovered the foundations of the original stone Customs House of the fourteenth century.

It was in this vanished building that the first of the great English poets, Geoffrey Chaucer, worked as a royal customs officer. Chaucer, the son of a London vintner, was born, it is believed, in a house in Thames Street at the foot of Dowgate Hill. In 1374 he was appointed Comptroller of the Customs of Wool, Skins, and Tanned Hides, which were in those days England's principal export. The people Chaucer met in his work in the Customs House contributed to the characters of his Canterbury pilgrims; for example, the Shipman:

> Hardy he was and wise to undertake,
> With many a tempest hath his beard been shake,
> He knew well all the havens, as they were,
> From Scotland to the Cape of Finisterre,
> And every creek in Britanny and Spain;
> His bark y-clepèd was the *Magdalene*.

A little upstream an excavation during the redevelopment of New Fresh Wharf site in 1974 uncovered more extensive remains of the early medieval and Roman waterfronts. At the same time a large wooden boat unique to British and probably to world archaeology was found on the river bed beside the quay, having been built into the structure. Its construction was unique because it was made of planks of pine, the plank overlaps being held by wooden pegs and made watertight by moss. The four previous ancient boats found, the oldest dating from the sixth century, were made of oak and had iron rivets holding their overlapping timber planking. Large quantities of red gloss pottery imported from France in the first and second centuries A.D. were found at the same dig and supply supporting evidence to Tacitus's account of the extensive trading activities of Londinium. The biggest prize of all, identifiable remains of the Roman and Saxon London Bridges, continues to evade the spades of the archaeologists. But they live in hope. Perhaps something will turn up when Billingsgate Market is eventually redeveloped.

The Pool, for many centuries so thick with shipping that it looked like a

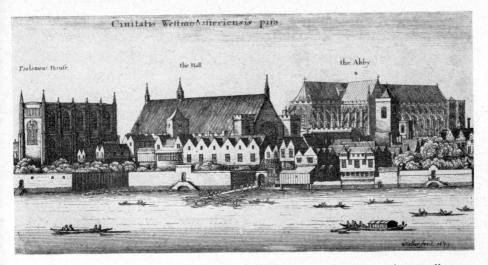

9a. Westminster Palace in 1644, drawn and engraved by Wenceslaus Hollar

9b. Whitehall Palace, 1645, drawn and engraved by Wenceslaus Hollar

10a.   The Adelphi, engraved by B. Green, 1771

10b.   The Savoy and Old Somerset House seen across the river from the water entrance to Cuper's Gardens, engraved by Fellows from a picture of 1770 by S. Scott

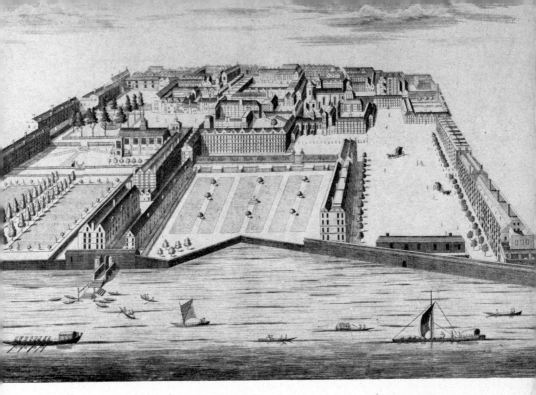

11a. Bird's eye view of the Temple in 1720, drawn and engraved
by Sutton Nicholls

11b. The National Theatre on South Bank

12. London Bridge in 1647 from Hollar's view of London

13a. St Paul's from Bankside, with sailing barges on the river, photographed in 1895

13b. View of the quays of the Port of London in the 1950s before the docks moved downstream

14a. Sir Joseph Bazalgette, president of the Institution of Civil Engineers, 1883–4, by Alessandro Ossani, 1878

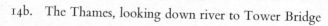

14b. The Thames, looking down river to Tower Bridge

15. The Queen's House, Royal Naval College, Greenwich, and the river beyond

16a. West India Docks near Blackwall, engraved by Black from a drawing
by Rowlandson and Pagin, 1810

16b. Isle of Dogs and palace of Royal Naval College, Greenwich,
viewed from Rotherhithe

floating forest of masts, is today empty of big ships except for H.M.S. *Belfast* moored off the south bank opposite to the Tower, as vastly incongruous as a pike in a goldfish bowl. She was the largest cruiser ever built for the Royal Navy (11,550 tons) and the last of Britain's big-gun warships. Built by Harland and Wolff and named for her native city, she was launched in 1938 by Mrs Neville Chamberlain. In her speech Mrs Chamberlain rashly prophesied that the *Belfast* would contribute to the peace of the world. On the contrary, as it happened, her back was broken in the following year by a magnetic mine off Rosyth. After she had been rebuilt and recommissioned her war service was thunderous. *Belfast* fired the first salvo in the battle that sank the *Scharnhorst* in 1943. She was chosen by Churchill as the ship on which he would embark, in a grandiose crusader's gesture, to lead the invasion forces into Normandy. Fortunately for the success of D-Day and the sanity of the generals he was dissuaded from his adventure by King George VI.

When the time came for *Belfast* to pay off in 1969, the Navy's ancient mariners could not bear to scrap the last of the line of their big ships. Money was raised to preserve her as a floating museum on the Thames. And there she sits in the mud of the Pool, a big fish out of deep water, a tourist attraction, and one of the oddest watermarks of the Thames. She is the biggest ship ever to penetrate the Pool of London, and one of the last big ships to do so.

The north bank of the Pool from London Bridge to the Tower is occupied partly with redevelopment and partly with buildings connected with the heart of the London River's history. On the eastern side of the approach to London Bridge rise the forbidding and vast, neo-Egyptian square cliffs of Adelaide House, built in 1924–5 as the offices of Her Majesty's Customs and Excise and Immigration office.

Next, in the dark canyon beneath the cliffs, comes the church of St Magnus the Martyr, rebuilt from 1671–6 by Christopher Wren. The Great Fire destroyed eighty-eight of the hundred and eight churches of the medieval City. Of these thirty-seven were not rebuilt. The remaining fifty-one were all designed by Wren with an intricate tracery of phoenix spires and towers encompassing the great football dome of St Paul's. The spires balanced the masts in the Pool, and made the skyline of the City from the river one of the most spectacular urban panoramas of the world, before the philistine office-block developers of the twentieth century got their cranes on it. St Magnus's glorious peculiarity is a massive stone tower with an octagonal lantern surmounted by a lead dome and spirelet and clock to welcome travellers across Old London Bridge to the City. The interior is richly furnished with what T. S. Eliot described as 'Inexplicable splendour of Ionian white and gold'. The whole district smells of fish from Billingsgate, but inside the church there is the abrupt change to a smell of incense.

Behind St Magnus's and with its golden brass dome and urn glittering on top rises the Monument erected by Wren to commemorate the Fire of London, or, more precisely, the incredibly rapid rebuilding after the fire. Wren wanted a statue of Charles II or an allegorical female figure on the top, and the urn was introduced 'contrary to his opinion'. The Roman Doric column is two hundred and two feet high, and is built close to the house of the baker called Farryner in Pudding Lane, where the fire broke out. John Evelyn left a long and vivid eye-witness account of the disaster that destroyed the medieval City: 'A resemblance of Sodom, or the last day. London was, but is no more.'

On the east side of the pedestal of the Monument is a relief by C. G. Cibber, the father of Colley Cibber the actor, author, and acquaintance of Dr Johnson, representing Charles II in Roman costume 'affording protection to the desolated City and freedom to its rebuilders and inhabitants'. One of the Latin inscriptions surrounding the pedestal originally attributed the fire to 'the treachery and malice of the Popish faction, in order to carry out their horrid plot for extirpating the Protestant religion and old English liberty, and introducing Popery and slavery'. This absurdity was obliterated in the nineteenth century, but its memory is a reminder that blockheaded bigotry was not always an exclusively Irish property.

Up the hill above the Pool, where the first colonists found dry land to build a settlement, the offices and empires of the masters of the river rise. The Port of London Authority was there, until it sold its grandiose headquarters in Trinity Square in 1971. There is Trinity House, which started as a semi-religious fraternity at Deptford to say masses for the souls of shipwrecked mariners, and has become the body responsible for all pilots, lights, and buoys. There also are the ship-owners, the shippers, the merchants, and other houses made rich by the trade that used to arrive in the Pool. The Lord Mayor of London himself is still entitled to the style of 'the Admiral of the Port'.

Next on the waterfront comes Billingsgate, one of the river-gates of London and hence the name of the fish market that has been established there since before William FitzStephen wrote his life of Thomas à Becket in the twelfth century. It is still London's fish market, handling about three hundred tons of fish a day and distributing them to shops all over the Home Counties.

The name is said to be derived from that of Belinus, the legendary British king and Celtic sun-god, possibly the same man as Cassivellaunus. This derivation is probably as fanciful as that which derives Ludgate from the mythical King Lud, who, according to that notorious liar and forger, Geoffrey of Monmouth, built the walls round the City founded by the refugee from Troy, Brute, which subsequently became London. Stow, magnificently prosaic, prefers the explanation that it has taken 'that name of some later owner of the place, happily named Beling, or Biling'.

The present market building, destined for redevelopment, is an incongruous early Victorian pavilion of yellow brick with a statue of Britannia seated on the apex of the pediment, surrounded by golden vanes in the shape of fish to show which way the wind is blowing. Morning starts early at Billingsgate, with the scent of fish and the bustle of fixing the latest prices of everything scaly in the world, from soles and plaice to such exotically named creatures as monkfish (skinned), witches (small), and hun saam (frozen).

Richard Church described the Billingsgate porters in action with sharp precision in *The Golden Sovereign*:

'Over their heads they sported a long grey linen garment like a frock-coat, and on their heads they wore a wooden helmet with a platform top, for carrying heavy burdens. Both overalls and helmets were saturated by fish-slime, a dreadful, glutinous fluid that pervaded the market, its buildings, its pavements, hanging in viscous skeins through the grids of its gutters and from the edges of boxes being carried at a slow trot by the porters, whom it festooned in a hideous travesty of bridal veiling.'

'Billingsgate' is a synonym for foul language, though the language of the bummarees and fish-porters today is not conspicuously fouler than anybody else's. But there are frequent references in seventeenth-century literature to the abusive language of the market; for instance, the third Earl of Shaftes-bury: 'Philosophers and Divines, who write in learned Billingsgate.'

Billingsgate was made a free fish market in 1699, the relevant Act specifying that mackerel only must be sold on Sundays, presumably because mackerel is the fishiest of all fish with a notorious proclivity to go bad fast.

Next to Billingsgate on the north bank comes the Custom House, head-quarters of Her Majesty's Customs and Excise, and the descendant of the building from which Chaucer and other medieval 'scavengers', or customs officers, inspected the unloading and unpacking of all goods imported into the Pool. The modern scavengers have a double-decked floating platform called the *Harpy* moored in front of their house from which they leave in launches to search incoming vessels and, in the ancient jargon of the business, to rummage. The uncomfortably apt name is taken from an old Government sloop called the *Harpy*, in which the customs men used to live. Their present building, with its massive Ionic portico confronting the river and potential smugglers, was built by David Laing early in the nineteenth century.

Behind the Custom House until 1962 stood one of London's great vanished buildings, the Coal Exchange, the most famous of the Victorian exchanges. With its circular hall, with three tiers of galleries surmounted by a glass and cast-iron rotunda and decorated with encaustic interior panels showing jolly miners and improbably picturesque views of collieries, it was the prime City monument of the early Victorian period. Its destruction, in order to widen Lower Thames Street, has become one of the great conservationist horror stories, comparable to the demolition of the Adelphi and the Euston Arch.

Next on the north bank comes Tower Pier. Sir Winston Churchill's body left from here in February 1965, on the state funeral that he had planned as carefully as Queen Victoria, who in her old age enjoyed nothing so much as arranging a funeral. The coffin of the Former Naval Person was carried down Tower Pier to the *Havengore*, the Port of London Authority's survey launch, which was flying Sir Winston's elaborate flag as Lord Warden of the Cinque Ports. The most memorable and unexpected moment of the stately ceremonies that marked the end of the Churchillian era then occurred, making the hair bristle on the napes of the necks of those present. All the cranes on Hay's Wharf on the opposite bank started dipping their long necks, like dinosaurs bowing, in an eery, unforgettable civilian salute.

The cranes have gone from the south bank of the Pool, the wharves are closed, and the Victorian warehouses are being redeveloped. Behind the waterfront wasteland runs Tooley Street, with offices still largely occupied with the business of the Port, particularly those of the wine importers, who find suitably cool space to store their bottles beneath the arches of the viaducts of London Bridge Station. Tooley Street gets its unusual name from St Olave's Street, after the twelfth-century church that once stood in it. This contractive process, dropping a letter or a syllable at the beginning of a word, is known as aphaeresis. It can be illustrated also by the case of St Audrey, at whose fair cheap and pretentious trinkets that came to be called 'tawdry' were sold.

The riverfront of the whole Pool is the heartland not only of Dickens, but of that other great Victorian reformer, Henry Mayhew. Mayhew lacked Dickens's imaginative flair, but he also avoided his lapses into maudlin sentimentality. He was the father of modern sociology, the ethnologist of London's forgotten tribes, with a genius for entering into and reporting upon the lives and feelings of classes and sub-cultures ignored by the official enumerators.

Mayhew was the son of a London solicitor, who turned from a legal apprenticeship to writing plays and popular journalism. He was one of the founders and co-editors of *Punch*, and responsible for that proud old crusading magazine's oldest joke: 'Advice to a young man on getting married: Don't.' Mayhew's masterpiece was his great sociological survey, *London Labour and the London Poor*, begun as a series of newspaper articles, and continued in four volumes as a report, often in their own unvarnished words, of the life and work of the people that respectable Victorians preferred not to think about. Mayhew was a pioneer explorer of the dark places of mid-nineteenth-century society, and the reports he sent back, like the work of great writers such as Dickens, helped to intensify the sense of guilt that accelerated reform. Much of his exploration was concentrated on the London River, the docks, and the waterfront, which, as they were the heart of London's trade, were concomitantly the heartland of London's labour, poverty, and crime. His style was non-literary, but acutely and photographically realistic and authoritative with observed detail. He had a true sociologist's hopeless and endearing passion for classification. His attempts to classify London prostitutes into league tables of different classes are ludicrous in their precision.

He divided those who scratched a living illegally on the Thames into an army ranging by minute distinctions from river pirates and felonious lightermen to smugglers, sweeping boys, and mudlarks. Here is a small part of a long narrative given to him in 1860 by an Irish-born mudlark aged thirteen:

'I generally rise in the morning at six o'clock, and go down to the river-side with my youngest brother you saw beside me at the barges. When the tide is out we pick up pieces of coal, iron, copper, rope, and canvas. When the tide is in we pick up chips of wood. We go upon logs, such as those you saw me upon with my basket, and gather them there. In the winter time we do not work so many hours as in the summer; yet in winter we generally are more successful than in the long days of summer. A good number of boys wade in summer who do not come in winter on account of the cold.'

The greater compassion of the Welfare State and the decline of metropolitan London as a great port have made mudlarks and most of Mayhew's other river characters almost as obsolete as bowyers and fletchers.

The Pool is cut in half by Tower Bridge, whose twin barren and high Victorian Gothic towers are as symbolic a London landmark for tourists as the Eiffel Tower is in Paris. They are steel skeletons clothed with stone to blend with the Tower of London at the Bridge's north-west end, though, in fact, they diminish and distort the scale of the Tower. But worthy or not, Tower Bridge as part of the Tower ensemble has become the most famous epitome of the London River scene. The Bridge was opened in 1894, designed by Sir John Wolfe Barry with 'Gothic styling' by Sir Horace Jones. The central bascules of the main bridge, each weighing eleven hundred tons, can be raised and lowered by a pint of water in a marvel of Victorian hydraulic engineering. They are no longer raised, since after the *Belfast* big ships no longer come into the Upper Pool. But their majestic machinery is to be preserved as a museum and a memorial to Victorian engineering. The two catwalks high above the main bridge were intended for use by pedestrians while the bascules were open for a ship. So many committed suicide by jumping from them that they had to be closed. In a notable piece of Thames eccentricity, Tower Bridge is registered as a ship with Lloyd's, and used to be run by a captain, a mate, and an engineer.

The Tower, the oldest, most historic, and most symbolic extant building beside the Thames, was erected by William the Conqueror to hold and

guard the east of London, as he built Baynard's Castle on the western bound-
ary. It is the oldest fortified building still in occupation, far more ancient
than such comparable fortresses as the Kremlin, the Vatican, and the Doge's
Palace. Popular tradition attributed the building of the Tower to Julius
Caesar, and the White Tower was for centuries referred to erroneously as
Julius Caesar's Tower. In *Richard III* Shakespeare makes the little Prince of
Wales, later briefly Edward V, ask his wicked uncle:

Did Julius Caesar build that place, my lord?
Gloucester, soon to be Richard III: He did, my gracious lord, begin that
place, Which, since, succeeding ages have re-edified.
Prince: Is it upon record, or else reported
Successively from age to age, he built it?
Buckingham: Upon record, my gracious lord.

Wise old John Stow knew better. He notes the legend, and dismisses it:
'*Caesar* remained not here so long, nor had hee in his head any such matter,
but onely to dispatch a conquest of this barbarous Countrey, and to proceede
to greater matters.' What is the case and perhaps also the reason for the
legend is that the Tower was originally built in the south-east corner of the
Roman City wall.

First built as a fortress, in its long history the Tower became also a royal
palace and a state prison: it was always found more useful for keeping people
in than keeping them out. The great stronghold has in its time also housed
the Royal Mint, the Public Records, and the Royal Observatory. For centuries it was the chief arsenal for armour and small-arms, and, because it is
the strongest fortress in England, it has always been the secure repository of
the Crown Jewels. Until 1834 it housed the Royal Menagerie, the predecessor
of the London Zoo. Its antiquity and its gruesome and bloody use as a
prison and place of execution, particularly under the Tudors, have given the
Tower its latest role: the British building that attracts by far the greatest
annual number of tourists. Macaulay captured the essentially dark side of
the Tower's history, writing of its Chapel of St Peter Ad Vincula, than which,
he said, there was no sadder spot on earth: 'Thither have been carried
through successive ages, by the rude hands of gaolers, without one mourner
following, the bleeding relics of men who had been captains of armies, the
leaders of parties, the oracles of senates, and the ornaments of courts.'

It is this pervading atmosphere of darkness, decay, and decapitation, these
folk memories of the state prison into which many top people entered but few
came out except head first, that most people first think of it in connexion
with the Tower. However it is also a most important building architecturally
and historically as well as penitentiarily, standing as the great paradigm of
all styles of fortification from the Norman to the time when the perfection
of gunpowder made fortresses of masonry obsolete.

William the Conqueror began the building of the central White Tower, a typical Norman hall-keep with its main entrance on the first floor up stairs that could be removed in time of danger. It is one of the earliest and largest keeps in Europe. Its purpose was to terrorize and hold London, which had surrendered to William reluctantly and remained restless for many years. The distance of time may make the Norman Conquest seem superficially a quick and tidy business. In fact it was slow, bitter, and brutal. A generation was wiped out by genocide so that, when the *Domesday* survey was carried out in 1086, Yorkshire was still a desert, infected with starvation, pestilence, massacre, and cannibalism. William began the Tower immediately after his coronation in Westminster Abbey at Christmas 1066, when lines of armed men had to protect him from his new subjects. William of Poitiers writes that, after the coronation, the King withdrew to Barking, 'while certain strongholds were made in the town against the fickleness of the vast and fierce populace'.

His architect was Gundulf, a monk from the Abbey of Bec in Normandy, who was later appointed Bishop of Rochester and built the Cathedral there. The materials he used were white limestone like marble imported from Caen and Kentish ragstone. Stow, following an ancient source in Latin, says that Gundulf lodged in the house of Edmere, a burgess of London, while he supervised the building.

The Tower is vast, ninety-two feet high from floor to battlements, with walls fifteen feet thick for most of their height, tapering to eleven feet at the top, and originally pierced only by narrow arrow-slits. It looks square from the river, but in fact its plan is irregular, its four sides all being of different lengths, and three of its corners not being right-angles. There is a semi-circular bastion at the south-east corner to accommodate the apse of St John's Chapel and the crypts beneath it. It is capped by turrets at the four corners, three of them square and the one at the north-east being circular. The royal apartments were on the second and third floors, with the royal Chapel of St John rising through both floors to the top of the Tower. With its massive columns, gallery for the women, and clerestory it is a masterpiece of Norman ecclesiastical architecture, and has the earliest barrel-vault in England.

The only staircase in the White Tower is in the circular turret in the north-eastern corner, leading the whole way up from the dungeons to the top. It rises in a clockwise spiral, so that any attackers would be at a disadvantage, unless they happened to be left-handed. The works at the Tower were still going on in 1097 under William Rufus.

The Constable of the Tower was one of the great magnates of the realm. Because of his impregnable base a treacherous Constable like Geoffrey de Mandeville could threaten the King with as much force as Warwick the Kingmaker did from the same base four hundred years later. Constables had a fixed salary and traditional perquisites such as the rent they charged prisoners, who, if they were of high rank, tended to bring large retinues of servants with them, for whom rent also was paid. Every ship passing the Tower on the river paid the Constable a toll, a wine ship, for example, being charged two flagons and a rush-boat a bundle of rushes. All the swans below London Bridge were the Constable's, and any cattle that fell into the Thames while crossing the bridge, and flotsam and jetsam of all kinds. The Constable also had extensive fishing rights; one of the grievances mitigated by Magna Carta was the custom of the Constables of putting *kiddles* or weirs across the Thames made of such fine nets that not even a minnow could slip through.

Many kings made improvements to their greatest fortress. But Henry III was responsible for the next major development. The experience of the crusades and the loss of Normandy to the French had demonstrated conclusively that the Norman keeps were unable to withstand modern techniques of siegecraft. Henry's plan, begun for him in 1220 when he was thirteen, was to encompass the White Tower with a high wall fortified with strong mural towers, with a moat beyond it. He also built the royal residential rooms inside the wall and south of the White Tower. The Great Hall and the King's Chamber are often mentioned in the Rolls. This ancient palace was pulled down by Oliver Cromwell and all traces of it have vanished. Henry also introduced the custom for the new King to spend the night before his coronation in the Tower and go from it in procession to Westminster Abbey.* Jean Froissart, the chronicler from Hainault at the English court, gave a description of a typical coronation procession, this one in 1399:

'The Duke of Lancaster [Henry IV] left the Tower this Sunday after dinner on his return to Westminster; he was bare-headed and had round his neck the order of the King of France. The Prince of Wales [the future Henry V], six dukes, and eighteen barons accompanied him. The whole cavalcade amounted to six thousand horse that escorted the Duke from the Tower to Westminster.'

Before his doubtfully valid coronation Henry IV introduced another curious ceremony that was to survive for some centuries at the Tower: the Order of the Bath. He conferred this new order of knighthood on forty-six of his faction while they were actually sitting in ceremonial baths in the White Tower for purposes of ritual and quite possibly physical purification. Afterwards the new knights spent the coronation eve in vigil in St John's Chapel before escorting the King to Westminster. Knights of the Bath are no longer made to take a bath before they are invested.

The last main stage in the construction of the Tower, the outer wall with its towers and moat, was built by Henry III's son, Edward I, that distin-

* The custom survived until Charles II.

guished soldier who was a leading contemporary expert on fortresses. His design was to make the Tower a great concentric fortress with a double ring of walls around the central keep, rendering it far stronger than any other fortress in Europe. Once again, to the annoyance of Londoners, its walls were pushed out into the City and beyond the old City walls. With its moat it now covered eighteen acres. Henry VIII reorganized the palace buildings in the Tower and surrounded its moat with a wall with embrasures for cannon. But the day of the old moated fortress-palace was over, and Henry built a new generation of unfortified manor-house palaces.

The development of gunpowder and the introduction of cannon in the fifteenth century made the great defensive works obsolete as a fortress, but it found an increasing use as a prison and place of execution. The first recorded prisoner incarcerated in the Tower was Rannulf Flambard, the extortionate and simoniacal chief minister of William Rufus. When Henry I finally threw him in the dungeons of the White Tower, all England rejoiced 'as if over the captivity of a raging lion'. The latest prisoners were German prisoners-of-war including Rudolf Hess during the Second World War, and William Joyce, 'Lord Haw-Haw', after it. In between the two periods prisoners in the Tower comprise a national roll-call of the famous and unfortunate, from John Oldcastle, the original name and possibly a model of Shakespeare's Falstaff, and Sir Thomas More to Sir Walter Raleigh, Guy Fawkes, Judge Jeffreys, and John Wilkes. Three Queens of England were beheaded on Tower Green. Many other prominent people were executed there, if they were of royal descent; and on Tower Hill outside the walls, if they were not. A King of Scotland (John Baliol), William Wallace, Llewellyn the Great of Wales, and Charles Duke of Orleans, nephew and son-in-law of the King of France, were imprisoned in the Tower, the last for twenty-five years.

While inside Charles wrote hundreds of roundels and other short poems instinct with the chivalry of the last chivalrous age. After his release he said: 'In my prison of England, for the weariness, danger, and displeasure in which I then lay, I have many a time wished I had been slain at the battle [Agincourt] where they took me.'

Through Traitor's Gate, the sinister old river entrance to the Tower, a continuous procession of the highly born, the treacherous, or the unlucky went on their way to prison or the scaffold. On her passage through the gate, Princess Elizabeth, the future Elizabeth I, though nobody would have wagered much money on her succession at the time, sat down on the wet river steps and refused to budge. Apart from the generally gloomy ambience, she had the hideous personal memory that her mother, Anne Boleyn, had passed through the same gate on her way to an appointment with a swordsman executioner specially imported from St Omer. The Lieutenant of the Tower expostulated: 'Madam, you had best come out of the rain, for you sit unwholesomely.' Elizabeth replied in a characteristically forthright sentence: 'Better sit here than in a worse place.'

Two Kings were deposed at the Tower: Richard II and Henry VI. There is a curious story in the *Annales Ricardi* that when Richard in the White Tower was visited by lawyers, representatives of the Estates, and certain Lords, he abdicated from his Kingship *vultu hilari* (with a smiling face). It may have been a cynical smile of defeat. Or he may have been fooled into believing that he was only resigning the *regimen* (the rule of the Kingdom) not the *regnum* (the Kingship). Such an arrangement would have given him a chance to resume power later in a *coup d'état* by magnates still loyal to him. The presence of Richard's faction among the magnates would have made such an offer too dangerous for Henry to accept.

Two Kings were almost certainly butchered in the Tower: the catalogue is as brutal as one of the more sensational chapters from Tacitus. Henry VI died in mysterious circumstances while at his devotions in the little oratory in the Wakefield Tower. His body was taken from the Tower to St Paul's, and lay in state there, with only his face uncovered: 'and in his lying he bled upon the pavement there.' Polydore Vergil and the other historians of the next generation, following the official line of Tudor propaganda, unanimously accuse Richard, Duke of Gloucester, later Richard III, of complicity in this foul and midnight murder.

Henry's two great educational foundations, better memorials than most kings manage to leave, place flowers in the Wakefield Tower oratory each year on the anniversary of his death: Eton College gives lilies and King's College, Cambridge, white roses.

The most notorious regicide in the shambles of the Tower was the murder of the princes, King Edward V and his brother, Richard, Duke of York. The account of their smothering in the Bloody Tower by agents of their uncle, Richard of Gloucester, is familiar from Shakespeare's *Richard III*, which was closely derived from Thomas More's life of Richard III. More was too young to have been politically active at the time of Richard, and it is probable that he got his information from Cardinal John Morton, the strawberry-growing Bishop of Ely, who was an eye-witness of many of the savage events and a minor participant in them. More served in Morton's household for a time in his youth, and Morton was a witness, though a prejudiced one with a bias towards justifying the revolutionary new dynasty from Wales.

Romantic royalists and diehard supporters of the Yorkist cause still try to carry on fighting the Wars of the Roses and exculpate Richard III. Some of his apologists go so far as to accuse Henry VII of the murder of the princes, which entails believing that they languished in the Tower, unnoticed and unrecorded, for another two years after their incarceration, until Henry was in a position to harm them. The argument is an engagingly eccentric minor national pastime, like the cult of Sherlock Holmes or the efforts to demonstrate that 'Shakespeare' is a pseudonym for somebody more suitable and upper-class, who really wrote the plays, sonnets, and poems, and left cryptograms revealing his identity cunningly concealed around the works. The appropriate reply to all such is *Honorificabilitudinitatibus*.

In the reign of Charles II the staircase leading to St John's Chapel in the White Tower collapsed, and the skeletons of two boys of the right age to be the vanished princes were discovered in the rubble. The royal surgeon and learned antiquaries examined the remains and pronounced that they were those of Edward V and his brother. The King therefore had them placed in a marble urn and reburied in Henry VII's Chapel in Westminster Abbey, with a Latin inscription accusing their uncle of murder. The bones were re-exhumed and re-examined in 1933, and the report corroborated the finding that they belonged to boys who were of the right age to be the princes and had probably been smothered to death.

The greatest political importance of the Tower was in the early Middle Ages, when it was often the master-key of the kingdom, giving power to whoever held it. In the civil war between King John and his barons about the validity of Magna Carta, the Tower was occupied for a year by Louis, Dauphin of France, with a French contingent, who were intervening on the side of the barons and in the interest of booty for the French. It is the only time that it has ever been taken by a foreign power. Wat Tyler's revolutionary peasants broke into the Tower by bluff, sacked the royal apartments, and, in dramatic political gestures, grabbed and kissed the Queen Mother and struck off the heads of the two men whom they held particularly responsible for their economic distress: Simon Sudbury, the Archbishop of Canterbury who was also Chancellor, and Sir Robert Hales, the Treasurer. Two generations later Jack Cade's men from Kent, following in the footsteps of the Peasants' Revolt, attacked the Tower, but were repulsed by its strength and the garrison. During the Wars of the Roses the Tower was occupied by the opposing sides and their alternate sets of prisoners including the poor puppet King in a bewildering series of alternations.

But, in general, the greatest military building in England has seen surprisingly little military activity in its nine hundred years of continuous occupation. It has had more action as a prison, and in its curious contingent uses, as, for example, the London zoo. This function started in the thirteenth century, when Henry III had an elephant house built in the Tower to accommodate an elephant that had arrived as a present from King Louis of France. The elephant was joined by a lion, a Norwegian bear provided with a long chain to enable it to fish in the river, and three leopards previously kept at Woodstock, a nicely judged present from the Holy Roman Emperor, Frederick, in compliment to the English royal coat of arms. The public loved the first elephant to visit London since the Roman invasion. Matthew Paris says 'they flocked together to see this novel sight'. The number of animals behind bars steadily increased: there were 627 animals in cages in the Tower in 1829. Dr Johnson asked visitors to London whether they had been to see the lions in the Tower. The London zoo was transferred to Regent's Park by George IV in 1834.

For many centuries the state papers were kept in the White Tower, but they were transferred to the Public Record Office in Chancery Lane from 1838 onwards. The Royal Observatory was first established in one of the turrets of the White Tower by Charles II, and presided over by the first Astronomer Royal, the Reverend John Flamsteed. It removed from there when the Royal Observatory was built at Greenwich in 1675. The Mint was established in the Tower by Edward I in the thirteenth century; it was the most secure place in the kingdom for such a vitally important and vulnerable activity, and was used to mint the currency for five centuries until 1810, when a special building was made for it beyond the north outer wall of the Tower.

Many other ancient functions of the Tower have left it, though the Crown Jewels are still there in a huge new underground vault opened in 1967. Monarchs no longer live there, not even on the eves of their coronations. The Courts of Justice have moved out centuries ago, and the Privy Council meets wherever the Queen is, usually at Buckingham Palace, never in the Tower. No prisoners languish in the dank, dark dungeons in the basement of the White Tower, one of which was known grimly as 'Little Ease', because it was impossible to lie down in it. But it is still officially a potential prison for traitors and spies. The trades of bowyers, fletchers, and gunsmiths have gone from the precincts. But the Armoury remains in the White Tower and the New Armouries, containing the finest collection of historic arms and armour in the world.

Somebody, presumably a faction of the Irish Republican Army, recognized the still potent symbolic significance of the Tower by exploding a bomb without warning in the basement of the White Tower in the summer of 1974. The explosion killed one woman and injured thirty-six other people, many savagely. The old Tower itself rode the shock as staunchly as it has survived the vicissitudes and storms of nine centuries.

Today the Tower is still ceremonially held for the Queen by a Constable, always a distinguished old soldier. In addition there are a Resident Governor and a Lieutenant, also retired military officers, and, of course, the Yeomen of the Guard, commonly called 'Beefeaters'. The conjecture that the name has some connexion with the French buffet, and that the original function of the Beefeaters was to guard the King's buffet, is as baseless as it is absurd. It is in fact derived, almost as absurdly, from an Old English word for 'loaf-eater', which came to mean a menial servant.

Henry VII formed this remarkable corps from members of his private bodyguard after he had won the kingdom at the Battle of Bosworth. Today they are recruited from retired warrant officers of the Army and Royal Air Force, but dressed up in ornate scarlet and gold Tudor costumes including frocks, ruffs, skirts, knee-breeches, and all the trimmings. In 1974, in a minor triumph for Women's Liberation, women won the right to be Beefeaters. The Beefeaters are armed with eight-foot Tudor pikes called partizans, and led by a Chief Warder and a Yeoman Gaoler, who carries the historic ceremonial axe. They live in the Tower and their job is to act as custodians, guides, and tourist attractions. Tourism has become the principal and most profitable activity of the Tower: it is visited by well over two million people a year.

The old grey Tower encircled by walls and turrets is one of the chief historic monuments of England, keeping watch beside the Thames as it has for nine centuries. In *The Yeomen of the Guard*, his heaviest light opera, W. S. Gilbert summed up its ancient purpose succinctly:

> O'er London town and its golden hoard
> I keep my silent watch and ward.

CHAPTER NINE

The docks to the sea

LONDON River east of Tower Bridge is dockland and, in many ways, the heartland of London. It is not simply patronizing sentimentality that asserts that true Londoners are born within the sound of Bow bells. The people of the traditionally working-class communities of the East End have been less mobile geographically and socially than the shifting tribes of other districts, partly because they have had less money to move out to the suburbs with. They also seem to have more independence, stronger roots, and fiercer tribal loyalties.

The colonization of the East End is a comparatively recent phenomenon. It happened in a rush in the industrial revolution, when heavy industry and a vast system of docks were planted in what was until then an irredeemably marshy and unhealthy suburb. Before that there had only been ribbon development on either bank of industries connected with the port and the sea. London was until recently a long, narrow City extended along its *raison d'être*, the river. As recently as 1724–7 Daniel Defoe in his *Tour through the Whole Island of Great Britain* considered Limehouse the farthest possible eastern suburb of London, and made it clear that it was a remote and new sort of place.

A hundred and fifty years before, John Stow complained that building was starting to encroach on the open fields of the East End, just outside the City wall: 'Without the bars [sc. outside Aldgate] both sides of the street be pestered with cottages and alleys, even up to Whitechapel Church, and almost half a mile beyond it, into the common field; all of which ought to be open and free for all men. Which is no small blemish to so famous a city to have so unsavoury and unseemly an entrance or passage thereunto.'

There is an old tradition of the newest and poorest immigrants to London settling in the marsh outside the eastern wall of the City, which until legislation restricting immigration in the second half of the twentieth century was proud to be the hospitable haven of immigrants from all over the world. London grew rich on the exotic talents of Hanse traders, Flemings, Huguenots, Jews, Germans, Poles, Russians, and other dispossessed and persecuted outcasts from all over the world who came to her East End. Their place today has been taken by new waves of Indians, Pakistanis, and West Indians.

By the end of the eighteenth century it was clear that the port would have to move down-river towards the sea to contain the increased volume of traffic and the increased size of ships. A system of enclosed wet docks, where ships could lie in safety and unload directly to the shore, was needed to replace the chaos of unloading in mid-stream of a tidal river, or at the Legal Quays hampered by congestion, collision, struggles for moorings, and continuous plundering by armadas of petty water thieves and armies of their colleagues on shore. In a renaissance of the port during the nineteenth century, particularly its first half, private companies built the great complex of London docks covering nearly three thousand acres of the East End littoral. These docks are now once again inadequate for the vast super-ships of the future and the container system of traffic. The port is at the beginning of another renaissance and another lurch down-river. It will leave behind the ugly industrial wasteland of the nineteenth century, and the best opportunity since the Great Fire to redevelop a whole area of London and transform it into a handsome and agreeable place to live in, worthy of its great riverine setting. It is still doubtful whether the great opportunity will be worthily taken, but it is one of the most important questions for the future of London for the next few centuries.

Today it is only possible to imagine from paintings, early photographs, and contemporary accounts what the docks were like in the heyday of sail. Hippolyte Taine, the French historian whose theories of 'la race, le milieu, et le moment' were concerned with environment and heredity and their effect on human character, sailed through the docks in 1861: 'The sea reaches London by the river; it is an inland port; New York, Melbourne, Canton, Calcutta are in direct connexion with this place. On the river to the west rises an inextricable forest of yards, of masts, of rigging; these are the vessels which arrive, depart, or anchor, in the first place in groups, then in long rows, then in a continuous heap, crowded together, massed against the chimneys of houses and the pulleys of warehouses, with all the tackle of incessant, regular, gigantic labour.'

Byron looked at the same scene in 1819 with the colder and less enthusiastic eyes of his hero, Don Juan:

> A mighty mass of brick, and smoke, and shipping,
> Dirty and dusky, but as wide as eye
> Could reach, with here and there a sail just skipping
> In sight, then lost amidst the forestry
> Of masts; a wilderness of steeples peeping
> On tiptoe through their sea-coal canopy;
> A huge, dun cupola, like a foolscap crown
> On a fool's head—and there is London Town!

There was an even darker side to the picture. The gigantic works and prosperity of the nineteenth-century expansion of dockland were founded on *laissez-faire* and gross exploitation of labour on the river. Poor immigrants flooded in from the countryside, Ireland, and the Continent to provide a ready supply of cheap labour for the docks. They were housed in squalid, overcrowded warrens in the marshy, unhealthy land along the river, working wretchedly long hours to earn enough money merely to exist and escape the grim alternatives of unemployment or the workhouse. Taine, the perceptive Frenchman, noticed what many native Victorians preferred to be oblivious of: 'Nowhere is the division between rich and poor more horrifying and dramatic than in London.'

The Ratcliff Highway in Wapping, just east of the Tower, demolished in the Blitz, was the notorious paradigm of the poverty, degradation, and cosmopolitan debauchery of the dockland slums. It was a hideous jungle of clip-joints, brothels, opium dens, perpetual drunkenness, and cheap lodging-houses where many a poor sailor shipwrecked. Montagu Williams, an East End magistrate, described it in the 1860s as 'a scene of riots, debaucheries, robberies, and all conceivable deeds of darkness. From the public houses there constantly issued the sounds of loud laughter, mingled with shouting and fearful imprecations. Far into the night the women and the drunken sailors danced and sang to the accompaniment of screeching fiddles. If the sailors were not entirely fleeced inside the saloons, the process was completed by bullies and fighting men when they staggered out into the streets.'

The Sailors' Home and Red Ensign Club was originally formed in 1827 to protect poor seamen from the crimps and other two-legged land sharks of London. It met ships at the docks with horse-drawn vans driven by tough drivers to rescue sailors and their pay and kit from the parasites and take them home to a safe, cheap, respectable, and non-profit-making hotel. The home from home for sailors stranded in the perilous seas of the East End only finally closed its doors in 1975, having been for many seamen the only home in England, or even on dry land, that they had. Within living memory policemen patrolled the district around Cable Street normally in pairs and on bad nights in fours.

Some idea of what the East End was like within living memory is given in the terrible pictures of the docks by Gustave Doré, and in the photographs that Dr Barnardo took of the 55,000 destitute, starving, and abandoned children that he removed from the streets of the East End in thirty years. The vast gallery of a whole class of children, which would otherwise have been visually lost, is overwhelming in the impact of its numbers. Occasional angry, brave, fierce, petrified, or marvellously obstinate faces stand out. But it is not the exceptions that make the chief impression. It is the procession stretching out to the crack of doom of ordinary, deprived, plain children, who would not normally get a second, or even a first glance. Who would

have thought that poverty and the industrial revolution could have undone
so many? Without Dr Barnardo they would have sunk without trace in the
alleys and 'lays' along the river-front; and without Dr Barnardo and his
camera there would be no memorial of them.

One of the chief causes of hardship in the Victorian docks was the almost
universal system of casual labour. Sail and early steam-ships were less
predictable in their passages than modern ships. Traffic was seasonal and
fluctuated wildly from week to week. Dockers were therefore taken on by
the day to unload whatever had come into the docks. There was a hideous
physical competition for work at the dock gates, with the weak and the
unlucky going to the wall. If he was unlucky, a docker could be out of work
for weeks or months in an age when there were no social security or unemployment payments. As often, Mayhew is the best witness of the under-
world beneath the mighty edifice of Victorian prosperity:

'He who wishes to behold one of the most extraordinary and least-known
scenes of this metropolis, should wend his way to the London Dock gates at
half-past seven in the morning. There he will see congregated within the
principal entrance masses of men of all grades, looks, and kinds. Indeed it is
a sight to sadden the most callous, to see thousands of men struggling for
only one day's hire; the scuffle being made the fiercer by the knowledge that
hundreds out of the number there assembled must be left to idle the day out
in want. To look in the faces of that hungry crowd is to see a sight that must
be ever remembered. Some are smiling to the foreman to coax him into
remembrance of them; others, with their protruding eyes, eager to snatch at
the hoped-for pass. For weeks many have gone there, and gone through the
same struggle—the same cries; and have gone away, after all, without the
work they had screamed for. What wonder, then, that the calling foreman
should be often carried many yards away by the struggle.'

Those lucky or favoured enough to catch the foreman's eye were grateful
for a long day of pitifully paid, heavy, dangerous, and degrading work,
tramping endlessly on treadmills to raise the cranes, burrowing into filthy
holds, or carrying heavy loads of deal up mountains of timber, balanced as
precariously as funambulists. Those who could not get work had to 'hang
about the docks and starve', as a witness explained to the Royal Commission
on Labour a few years after Mayhew visited the London Dock gates. It is
not surprising that such conditions were prolific of class bitterness and industrial unrest. The first dockers' strikes took place in the 1870s, shortly after the
Paris Commune uprising, and achieved an increase in dockers' wages from
fourpence to fivepence an hour. In the 1890s more famous strikes for 'the
dockers' tanner' to raise the hourly wage to sixpence were led by the great
Ben Tillett, first secretary of the Tea Operatives' and General Labourers'
Association, and a founding patriarch of the Labour movement. After a

bitter struggle the dock employers were persuaded to give what John Burns described with satisfaction as 'the full round orb of the dockers' tanner'.

By the end of the century the private Dock Companies were demoralized and unprofitable, partly because there was for the first time a surplus of dock and wharf accommodation, and partly because of the ancient Free Water Clause in Acts of Incorporation of the Docks. This anti-monopoly provision granted freedom from dock charges to all lighters and other river craft engaged in delivering, discharging, or receiving ballast or goods to or from sea-going vessels in the private docks. The Dock Companies began to feel the full effect of this privilege of free access and egress given to all lightermen in all dock legislation. There was an irresistible movement towards rational-izing the London Docks and bringing them under control of some public body, as the river and Pool used to be administered by the Corporation and Lord Mayor of London until the docks were built. In 1908 a Bill was passed setting up the Port of London Authority, a self-governing public trust, which took over the ownership and control of the 2,700 acre estate containing the docks from the private Dock Companies. The Port of London Authority also took over from the Thames Conservancy the control of the sixty-nine miles of tidal river from Teddington to the sea, and from the Watermen's Company the power to register and license craft and boats, lightermen and watermen.

Almost immediately there was another major dock strike over proposals to raise the day rate for dockers from sixpence to sevenpence an hour, and overtime from sevenpence to eightpence. The first chairman of the Port of London Authority, Lord Devonport, refused to budge, declaring that he would starve the men into surrender rather than compromise. There was great bitterness during that long hot summer of 1911, culminating with Ben Tillett leading a vast crowd of dockers in prayer on Tower Hill: 'Oh God, strike Lord Devonport dead.' The strikes failed, and the men went back to work without their extra penny. But chronic industrial trouble continued to plague the docks, with such periodic climaxes of fever as the long *Beaverbrae* strike just after the Second World War. The root of the disease was not eradicated until the ending of casual labour ('decasualization' was the rebarbative official gobbledegook) in the 1960s, the payment of handsome redundancy money to encourage surplus dockers to retire to other work, and the automatization and containerization (in two other admirable operations but repulsive abstract nouns) of the docks, which ended the brutal manual labour.

At the same time the atrocious slums of the East End, which had borne the brunt of the Blitz, were redeveloped with great council estates and 'high-rise' blocks. Many of the people forced to live in these tall modern concrete and glass boxes beside the Thames missed their squalid old village slums and the tribal solidarity and pride of communities at the bottom of the national pile. There were fine new comprehensive schools for the children; National

Health and Social Security for all; even a large and magnificent national park, offering every sport in the calendar from golf to horse-riding, up the valley of the Lea, once a grossly polluted tributary of the Thames. To feel nostalgia for the harsh old days was irrational and sentimental. But the East End has always been famous for its sentiment, the soft heart beneath the tough exterior.

The redevelopment of dockland gave the generation of 1970 to the end of the century its best chance of changing the face of London, without destroying too much of value from the past. The Docklands Study of 1973 outlined five options for the future of the area. Their pretentious names suggest the general flavour of the plans: *Waterside* proposes a kind of cockney Venice, with houses built round the water areas of the existing docks; *Thames Park* proposes over seven hundred acres of wooded parks; *East End Consolidated* emphasizes the use of the docklands for industry and public housing; *Europa* proposes a large amount of new private housing; and *City New Town* proposes a self-sufficient new town with a large population.

Whatever choice, or more probably compromise mixture of choices, is made, it will rescue the East End from the dark side of its past. It is to be hoped that the baby is not thrown out with the dockwater, and that the area retains its many virtues and idiosyncrasies.

East of Tower Bridge the south bank is Bermondsey, the ancient village that became a Victorian slum. The name is first recorded in A.D. 708 as *Vermundesei*, the 'ei', or marshy land, of Beornmund. In *Oliver Twist* Dickens described what it was like in the nineteenth century, when the centripetal force of the industrial revolution had created some of the worst living conditions in London:

'Tottering house fronts projecting over the pavement, dismantled walls that seem to totter, chimneys half crushed hesitating to fall; windows broken and patched, with poles thrust out to dry the linen that is never there, rooms so small, so filthy, so confined that the air would seem to be tainted even for the dirt and squalor which they shelter; every repulsive lineament of poverty and every imaginable sign of desolation and neglect.'

The slums have been replaced by huge tenements and new council estates, but the buildings, transport, and living conditions of Bermondsey remain worthy of improvement. If they are not improved the ancient class division between east and west London and north and south of the river will be perpetuated.

Rotherhithe, or Redriff as it used to be called, where the river begins a great loop south, is the site of one of the earliest of the London docks. A dry dock was built here as early as 1599. The precursor of all the modern wet docks was begun in 1696, when a Bill received the Royal Assent for the construction of a great wet dock at Rotherhithe covering ten acres. It was named the Howland Great Wet Dock after the woman (a daughter of Sir Josiah Child, the East India merchant) who owned the land on which it was built. Its builders claimed that upward of a hundred and twenty sail of the largest merchant ships could lie in it, 'being much larger than the famous bason of Dunkirk or any pent water in the world'.

The dock was used as a harbourage and fitting out place for ships, not for commercial purposes. Trees were planted around the edge as a protection against the wind. Their value was proved, and conservatives were converted to the new system of docks, by the great gale of November 1703, one of the worst ever recorded in England. Almost seven hundred ships anchored in the Pool were smashed, driven ashore, and damaged in other ways. An account of this storm attributed to Defoe says: 'The damage was incredible. The posture is not to be imagined but by those who saw it; some vessels lay heeling off with the bow of another ship over her waist and the stem of another upon her forecastle, the boltsprits of some drove into the cabin windows of others.' Only one vessel in the Howland Dock received any injuries, and they were trivial.

During the eighteenth century the dock was adapted for the whaling trade by being equipped with boilers and tanks for extracting oil from blubber. Renamed the Greenland Dock it became the home of the whaling fleets. Bones of whales still sometimes emerge from the mud.

As the whaling industry declined, the growing complex of docks gradually became used for timber and renamed the Surrey Docks. These were finally closed in 1970, and their four hundred and fifty acres await redevelopment. This is therefore the last generation of that ancient and proud occupation, a Surrey docker. You can still meet in Rotherhithe ancient mariners with glittering eyes and horny hands, who worked in the docks all their lives and lived in a council estate outside the dock wall. They reminisce about the great days before the Second World War, when the fleets of ships bringing timber from the Baltic and Scandinavia covered the waters, so that a man could walk across without getting his feet wet. Horses and carts loaded at the dock gate. In those days before mobile cranes, acrobatic porters used to carry the timber from the quays, swaying up precarious gang-planks to pile it forty feet high at the top of a shed. In the great days of the timber trade about two thousand dockers were employed in the Surreys. You could recognize a deal porter from the Surrey Docks because he had a permanent list to port or starboard and the fixed smile of a tightrope walker, even when not carrying wood.

The Surrey dockers invented their own hat, a trilby with a leather flap down the back to take the pain out of walking the plank. Their name for their ten minute official tea-break every hour was *Beer-O*, which suggests something significant about the stamina of dockers. 'A badger' was Surrey Docks slang for a temporary loan, a literally vital arrangement before the last war, when a porter was not paid for his piecework until the whole job was finished, which could take months.

The past clings and lingers around place names in the deserted docks. There is Cowhouse Corner, where a milkman kept his herd in the days within living memory, when the clear Thames was bordered by gardens green. Rice-mill Corner marks the site of a vanished mill beside the banks of the Grand Surrey Ship Canal. This ambitious project was started in 1801. The prospectus stated that a line had been found by which the Thames at Rotherhithe could be connected with Portsmouth Harbour by way of Deptford, Peckham, Clapham, Croydon, Kingston, Ewell, and Epsom. This tidal canal without locks was to be navigable by ships of the largest size, fully equipped and laden. The best laid canals of mice and men seldom get dug. Only four miles of the Grand Canal were ever built.

Now the docks themselves, ancient, unprofitable, out of date, and inconvenient, have been closed, and have left London an opportunity to build something newer and better on the great loop of the Thames. But the closure has also removed Rotherhithe's occupation and left it like a ghost village or a mining town that has lost its pit. It was always an insular community, partly because everyone worked in or had some connexion with the docks, and partly because public transport to the rest of London was so inadequate. People were brought together by their work and by hardship and poverty. Strangely and sadly, people still say that Rotherhithe's greatest and most cohesive days were during the wartime bombing, when the Greenland Dock was turned into a lake of fire that burnt for a week, and the Cockney community spirit survived the horror of the bombs.

The backbone of Rotherhithe is Rotherhithe Street, the longest street in London, stretching between the docks and the Thames right round the great curve of river from the Pool to Limehouse Reach. Most of the wharves and tall warehouses, with incantatory names like Fisher's Sufferance and The Red Lion and Three Cranes are closed. From dank alleyways leading to river stairs there are sudden prospects of the broad brown river and the derelict warehouses of Wapping and Shadwell opposite. Dead cranes stand against the skyline like a valley of dinosaurs' bones. The riverside village church of St Mary is early Georgian, built of yellow brick trimmed with red brick and stone. Christopher Jones, captain of the *Mayflower* is buried here. The graveyard also has the tomb of Captain Wilson, of the East Indiaman *Antelope*, and the young Polynesian prince Lee Boo, whom he brought home with him from the South Seas to die of smallpox in Rotherhithe.

Rotherhithe holds the southern exit of the first tunnel built beneath the Thames. There had been several unsuccessful attempts to tunnel beneath the Thames at Rotherhithe from 1799 onwards. The great enterprise was finally achieved by Marc Isambard Brunel, the elder of the two great nineteenth-century engineers who emigrated from France. Brunel had an inspiration as suddenly as Archimedes one day walking through Chatham dockyard, when he saw a ship's timber tunnelled by the woodworm *teredo navalis*. Imitating the worm he constructed a cast-iron shield that bored like an auger by means of hydraulic screws. As the earth was screwed away, bricklayers would replace it with an arch. He patented his plan, and revived the old dream of a road under the Thames. The Thames Tunnel Company was formed in 1824 and tunnelling began in the following year, hampered by persistent explosions of gas and irruptions of water. In 1828, when six hundred feet of the tunnel were completed, the river burst in; six men were drowned; and Brunel's son, Isambard Kingdom, that other master engineer and the pioneer of ocean steam navigation, only escaped by being washed up the shaft.

The tunnel was emptied of water, but the company's funds were also empty. In *Ode to M. Brunel* Thomas Hood wrote, with a characteristically awful pun:

> Other great speculations have been nursed,
>   Till want of proceeds laid them on the shelf:
> But thy concern was at the worst
>   When it began to *liquidate* itself.

Work was suspended for seven years, and the incomplete tunnel became a sideshow known derisively as 'the Great Bore'. Then the Duke of Wellington persuaded the government to make the company a loan of quarter of a million. The entire twelve hundred feet from Wapping to Rotherhithe were then finished. The subterranean breakthrough was made in 1841, the first person to pass through the narrow hole being Marc Brunel's three-year-old grandson. The tunnel was ceremonially opened in 1843, and the official procession with brass band playing marched through the western arch of the tunnel, which was divided internally although it had been dug as one hole, and back along the eastern arch.

Brunel's name was made. He was knighted by Queen Victoria. His tunnel was a prodigy of inventive engineering, but a commercial failure. It remained a pedestrian subway and a white elephant, because there was no money to build approach roads for vehicles. In 1865 its two parallel arched passages were bought by the East London Railway Company, and its use restricted to the railway. The Rotherhithe tunnel for pedestrians and cars and lorries was built in 1908.

On the north bank in Wapping immediately east of the Tower and the old City wall two other early docks have now been closed: St Katharine Dock, the nearest to the City, opened in 1828, and the London Dock opened in 1805. They were both built by private Dock Companies, amalgamated in 1864, and closed to shipping in 1969. These docks with their fortress-like bonded warehouses specialized in particularly valuable cargoes. St Katharine's was the dock for indigo, opium, marble, tortoise-shell, and scent. London Dock was the home of the tea and wool trades, the iodine trade, and most of the wine and spirits imported into England. Their impregnable warehouses were accurately described in their busy days as 'the world's greatest concentration of portable wealth'. The two docks are being redeveloped. St Katharine's has become a marina, a conference and trade centre, the new home of the Port of London Authority, and the site of a huge new hotel, with appropriately military architecture, named after the Tower.

The dock era was introduced to this part of London by the Limehouse Cut, one of the first English canals. It was finished in 1770 and links the River Lea with the Thames at Wapping. The Regent's Canal, connecting the Grand Union Canal and concomitantly Birmingham and the Midlands to the lower Thames at Wapping beside the Limehouse Cut, was built between 1812 and 1820.

Before the canals, docks, and slums arrived, the ancient parish of Stepney, originally Stebunheth, on the eastern fringe of the City was famous for its farms and the monastic houses that had settled there. Thomas More in a letter of 1504 described Stepney: 'Wherever you look, the earth yieldeth you a pleasant prospect. Here you find nothing but bounteous gifts of nature and the saint-like tokens of innocence.' John Stow remembered the country lane in Stepney of his youth, with hedges and stiles into the fields on both sides, which had been changed in his life-time to 'a continuous building throughout'.

The most famous of the monastic foundations that once occupied this bank of the river survives as England's oldest subsisting charity, still performing its original function in the East End. The Royal Foundation of St Katharine, which gave its name to the dock, was founded as a hospital for the poor beside the Tower by Queen Matilda in 1148. The present Chapter of Anglican brothers of the Community of the Resurrection and deaconesses of the Community of St Andrew still pray regularly for the souls of Matilda and her cousin and rival for the throne, Stephen. The hospital was granted a charter of independence in 1273 by Eleanor of Castile, Edward I's Queen, for whom he built Charing Cross and the line of other stone crosses to mark the slow route of her funeral cortège from Lincoln to Westminster Abbey. This makes St Katharine's the oldest Royal Peculiar in the realm after Westminster Abbey and the Tower of London.

From its beginning, in an early example of women's liberation, brother and sister members of the Chapter have been equal in everything, including voting rights. With one exception a Queen of England has always been the patron of the foundation. This aberration occurred when George IV, having discarded but failed to divorce his incompatible Queen Caroline, became the only male patron of the hospital. By then it had become a refuge and a very present help for about three thousand immigrants and other poor of the East End. But George, characteristically hard up, sold the hospital's land adjacent to the Tower to make room for the new St Katharine Dock, and the hospital was removed to a site in Regent's Park. There it became little more than a grace-and-favour lodging for superannuated royal servants. In 1948 St Katharine's was re-established in its old function and as near to its old position as possible, off Cable Street in a large Georgian manor house once owned by a shipwright. It is an unexpected oasis of religious life and welfare work in the heart of the Borough now called Tower Hamlets, beside the river.

The Chapter continues to perform its medieval work of prayer by celebrating the Eucharist and reciting four offices daily. It is caretaker of a priceless repository of treasures given by the unique line of royal patronesses. These include contemporary statues of Queen Philippa and Edward III still showing traces of their medieval paint; embroidery stitched by Catherine of Braganza; William and Mary chairs given by Mary; and a putative Correggio from the royal collection given by good Queen Caroline. The modern chapel houses the original fourteenth-century stalls with their finely carved misericords. Another marvellous piece of medieval carving, depicting an angelic pop group, is one of the surprisingly few recorded examples of angels shown smiling. St Katharine's is still a hospital in the original sense of the word for unfortunates like depressives and meths drinkers; though in the twentieth century these tend to be passed eventually to the local authorities, who have greater physical facilities for rescuing them. Remarkably, the descendants of the community founded beside the Thames by the medieval Queens carry on with the good work in the East End of London of praying for the world and looking after those who are oppressed by it.

In one of those incongruous juxtapositions that gave medieval London its strong flavour, Execution Dock, where pirates were put to death, stood next to St Katharine's on the waterfront of Wapping. Captain William Kidd and many other notable villains were 'turned off' here on a gibbet erected at low water mark and left to be covered by three tides. John Taylor, as usual, had some poor rhymes for it:

> There are inferior gallowses which bear
> (According to the season) twice a year:
> And there's a kind of waterish Tree at Wapping,
> Whereas sea-thieves, or Pirates are catch'd napping.

A formidable Scottish pirate called Sympson uttered the famous last words at Execution Dock, on recognizing a prostitute in the crowd of spectators: 'I have lain with that bitch three times, and now she has come to see me hanged.'

The Isle of Dogs is the great peninsula jutting south into the loop of the Thames bounded by Limehouse, Greenwich, and Blackwall Reaches. The land is also called Limehouse and Millwall, and is inundated and channelled with the interlocking complex of the East and West India Docks system and the Millwall Docks, which are still in use but will be obsolescent before the end of the century.

At the end of the eighteenth century congestion in the Pool persuaded Parliament to appoint a committee 'to enquire into the best mode of providing sufficient accommodation for the increased trade and shipping of the Port'. The committee recommended the construction of a dock on the Isle of Dogs 'for rendering more commodious and better regulating the Port of London', and in particular to ensure that 'West India produce might be effectually secure from loss by theft or other causes and the public revenue greatly benefited'. The Dock Company, composed of West India merchants and the City Corporation, was given leave to enclose 295 acres between Limehouse and Blackwall on the Isle of Dogs. Across it the Company built two parallel wet docks, each half a mile long, connected with the river by basins and locks at either end, and providing accommodation for six hundred vessels.

The docks were flanked by nine huge five-storey warehouses capable of storing the entire annual sugar imports of London, and the complex was surrounded by a high wall with a guard-house and a wide ditch. Some idea of the disturbed condition of the times and the district is given by the fact that the West India Docks Company in conjunction with the Government organized an armed watch of a hundred men, equipped with muskets and reinforced by another hundred men sworn in as special constables. The foundation stone of this titanic project was laid in 1800 in the presence of the Prime Minister, William Pitt. The West India Docks were ceremonially opened two years later by Pitt's successor, Henry Addington. Two provisions of the legislation enabling the construction of the West India Docks are of particular significance. The Company was given a monopoly for twenty-one years to unload all West Indian imports and load all exports to the West Indies. Another clause gave the right to wharfingers and lightermen to send lighters and other craft into the docks to collect goods for the riverside wharves, or to deliver exports to ships in the dock without payment of dues. This became known as 'the Free Water Clause', and was retained in all subsequent legislation enabling the construction of docks. It has influenced the affairs of the Port significantly, for example making it difficult for a private dock company to make a profit once its initial monopoly had expired.

Under the same legislation the Corporation of London was given powers to build a canal from Limehouse to Blackwall Reach, the idea being to save sailing vessels the time and hazard of circumnavigating the Isle of Dogs. The canal was not a success and was bought by the West India Docks Company and turned into a timber dock.

The East India Docks were opened in 1806 on the eastern side of the Isle of Dogs at Blackwall, and incorporated the Perry or Brunswick Dock, built in 1789 to fit out East Indiamen. The new docks were made large enough to hold the East India Company's twelve hundred ton vessels, the largest in the port at that date.

The Millwall Docks were built on waste land south of the West India Docks and opened in 1868. Their particular contemporary purpose was to unload the imports of cheap foreign grain that began to pour into England after the repeal of the Corn Laws, and, in a greatly accelerated flood, after railways had been built to the mid-Western prairies of North America.

The unrestricted *laissez-faire* and free trade on the river made life increasingly difficult for the older docks. In any case they were inadequate to house the big new steamers that were capturing the prime trade to the Americas and the Far East. The average size of ships coming to London increased prodigiously during the middle decades of the nineteenth century, faster than at any period until the later decades of the twentieth century. The steamship made its first appearance on the Thames in 1815, but it was not until 1875 that steam (5·1 million tons) finally overtook sail (3·6 million tons) in the tonnage of vessels that used the port. The docks were forced into amalgamation and rat-race competition that depressed dockers' wages and created the dreadful conditions in the East End slums. The West India Dock Company took over the adjacent East India Docks, and became by shorthand the India Docks. The London and St Katharine Dock Companies merged, and later took over the Victoria Dock.

Once again that devoted riverman, Dickens, is a perceptive witness of what this part of the river was like in the heyday of its youth. His godfather, Christopher Huffam or Huffham, lived in Limehouse, and Dickens transmuted his visits as a small boy to him into golden descriptive pieces in his fiction. Here is the approach to the lodgings of Captain Edward Cuttle, that very salt-looking man indeed, who had been a pilot, or a skipper, or a privateer's man, or all three perhaps, and who had a hard time evading the matrimonial advances of his landlady, Mrs MacStinger. It comes from *Dombey and Son*. The Captain clearly lived just down the river from Mr Huffam:

'Captain Cuttle lived on the brink of a little canal near the India Docks where there was a swivel bridge, which opened now and then to let some wandering monster of a ship come roaming up the street like a stranded leviathan. The gradual change from land to water in the approach of Captain Cuttle's lodgings was curious. It began with the erection of flagstaffs as appurtenances to public-houses, then came slopsellers' shops with Guernsey shirts, sou'wester hats, and canvas pantaloons, at once the tightest and the loosest of their order, hanging up outside. Then came rows of houses with little vane-surmounted masts uprearing themselves from among the scarlet beans. Then ditches, then pollard willows, then more ditches, then unaccountable patches of dirty water hardly to be descried for the ships that covered them.

'Then the air was perfumed with chips, and all other trades were swallowed up in mast, oar, and block making and boat-building. Then the ground grew marshy and unsettled. Then there was nothing to be smelt but rum and sugar. Then Captain Cuttle's lodgings—at once a first storey and a top storey in Brig Place—were close before you.'

Lucky Captain Cuttle; except that when Brig Place comes, can Mrs MacStinger be far behind?

The ecclesiastical landmark of dockland, impending above the docks and cranes, is the dockers' church of St Anne, Limehouse. It was begun in 1712, when an Act of Parliament provided for the building of fifty new churches in and around London and Westminster to meet the needs of the growing cities and their suburbs. Christopher Wren, one of the Commissioners for the project, wrote a pragmatic directive on church-building to guide the Commission: 'A church should not be so filled with pews but that the poor may have room to stand and sit in the alleys, for to them equally is the Gospel preached. It were to be wished that there were to be no pews but benches, but there is no stemming the tide of profit and the advantage of pew-keepers, especially since by pews in the chapel of ease the minister is chiefly supported.'

The architect of St Anne's was Nicholas Hawksmoor, one of Wren's pupils and his clerk of the works at St Paul's Cathedral. It is notable for its spectacular west tower, rising in layers like a wedding-cake. Beneath the tower there is no portico but a grand entry with flights of approach steps and an apsidal projection that holds the main door. J. P. Malcolm in *Londinium Redivivum* written early in the nineteenth century described St Anne's: 'This strange jumble of architecture has a majestic outline. A sailor might be deceived by a distant view in supposing it a very large ship coming towards him, under easy sail, with a flag flying at her main-top.'

From the head of the Isle of Dogs the prospect of Greenwich on the south bank is one of the noblest sights on the Thames. But it was not until the 1970s that anybody had the obvious idea of building a housing estate there instead of warehouses so that people could enjoy the view. The focus of the view is the grand square of the Royal Naval College, the navy's university. In the distance the Queen's House, home of the National Maritime Museum, is framed in the long perspective between the classical symmetrical blocks and domes of John Webb and Christopher Wren. On the summit of the park rising behind the stately architecture stands the first

Royal Observatory, built by Charles II for the Reverend John Flamsteed. This was the birthplace of the Prime Meridian and Greenwich Mean Time.

Greenwich looks more like a palace than any other building in England. It once was: the sea palace on the Thames below London, as Hampton Court was the inland river palace above London. Like Hampton Court, Greenwich's greatest period was under the Tudors. But unlike Hampton Court, its history stretches back beyond the Tudors into the black past of pre-history.

The site on the huge loop of the Thames was of great strategic importance. It dominated both the sea and the land approaches to London. Watling Street and the pre-Roman roads from the Channel ports crossed the high plateau of Blackheath above the Thames at Greenwich. Looking towards London from here, Marshal Blücher is supposed to have made his honest but tactless remark: 'Was für plündern': what a place to plunder. Enthusiasts have tried to identify Greenwich as Trinovantum, the legendary prehistoric capital of south-east England. The archaeological evidence is too slight and the documentary witnesses, like Geoffrey of Monmouth, too mendacious for the identification to be positive. There are better grounds for asserting that the lost Roman city of Noviomagus, placed by the *Antonine Itinerary* ten miles from London on the Kent road, was situated somewhere near Blackheath.

The first verifiable appearance of Greenwich in history is when King Alfred gave the place he called Gronovic to his youngest daughter Aelfthryth (Elftrudis) as her marriage portion. She married Baldwin II, the Bald, Count of Flanders and one of Alfred's allies against the Danes at the end of the ninth century. Count Baldwin died in 918 and was buried in the Abbey of St Peter, Ghent. His widow gave her manor of Greenwich, together with Woolwich and Lewisham, to the Abbey as a memorial to her husband 'for the good of his soul'. The Abbey tenaciously retained its title to the manorial rights of Greenwich throughout the great upheavals of the next five centuries, though it found it increasingly difficult to collect its rents, tolls, and port dues.

In the eleventh century the Danes demonstrated that the Thames was a dagger pointing at London, and that Greenwich should be London's shield, by anchoring in the river and making Greenwich their base for raids and plunder for several years. During these incursions they kidnapped Alfege, the Archbishop of Canterbury, from his Cathedral and took him back to Greenwich, hoping for ransom. After a feast they were provoked by drink, disappointment at getting no ransom, and Alfege's infuriating habit of quoting the scriptures at them into throwing insults at him. Other missiles followed the insults. Alfege was felled by the skull of an ox and murdered.

Greenwich Parish Church, the latest building being early eighteenth century by Nicholas Hawksmoor and John James, commemorates the martyrdom of the unfortunate Archbishop. Tradition asserts that the church is built on the site of the murder. The awfulness of the sacrilege of killing an Archbishop lingered in the popular memory. Thomas à Becket, when struck down at his altar at Canterbury, is said to have called on Alfege at the moment of death.

The monks of Ghent continued nominally to own Greenwich, though, as the feudal system crumbled and nationalism grew, there were understandable English jealousies about alien Flemings holding such a key place. In 1414 Henry V confiscated and nationalized the possessions of alien monasteries. His uncle Humphrey, Duke of Gloucester, who was Regent and Protector during the long minority of Henry's son, acquired the site and built the first Greenwich Palace of which we have any reliable documentary and archaeological record. In addition to its strategic importance, Greenwich was a good place for a house, because of its bracing sea air unpolluted by the smoke of the City, and because of its fresh water and tides, convenient for flushing drains twice daily.

A licence gave Humphrey permission 'to build a mansion, crennelled and embattled, and enclose it within walls, also to erect and turrelate a certain tower, all in stone and lime, within the park'. This tower was a small castle up the hill on the site of the Royal Observatory to guard the road from the south-east to London, as the main palace on the waterfront guarded the river approach. Humphrey called his palace Bella Court, and there he built his great collection of books of Latin and the new learning of the Renaissance, before bequeathing them to Oxford University.

For diplomatic reasons Humphrey opposed the marriage of his nephew, Henry VI, to Margaret of Anjou; though he lent them Bella Court, the finest modern house in England, for their honeymoon. However he was on the wrong side in the wrong place at the wrong time in the power struggle that historians were to call the Wars of the Roses. His mistress whom he had married, Eleanor Cobham, was imprisoned for life on charges of witchcraft. Humphrey was subsequently disgraced, imprisoned, and, according to Shakespeare and other more prosaic authorities, murdered.

Bella Court was promptly seized by the Queen, Margaret of Anjou; she was only seventeen, but already the wilful and greedy virago who was such a stormy activist of the Wars of the Roses. She changed its name to *Pleasaunce*, in the same way that Henry VIII changed the name of York Place to Whitehall when he seized it.

Henry VI and Margaret spent much time and money at Greenwich. A 'bridge' or pier was built to give better access to the tidal river. A vestry was made to house the Crown Jewels. The 1447 accounts show lavish expenditure on the Queen's apartments. Her chamber was to be paved with Flanders tiles, a great new door decorated with two hundred tin nails was to be made

for it, and a *tresans*, or dais, was erected at one end. The windows throughout
the Palace were glazed in the novel and luxurious Continental fashion. The
glass and plasterwork were decorated *cum margaritis*, the daisies that were
the eponymous but incongruous emblems of the she-wolf Queen.

It is difficult to recreate the appearance of Bella Court and its successor,
Pleasaunce. We know only that the complex of buildings was built of pink
brick and white stone; that they were considered the height of modernity
and luxury; and that daisies were a recurrent theme of the ornamentation.
Excavations of the Grand Square of the Royal Naval College in 1971 uncovered the foundations of Bella Court and its predecessor, the house of the
Abbots of Ghent. Among the rubble of the foundations the excavators found
pink brick and white stone, plaster daisies in perfect condition and a piece of
cloth of gold.

The first Tudor razed Pleasaunce to the ground and built a great new sea
palace on its foundations, renaming it once again, Placentia. It was the great
Tudor palace and at the heart of English history for most of the Tudor epoch.
Contemporary drawings and building accounts make it possible to recreate a
quite detailed and systematic plan of Placentia. It was built of red brick with
white stone dressings, like Hampton Court, with ranges of rooms and galleries arranged around three main courtyards and several smaller ones. The
state rooms extended along the river front to the chapel at the eastern end.

The sea palace was conveniently placed for those founding fathers of the
Royal Navy, Henry VII and Henry VIII. Just upstream at Deptford, where
the Ravensbourne joined the Thames, was one of their new naval dockyards;
just downstream at Woolwich there was another. From his Palace at Greenwich Henry VIII used to sally forth in his gilded barge, dressed in cloth of
gold, blowing upon his golden whistle 'as loudly as upon a trumpet' to glory
in his role as head of the navy.

Deptford was the home since the Middle Ages of a religious society of old
pilots and other seafaring people grouped together to say masses for the souls
of shipwrecked sailors. Henry VIII gave them their first charter, naming
them as 'the Guild or Fraternity of the Most Glorious and Undivided
Trinity of Saint Clement'. Their activities were to include 'the increase, the
encouragement of navigation, the good government of seamen, and the
better security of merchant ships on our coast'. The Corporation of Trinity
House is still the general lighthouse authority for England, Wales, the
Channel Islands, and Gibraltar, responsible for all pilots, buoys, lighthouses,
and associated navigational matters around the Thames and the other coasts.
It is a good example of the English capacity for reverencing and at the same
time modernizing ancient traditions. The Corporation removed from
Deptford to its present headquarters on Tower Hill in the eighteenth century. It is still administered by a Board of ten Elder Brethren, elected from
the Royal Navy and the Merchant Navy.

A less happy association of Deptford is that Christopher Marlowe, that extravagantly brilliant and erratic Elizabethan poet and playwright, was killed there. A man called Ingram Frisar killed him after supper in a Deptford tavern. The contemporary inquiry decided that there had been a quarrel about the bill. Subsequent researches have suggested that Marlowe was a government agent, and that his death had a political complexion.

Placentia was the stage for a remarkably large number of the great events, political, social, and personal, of Henry VIII's eventful reign. He married Katherine of Aragon there. Anne Boleyn became a lady-in-waiting at Placentia, and during most of the long-drawn-out drama of the divorce the classic triangle of the King, Queen Katherine, and Anne were living there. At Placentia Henry heard that Cardinal Campeggio and Cardinal Wolsey had been appointed to try the case; at Placentia in 1529 Henry ordered the former to leave the country and the latter to be dismissed from all offices of state. The opening shots of the power struggle between King and Church that led to the Reformation were fired by William Peto and other courageous members of the adjacent order of Observant Friars preaching before the King at Greenwich, and being angrily rebutted by obedient royal chaplains. Henry's two daughters who became Queens of England were born, brought up, and formed in their neuroses there. Anne Boleyn was disgraced there. Anne of Cleves, whom Henry decided on first view was 'no better than a Flanders mare', was married and hastily unmarried there.

But apart from the larger-than-life Tudor personality cult, some of the seemingly trivial events of the perpetual round of parties and pageants for which Placentia was famous cast long shadows before them. The Masque, which was to have such a formative influence on Shakespeare and the English stage, was introduced from Italy at Greenwich. Raphael Holinshed, who supervised the compilation of the *Chronicles* that bear his name a generation later, wrote that by 1511 the famous Christmas feast at Placentia was made open to 'all respectable comers'; and that the King with eleven others disguised themselves and put on an entertainment 'after the maner of Italie called a maske, a thing not seen before'.

But it was the sea connexion that distinguished Placentia from other palaces. An appropriate emblem of this link was the river ceremony in which Henry left from there to launch England's first battleship, the greatest ship ever built in the world at that date. The towering thousand-ton round ship, the first to have gun-ports for great guns to fire broadsides, had a crew of 350 soldiers and 300 mariners. It was built downstream at Woolwich. The King sailed there in procession and, after a vast banquet on board, splashed some wine on the deck from a silver-gilt goblet, and named the massive ship, with characteristic complacency, *Henry Grâce à Dieu*.

The ship would only have qualified as a 'second rate' in Nelson's fleet. But its size and armament were contemporary prodigies. Such great guns and great Tudor ships revolutionized naval tactics, substituting cannonading at short range with expert seamanship for the obsolete tactics of ramming, peppering with small arms, grappling, and boarding. They were justified at the defeat of the Armada, when an eye-witness on an English ship wrote: 'There was never seen a more terrible value of great shot, nor more hot fight than this was, for although the musketeers and harquebusiers were then infinite, yet could they not be discerned nor heard, for that the great ordnance came so thick.' By establishing a tradition of English naval supremacy the great ships built in the Thames by the Tudors led the way to English mercantile and imperial supremacy.

Another notable example of the sea connexions of Greenwich comes from the reign of Henry's son, Edward VI. In May 1553, Hugh Willoughby and Richard Chancellor sailed to search for the north-east passage to India, the voyage that led to the signature of the first English trading treaty with Russia.

The contemporary account records:

'Being come near to Greenwich where the Court then lay, the courtiers came running out and the common people flocked together standing very thick upon the shore; the Privy Council, they looked out at the windows and the rest ran to the tops of the towers; the ships hereupon discharged their ordnance and shot off their pieces after the manner of war, inasmuch as the valleys and hills gave an echo, and the mariners shouted in such sort that the sky rang again with the noise thereof.'

None of Henry's children spent as much time at Placentia, when they came to the throne, as their father. It was haunted by memories of Henry's tremendous and terrible presence. But many of the notable maritime events of Elizabeth's reign were staged in her maritime palace. She knighted Drake from there after his circumnavigation, while his *Golden Hinde* was anchored off Deptford. She finally signed the death warrant of Mary Queen of Scots there, and her messengers left for Fotheringay with it before she could change her mind. She signed the orders for resisting the Armada there.

Placentia is thought to have been the setting of the traditional scene of the ambitious young Walter Raleigh and his cloak laid across a puddle for the Queen at 'a plashy place' near the present Queen's House. Raleigh is also supposed by tradition to have scratched on one of the windows: 'Feign would I climb, but that I fear to fall.' The Queen scratched underneath: 'If thy heart fail thee, climb not at all.'

Placentia was high on the itinerary of those invaluable witnesses who begin to appear in the sixteenth century, worthy Germans on tour with their pupils and their diaries. Here is part of Paul Hentzner's deservedly famous description of Elizabeth at Placentia in 1598, written in Latin and first published by Horace Walpole. After noting that the Queen generally stayed at Greenwich for the summer because of the delightfulness of the situation, Hentzner wrote:

'Next came the Queen, in the sixty-fifth year of her age (as we were told), very majestic; her face oblong, fair but wrinkled; her eyes small, yet black and pleasant; her nose a little hooked, her lips narrow, and her teeth black, (a defect the English seem subject to, from their too great use of sugar); she had in her ears two pearls with very rich drops; her hair was of an auburn colour, but false (*crinem fulvum, sed factitium*); upon her head she had a small crown, reported to be made of some of the gold of the celebrated Luneburg table; her bosom was uncovered, as all the English ladies have it till they marry.'

Hentzner goes on to describe her clothes; her versatility in speaking English, French, Italian, Greek, Latin, Spanish, Scotch, and Dutch; her ceremonial dinner; and her park with its old square tower, called *Mirefleur*, presumably Duke Humphrey's watchtower at the top of the hill guarding the Dover road.

The only significant part of the Palace of Placentia that subsists is the crypt of Queen Anne block of the Royal Naval College. But close beneath the surface of the present buildings and lawns lie the massive foundations of the old buildings, occasionally exposed by excavation.

The new Stuart regime made Whitehall its headquarters. But James I surrounded the palace and park at Greenwich with a brick wall, and commissioned his arbiter of elegance, Inigo Jones, to build a summer pavilion for his Queen, Anne of Denmark. It was called the House of Delight and stood near the site of the old gatehouse. Its purpose was in part to bridge, like Raleigh's cloak, the notoriously muddy road from Deptford to Woolwich, which was a right of way that even the King could not annul. Inigo Jones was just back from one of his seminal tours of Italy, impressed and influenced by the originality and the refinement of classical detail of the Venetian villas of Andrea Palladio. He introduced the Palladian style to England with the Queen's House at Greenwich, so changing the face of English architecture. One of the most striking features of the new style was its replacement of the Tudor system of grouping rows of rooms around a central courtyard by a spacious covered entrance hall with symmetrical rooms and stairs to other storeys leading out of it.

The Queen's House, now the home of the National Maritime Museum, stands today largely as Inigo Jones built and decorated it, one of the masterpieces and landmarks of English architecture. But its peculiar purpose to act as a bridge from the Palace to the park over the road was found to be impractical. The traffic passing through the middle of the H-shaped house and beneath its bridge was, not surprisingly, too intrusive. The road was eventually diverted to the north.

Charles I and his Queen, Henrietta Maria, took over the Queen's House after Anne's death, and used it as a repository for their great collections of paintings and furniture. During the Civil War and the Commonwealth, Placentia and its summer pavilion were like their owners, in eclipse. The great collections were auctioned at bargain prices to such eminent and ac-quisitive connoisseurs as Louis XIV, Mazarin, and the Queen of Sweden. Attempts were made to sell the Palace and its park. But eventually Placentia was allowed to fall into ruins. Part was filled with squatters, part leased to a contractor for army biscuits, and part used as a camp for prisoners-of-war during the First Dutch War.

After the Restoration, Henrietta Maria returned to the Queen's House. Her son, Charles II, decided to revive the glories of Tudor Greenwich by building a King's House on the dilapidated ruins of Placentia. John Webb, the nephew and disciple of Inigo Jones, was the architect, and the plan was for a building forming three sides of a square, with the river making the fourth side. On March 4, 1664, Pepys recorded in his diary: 'At Greenwich, I observed the foundation laying of a very great house for the King, which will cost a great deal of money.' A year later he wrote that the King was 'mightily pleased with his new buildings'. However, entirely characteristic-ally of Charles, the money ran out. Only one side of the grandiose project was completed, known today as the King Charles block, the western, right-hand block in the foreground to the observer from the river.

Charles II also founded the Royal Observatory at Greenwich, which makes it the oldest and most famous scientific research establishment in Britain. Greenwich is, at first or even at second sight, an unlikely place to have become custodian of the Prime Meridian and official time-keeper for the rest of the world. The climate of the Thames valley is notoriously foggy and uncongenial for star-gazing. The night sky over the United Kingdom is seldom completely dark. There are no mountains protruding above the clouds for the astronomers to peer from.

But in the seventeenth century it was urgent for navigators to discover longitude, a method of measuring accurately a ship's position at sea in an east and west direction. The great Portuguese sailors had found a way of calculating north–south latitude from the sun and the stars. In 1674 a Frenchman, a friend of the King's mistress the Duchess of Portsmouth, claimed that he had discovered a method of finding longitude at sea by observing the positions of the moon against the background of the stars. What he claimed was theoretically possible. But contemporary instruments for measuring the time, the motion of the moon, and the position of the stars were not accurate enough to make it practicable. In the following year Charles II established the Royal Observatory at Greenwich, and instructed the Reverend John Flamsteed, the first Astronomer Royal, 'forthwith to apply himself with exact care and diligence to the rectifying of the tables of the motions of the heavens, and the places of the fixed stars, so as to find out the so-much-desired longitude for the perfecting the art of navigation'. Christopher Wren built the observatory at the highest point of Greenwich Park, on the site of Duke Humphrey's watch-tower, with 'lodging rooms for our astronomical observer'. The Great Room of Flamsteed House and the other apartments are some of Wren's finest interiors in their pristine state.

Flamsteed never did succeed in perfecting the means of obtaining the longitude. But his successors at Greenwich, with the telescopes, chronometers, and sextants of the observatory, did. Hunting the longitude is evidently conducive to longevity. Astronomers Royal naturally tend not to be appointed until they are of mature years. But there have only been eleven of them in the unbroken succession of three hundred years since Flamsteed. Until the coming of the railways each community kept its own local time around the world by the sun. But the development of communications around the world made it essential to agree on an international zero longitude and an international time. In 1884 an International Meridian Conference in Washington chose as the prime meridian of the world 'the meridian passing through the centre of the Transit Instrument at Greenwich'. There was some opposition to Greenwich, particularly from the French, who preferred Paris, and when they could not get that, with revealing chauvinism, the meridian 180 degrees away from Greenwich. Since then the world has marched in time with Greenwich, and the old hill beside the Thames is of prime importance to all navigators. The smoke of London, and the street lights reflecting off the smoke, made Greenwich increasingly inimical to astronomy. So after the last war the Royal Observatory removed to Herstmonceux in Sussex, but retained its old name of the Royal Greenwich Observatory with confusing English reverence for traditional nomenclature. The Old Royal Observatory, Greenwich, has been restored and is preserved as a museum of astronomy and navigation by the National Maritime Museum.

At the end of the seventeenth century, war with France broke out over the Glorious Revolution personified by the accession of William and Mary. The English fleet won a great victory off La Hogue, the peninsula at the tip of Cherbourg that the modern French call la Hague. In its decisiveness it was the Trafalgar of the century. London was filled with old and disabled seamen, for whom there was no national provision, as there was for old soldiers at the Royal Hospital, Chelsea. William III was away on campaign in the Low Countries against the great enemy of European freedom, Louis XIV. In his absence, Mary decided to complete the King's House, Greenwich, as a hospital for seamen on the lines of Chelsea or Les Invalides in Paris. Wren supplied the plans free. Queen Mary died before the building was started. William completed the hospital as a memorial to her.

Macaulay, who made William the hero of his *History of England*, wrote:

'Had the King's life been prolonged till the works were completed, a

statue of her who was the real foundress of the Institution would have had
a conspicuous place in that court which presents two lofty domes and two
graceful colonnades to the multitudes who are perpetually passing up and
down the Imperial river. But that part of the plan was never carried into
effect; and few of those who now gaze on the noblest of European hospitals
are aware that it is a memorial of the virtues of the good Queen Mary, of the
love and sorrow of William, and of the great victory of La Hogue.'

Nicholas Hawksmoor and Sir John Vanbrugh were responsible with Wren
for different stages of the vast project, comprising the greatest team of architects ever to work together in England. The most splendid room in the building is the Painted Hall, a masterpiece of English Baroque by Wren and
Hawksmoor, in which the body of Horatio Nelson lay in state.

Dr Johnson visited the newly completed buildings with Boswell. Boswell
insisted on declaiming the lines from Johnson's *London*:

> On Thames's banks in silent thought we stood,
> Where Greenwich smiles upon the silver flood:
> Pleas'd with the seat which gave Eliza birth,
> We kneel and kiss the consecrated earth.

Johnson judged that the hospital was too magnificent for a place of charity,
and agreed with Boswell that it was too far from Fleet Street and 'the busy
hum of men' for him: significant confirmation of how remote from the
sprawl of London Greenwich was until comparatively recently.

The hospital was closed in 1869. Old sailors by then preferred home
comforts and an out-pension to living in the magnificent but monastic conditions of the hospital. The Royal Naval College was established there a few
years later, to provide higher technical, scientific, and general education for
its officers. It is still there, aptly established on the site of the old Tudor sea
palace and the even older sea and river gate to London.

The *Cutty Sark*, last and greatest of the sailing ships called Clippers, is
preserved in dry dock beside the College as a museum of the great days of
sail. She was built in Dumbarton in 1869 and finished her days on the
Australian wool run. She broke the record by sailing from Sydney to London
in seventy-five days. Beside her stands *Gypsy Moth*, the small yacht in which
Francis Chichester made the first sole circumnavigation of the world. When
he had made the great circle, he sailed up the Thames to Greenwich, where
Queen Elizabeth II knighted him on the Grand Square of the College with
the sword with which Elizabeth I knighted Drake after his first circumnavigation.

From the Greenwich Reach the Thames bends north-west up Blackwall
Reach to complete the great loop of river that encompasses the Isle of Dogs.
At the head of the reach the twin Blackwall road tunnels pass under the river.

The Lea, indifferently spelled the Lee, which rises in Hertfordshire, joins the Thames on the north bank here. This is 'the sedgy Lea' on which Piscator instructs Venator in the arts of angling in Izaak Walton's *The Compleat Angler*, that admirably escapist recreation for the contemplative man, even if he does not actually want to go fishing. The Limehouse Cut and industry have polluted the Lea for fishing since the seventeenth century, and turned it into derelict and dirty wasteland. But it is gradually being purified and the fish restored as part of the plan to turn the whole Lea valley into a regional park and recreation centre for the East End.

The Thames bends south-east in Bugsby's Reach, then east in Woolwich Reach, where the Greater London Council are building a movable flood surge barrier to stop the high tides swamping London. The derivation of the Bugsby that gave its name to the reach and also the former marshes on its north bank is obscure. One tradition, unsupported by convincing documentary evidence, is that the name comes from a once famous or notorious Captain who commanded one of the prison hulks that used to be moored in this reach, like the one from which the convicts had escaped at the beginning of *Great Expectations*. A nicer and more recondite derivation is that Bugsby is a contraction of *Boggarts-by*, 'by the boggarts'. A boggart is a bogle or bugbear that causes fright. Before Bazalgette built the London sewers, the refuse of London was drained in open ditches into the Thames. Particularly when they passed through marshy ground such as Bugsby's marshes, the ditches gave off a foul effluvium thick with methane gas that flared and guttered with spontaneous bursts of flame. Mysterious lights flickering over lonely marshes are the favourite manifestation of boggarts.

Woolwich was a fishing village in the Middle Ages. The construction of the royal dockyard there by the Tudors brought it to prominence and caused William Camden, the antiquary, to describe it as 'the mother dock of our royal navy'. One of the many momentous maritime events starting from Woolwich was the dispatch from there, in February 1601, of the first trading fleet of the East India Company. It had been chartered by a meeting of London traders under the Lord Mayor to challenge the Dutch and Portuguese monopoly of trade to the Far East. From that beginning at Woolwich grew the British Empire in India and the whole Indian connexion.

The Royal Arsenal, which was also an important element in Woolwich until it was closed in the 1960s, originated in the ordnance stores kept there by the Tudors. The official Arsenal was moved to the safety of the open country there in 1716, after a calamitous explosion at Moorfields in the City, until then the chief foundry for the production of ordnance. The 'Brass Gun Foundry' was designed by Vanbrugh. Barracks and other military establishments, arsenals, and factories came to Woolwich in increasing numbers as, after the Crimean War, the machinery of warfare became ever more elaborate.

The Royal Military Academy was founded there in 1741 to train cadets for the Artillery and Engineers, as Sandhurst was to train cadets for the Infantry and Cavalry. Originally the Academy was housed in the Model Room in the Royal Arsenal, but appropriately grandiose barracks were built in Woolwich for it early in the nineteenth century. This separate school for regular officers was closed after the Second World War, and all officers are now trained at Sandhurst. The industrial revolution and the overflow of London suburbs swamped Woolwich with industry and buildings as they swamped so many other old Thames villages. But until the second half of the twentieth century Woolwich retained its individual village atmosphere, partly because of its strong military connexions, and partly because its Arsenal and associated factories provided work locally. Until the Arsenal closed, Woolwich was never a dormitory suburb.

The north bank of the long Woolwich Reach is called North Woolwich as well as Silvertown, and is the site of the Royal Docks, the largest and the last docks within the boundaries of Greater London. The Royal Docks, running parallel to the river, consist of the Royal Victoria, Royal Albert, and King George V Docks, and have a water area of 234 acres, constituting the largest sheet of impounded dock water in the world.

They handle approximately three million tons of cargo a year, importing most of the beef, lamb, butter, cheese, bulk grain, and tobacco that comes into the United Kingdom, and exporting most of the motor vehicles, machinery and steel, spirits and manufactured goods. The Royal Docks, with a depth of water of up to thirty-eight feet, are likely to remain navigable for some time even by the largest of the new generations of general cargo ships. But the men who built them anticipated a longer life for them than looks likely with the transformation of the shipping industry that is taking place.

The Victoria Dock was opened during the Crimean War on the previously marshy flats below Blackwall known as Bugsby's marshes. This gradual movement of the port downstream was part of the ancient and continuing process in order to handle the growing volume of trade and size of ships. The Victoria, built for the swelling trade of the industrial revolution, was the first dock to be linked to the new railways, with rails running on its quays.

The Royal Albert Dock was opened just east of the Victoria in 1880. It was one and three quarter miles long and specially designed to accommodate the large new iron and steam ships that were replacing sail.

Leap-frogging downstream, the East and West India Dock Company opened the Tilbury Docks in the Essex marshland in 1886 as a move in the fierce competition to provide more modern and therefore cheaper dock equipment. These were the last of the great docks built by private enterprise. The Port of London Authority merged the private dock companies and ended the cut-throat and ruinous competition that had made very few men rich and had impoverished the East End. In 1921 King George V opened for the Port of London Authority the great dock that bears his name in North Woolwich. This, the only major dock to have been constructed by the Authority so far, lies between the Royal Albert and the river, and completes the complex of the Royal Docks. The next logical step in the progress down-river, if money can be found to build it and if it can be done without despoiling the environment (a consideration that never hampered single-minded Victorian industrialists), is to move the port to the mouth of the Thames at Maplin sands off Foulness Island, nearer to Britain's trading partners of the European Economic Community and more accessible for the huge ships of the future. Even if circumstances prevent this happening, port activity is bound to be increasingly concentrated at Tilbury.

The Royal Albert and the King George V have entrance locks into the Thames at Gallions Reach, where the foiled, circuitous wanderer turns northeast again, before straightening east towards the sea. Gallions is presumed to be an ancient variant spelling of galleons. The north bank is Dagenham, a town in Essex until it was brought into London by the reorganization of London local government and the creation of the Greater London Council in 1965.

The most conspicuous monument and symbol of Dagenham is the titanic Ford Motor Works towering on the river bank. The name of Ford's, Dagenham, has become a synonym for stylish, efficient, cheap family cars that ordinary British people can afford—and for industrial unrest. Henry Ford, the great American mass-assembler, father of the Tin Lizzie, the Model T, and the saying that 'history is bunk', brought his industrial complex and his philosophy to Dagenham in 1929. It was the introduction to Britain of Ford's development of mass production, mechanization of productive operations, 'production flow', standardization and simplification, assembly-line methods, and scientific management. The vast Dagenham works beside the Thames are not generally considered beautiful, but they are an industrial and social portent, neatly moralized by the inextricable traffic jams on the roads out of the East End behind them.

On the Erith marshes and the site of the former Royal Arsenal Woolwich on the south bank opposite Dagenham the Greater London Council is making a notable experiment to turn its face towards the river again with a new town inside London called Thamesmead. The plan, to be completed by the 1990s, is to provide homes beside the Thames for about 45,000. It will be not just a dormitory suburb, but a self-sufficient community with factories and óffices, local and central shopping, and extensive educational, communal, and recreational facilities. There may be disagreement about some of the 'high-rise' architecture, but there can be none about building a whole new town instead of a suburb, or about giving people rather than industry the best places on the river bank again.

At present the Thames leaves the boundaries of Greater London just before

Purfleet on the north bank and at Crayford Ness, where the River Darent joins it on the south. Quite appropriately the capital's two main sewage treatment works, the Northern and Southern outfall drainage works, are at this eastern extremity of London.

If London is seen anthropomorphically as a giant, with his head in Westminster and County Hall, his heart in the East End, his belly and privates in Soho, his credit cards in the City, and his limbs sprawled asleep in the dormitory suburbs, then his principal excretory organs are at Beckton on the north bank and at Crossness in the Erith marshes. Beckton, the largest sewage treatment works in Europe, treats an average daily dry weather flow of 215 million gallons; Crossness, the largest completely modernized and automatized works in Europe, about 115 million gallons a day.

Until the middle of the nineteenth century London's drainage was simple and crude: sewers and the vanished rivers of central London disembogued and disgorged directly into the Thames; and the nightmen of the obsolete euphemism cleaned out the cesspools. Then Sir Joseph Bazalgette, who could be called the father of the effluent society, constructed the magnificent network of intercepting sewers parallel to the Thames and running down to Beckton and Crossness. The Prince of Wales started the beam-engine pumps to hoist the sewage into Crossness works in 1865. Prints of the period show men in top hats and women in crinolines admiring the marvels of modern science. The modernized works at Crossness today cover 168 acres with grit channels measureless to man and serried rows of sludge digestion tanks. To explain in detail the modern treatment of London's sewage would need schematic flow diagrams and a vast flush of technological terminology. Crudely, however, the sewage is first screened to remove solid rubbish that might obstruct the flow. It is then pumped to the detritus channels, where grit and sand sink to the bottom and are removed, washed, and used for land reclamation.

The sewage passes on to the primary sedimentation tanks, where solids settle to the bottom as crude sludge. This is pumped into what are known, picturesquely, as digestion tanks. Here the sludge is heated to ninety degrees Fahrenheit, and ferments for sixteen days. In the process it gives off each day millions of cubic feet of gas rich in methane. The gas is used to run the power-house that generates the electricity for the sewage works. After the sludge has been thoroughly digested and so made innocuous, it is carried down river to sea by sludge vessels and deposited in the Barrow Deep opposite Foulness.

Meanwhile, back at the farm, the liquid sedimented sewage, from which the crude sludge has been extracted, passes into aeration tanks. Here there is a Niagara of rushing waters, and the first faint scent of sewage does annoy the air. Air and a culture of bacteria are forced into what sewermen call 'the mixture' for about seven hours. The oxygen encourages the bacteria to break down the organic matter in the sewage. The mixture then passes to the final sedimentation tanks, and from there, purified and wholesome, it spills over weirs into the Thames.

William FitzStephen wrote that London water was sweeter than other water, and Thames fish more plentiful and fatter than in any other river. FitzStephen was a partial and enthusiastic historian. He also asserted that Londoners were more handsome than other men, and their wives more virtuous. But if the progress of cleaning the river were to be continued at the rate of the past two decades, it is not entirely inconceivable that one day the salmon would come back to the Thames. The first salmon for a hundred and fifty years was taken in the tideway in 1974.

CHAPTER TEN

The control of the Thames and its future

AT the dawn of geology, two hundred and twenty-five million years ago, the floating continents coalesced to form a single land-mass, aptly named Pangaea by the geologists, and a single ocean, Panthalassa. About a hundred and eighty million years ago, give or take a few million, Pangaea rifted initially into two parts, Laurasia on the north and Gondwana on the south, which drifted apart, split up, and collided to form the present geography of the world, its oceans, mountain ranges, and rivers. We can date these events across such a great backward gulf of time from the age of the oldest basaltic rocks along the margins of the oceans. Within the past sixty-five million years the continents attained their present positions, Britain separated from the rest of Europe, and the Thames ceased being a tributary of the river now called the Rhine and became a river on its own.

For almost all of its history the Thames has been its own master, flowing to the sea and being regurgitated twice daily by the tide, subject only to the laws of geology and hydrology. It was always the most spectacular natural phenomenon in southern Britain, and its freedom from restraint by man was what excited even the normally phlegmatic. Izaak Walton wrote: 'It flieth between Berks, Buckinghamshire, Middlesex, Surrey, Kent, and Essex: and so weddeth himself to the Kentish Medway, in the very jaws of the ocean. This glorious river feeleth the violence and benefit of the sea more than any river in Europe.' Walton's contemporary, the clergyman and miscellaneous writer, Donald Lupton, was similarly impressed by the unrestrained autarky of the London river: 'This is a long, broad, slippery fellow: rest he effects not, for he is always in motion: he seems something like a carrier, for he is still either going or coming, and once in six or eight hours, salutes the sea his mother and then brings tiding from her.'

This uncontrolled independence of the Thames did not stop Londoners, when they arrived on its banks, from trying to restrain and regulate it. For the last tiny fraction of the river's evolution man has tampered with the Thames, changing it from a broad, clear, shallow river, famous for its salmon, into a narrow, embanked river, so heavily polluted at the height of the industrial revolution that it was little better than an open sewer.

There are records from the Middle Ages of London apprentices complaining that they were given salmon to eat far too often. By the 1830s the Thames salmon were extinct; the thriving fishing industries based on whitebait, shad, and smelt in the lower estuary were driven out of business by the 1870s. Modern methods of sewage treatment combined with concern about pollution and the environment have brought about a dramatic change over the past decade, in the most beneficial piece of tampering with the river for many years. In 1965 several fish were caught in the cooling water intakes of riverside power stations, indicating that the water was becoming less poisonous. Since then over seventy species have been recorded in the tidal Thames. Flounder, plaice, and dab are commonly caught, and sprat and herrings are sometimes caught in shoals of hundreds.

Colonies of fish-eating birds have followed the fish back up the London river. And although there is no record yet of a London apprentice complaining that he is given salmon to eat too often for his luncheon vouchers, a live salmon was caught in the Thames in November 1974. It was trapped in the filters of West Thurrock power station, and was the first taken in the Thames since 1833. It weighed eight pounds, four and a quarter ounces. The Greater London Council has started an annual angling competition, partly to monitor the welcome return of fish to the Thames.

The Romans were the first to start to regulate the Thames with their wharfs and port buildings; their water channels and slow sand filter, which is still the main method of cleaning London's drinking water; and, above all, with their bridge, the most important man-made interference with the river for many centuries. In the Dark and Middle Ages river controls over such matters as fishing, customs duties, and tolls proliferated, as the Kings farmed out parcels of their ownership of the river to the City or to great magnates in return for political or, more usually, financial support.

From early times there was concern about pollution of the river, and ineffectual attempts were continually made to reduce it. Edward III in 1357 observed 'that dung and other filth had accumulated in divers places upon the banks of the river and noticed the fumes and other abominable stenches arising therefrom', and issued a royal order to clean the Thames. History does not record the efficacy of Edward's order, but it is unlikely to have been great, since similar complaints recur with regularity.

An official called the Serjeant of the Channels, responsible for supervising the drainage of the City, makes his first appearance in the *Letter Books* in 1385. A *Letter Book* ordinance of 1383 indicates the antiquity of the problem of pollution of the Thames:

'And whereas the watercourse of Walbrook is stopped up by divers filth and dung thrown therein by persons who have houses along the said course, to the great nuisance and damage of all the City, punishment may be inflicted upon the offenders. But it shall be fully lawful for those persons who have houses on the said watercourse to have latrines over the course, provided that they do not throw rubbish or other refuse through the same, whereby the passage of the said water may be stopped.'

The climax of pollution of the Thames came in June 1858, when an unusually hot summer and an unusually low rainfall combined to produce the phenomenon known to Londoners as 'the Great Stink'. It excited more comment even than the contemporary Indian Mutiny, and occupied more prominent space in the newspapers. Members of Parliament spoke of the pestilential condition of the Thames and 'the vile state of this magnificent river'. One said: 'It is a notorious fact that Honourable Gentlemen sitting in the Committee Rooms and the library are utterly unable to remain there in consequence of the stench which arises from the river.' The windows of Westminster had to be draped with curtains soaked in chloride of lime to enable Members to breathe. In the Lords the Earl of Hardwicke said that the Thames had been made 'the main sewer for the whole of London, and had been converted into a most abominable ditch'. They debated whether to remove the Law Courts to Oxford or St Albans, and a Select Committee was set up to investigate the Stink and recommend means of abating it. One witness, an inventive Mr Gurney, proposed sealing the ends of all the sewers in London, and piping the gas from them away to high places, where it would be fired and would burn away, he said, harmlessly.

He was particularly anxious to run a pipe from the huge new Victoria sewer through the Palace of Westminster to the top of the Clock Tower. He was allowed to do this, but a more practical engineer prevented the subsequent explosion from carrying out Guy Fawkes's ambition. The Great Stink was eventually cured by the use of large quantities of slaked lime and the heavy rainfall inseparable from an English summer.

Modern attempts to control the sanitary conditions of London and its river began with the Great Fire, which in five days swept away the accumulated filth of many centuries. Wren's revolutionary plan for the reconstruction of London included several imaginative schemes for improving sewers and drainage, which, like much else of his plans, he was not permitted to carry out. But the Act of 1667 'For Rebuilding the City of London' introduced the Commissioners of Sewers, who were responsible for the sanitary health of London and the Thames for the next two centuries.

The population explosion of the nineteenth century and the general introduction of that fundamentally momentous invention, the water-closet, altered the scale of the problem. Water-closets were originally made to discharge not into sewers, but into cesspools, which were emptied from time to time as necessary. The enormous addition that the water-closet made to the contents of cesspools necessitated the introduction of overflow drains running into street sewers and thence into the Thames. In 1843 the Metropolitan Commissioners of Sewers were appointed to improve the sanitary conditions of the London poor. In a few years they abolished about two hundred thousand foul cesspools, and compulsorily established water-closets draining to sewers. Consequently the Thames itself was transformed into an open sewer, and its old natural tributaries like the Walbrook and the Fleet became what they had threatened to become since the Middle Ages, branch sewers meandering haphazardly towards the river and emptying into it at low tide. Not surprisingly there were repeated epidemics of cholera: twenty-five thousand people died in 1849 and 1854.

In 1855 the Metropolitan Board of Works was founded to maintain main sewers and prevent sewage from entering the Thames within the London area. Under its chief engineer, Sir Joseph Bazalgette, the Board built a system of intercepting sewers running parallel to the river and disgorging a dozen miles below London at Beckton on the north bank and Crossness on the south. This system, with many of Bazalgette's original and elegant brick sewers, is still in use. The sewage was not treated, but held in large reservoirs and released into the river at ebb tide. In other words, the problem had not been solved, only removed from London, to the great annoyance of the local inhabitants near the outfalls.

Methods of treating sewage continued to improve. Covered sedimentation channels were built at Beckton and Crossness in the 1880s and treatment with lime was introduced. Six ships were built to carry the sludge out to sea. But the population of London and the concomitant pollution of the London river also continued to grow steadily. By 1934 more than a hundred and eighty disposal works were discharging into the Thames and its tributaries within twenty-five miles of central London.

The next great step forward in washing the River Thames was taken by the old Middlesex County Council, which from 1936 onwards rationalized its twenty-eight small sewage works into one giant treatment plant and outfall into the Thames above London at Mogden. Scientists had discovered twenty years before that it was possible to harness bacteria to purify organic waste, but Mogden was the first large-scale application of the activated sludge process. An entirely new treatment plant at Crossness, which had scarcely changed since the beginning of the century, was commissioned in 1964; and from then the condition of the tidal Thames began to improve noticeably. The Crossness plant is similar to the pioneering plant at Mogden, except that surface aeration instead of diffused air is used in the activated sludge process, and the sludge is disposed of at sea and not on land. In 1975 the major extension and improvement of the Beckton plant was finished, making it the largest full-treatment sewage plant in Europe, treating an average daily dry weather flow of two hundred and fifteen million gallons.

Pollution of the Thames has been notably reduced during the past decade. But the control of the river was parcelled out among a number of different authorities, many of them excellent and far-sighted in themselves, but having a natural proclivity towards an overall lack of coordination. Drainage was the responsibility of the Middlesex and London County Councils, united in 1965 to form the Greater London Council. The Port of London Authority was responsible for controlling pollution in the tidal Thames in addition to its port activities. The Thames Conservancy was responsible for the entire water cycle of the Thames from its source to Teddington, with conspicuous success that made it a model river authority for the world. The Metropolitan Water Board, formed at the beginning of the century, supplied the people of London with clean, safe, and palatable water for seventy years, with a lack of publicity that was a sure sign that it was doing its job efficiently. In the water supply business above all, no nuisance is good news; and no news-men is even better. A network of two hundred other smaller public and local authorities had their parts in the machinery of controlling the river on its journey from source to the sea.

Accordingly, in order to rationalize this diffused control, the Thames Water Authority was set up and, on April 1, 1974, assumed control of the entire water cycle throughout the five thousand square miles of the river basin and catchment area of the Thames. The Port of London Authority continues to control navigation in the tidal Thames; but the Thames Water Authority has taken over the use of water resources, sewerage, recreation, and improvement of the environment in the lower Thames. Above Teddington it is responsible for navigation as well, and everything else to do with the river.

Some twelve million people live in the basin of this comparatively small river, compared, that is, with such copious floods as the Nile or the Zambezi. Each of them uses on average more than fifty gallons of water a day for domestic purposes alone. At present the Thames, continually recycled on its passage to the sea, is sufficient to satisfy this demand. But scientific prognosticators calculate that the demand for water will double by the end of the century. Such projections and extrapolations are suspect and liable to gross error; and it is difficult to see how domestic demand can double if the population remains stable. Are people really going to start taking two baths a day?

However, if these calculations are roughly accurate, by the end of the century there is going to be a shortage of water in the Thames valley for the first time since Laurasia separated from Gondwana. One of the principal future preoccupations of the Thames Water Authority is how to meet this predicted shortage. There are several ways of doing this. One method being considered is to bring water from the wetter and less densely populated west of the country and feed it into the upper Thames. The engineering problems and the cost are formidable; and ecological difficulties or even disaster could result, for example from mixing western water, which is soft, with Thames water, which is hard.

A second method is to recirculate present supplies of water even more than at present, passing them through more houses, more factories, and more bodies before they are allowed to disembogue themselves to sea. This is also expensive, but the techniques for carrying it out have been well established.

Recycling water round and round inside a house in a kind of domestic perpetual water machine is ruled out as too dangerous, because there would be no warning system against break-down and pollution. In its present huge regional water cycle the Thames Water Authority has men employed tasting and sampling water scientifically around the clock to make sure that the water stays pure.

A third or complementary method is to encourage people to economize with water by pricing policy or some other system. The danger of such a policy is that, by discouraging people from washing or flushing their lavatories, diseases like cholera and dysentery that were endemic in Thames water in the Middle Ages, might be reintroduced.

Economies could be made by encouraging people with advertisements and perhaps with building policy to have showers instead of baths. Ingenious water ergonomists have proposed designing lavatories with a dual system of flushing. For modest matters a single push of a button or pull of a lever would flush a small quantity of water. Where necessary, a double push or pull would flush a larger quantity. Unfortunately for these best laid schemes of sluice and men, even more ingenious water psychologists have suggested that what would happen in practice would be that people would flush once, and then decide that their lavatories still looked inadequately purged. They would then flush twice to make sure, so using half as much water again as in an old-fashioned single-flush lavatory.

Another method of encouraging economy would be to instal domestic meters to measure how much water people actually use and charge them accordingly. The present system of charging for water by rateable value is crude and discriminatory. A household using fifty gallons a day can pay the same as a household using a thousand gallons, because they live in similar houses. The argument against such a pricing policy is that water is not just an ordinary commodity to be measured and sold like other things, but a social service on which public hygiene and health depend. If you discourage people from using water by your pricing policy, you risk disease. You could perhaps allow every household a basic minimum of water free, for example, a thousand gallons a week, and charge for any water in excess of this basic ration. But then households that would not normally use a thousand gallons might use up their ration like water, so as to be sure of getting their money's worth.

The tideway of the Thames is a large potential source of water not yet tapped. At present the water is brackish, and therefore unsuitable for the domestic water supply, because current filtration processes do not remove

salt from water. But if legislation were passed to enable the Woolwich barrier
to be used as a barrage, so stopping the tide in the Woolwich Reach, the
water in the tideway would become fresh and available for the water cycle.
This is not likely to happen so long as the Royal and the India and Millwall
Docks are important parts of the Port of London. Commerce is more vital
to London than an additional source of water. But, far from being immutable,
the pattern of dock activity is changing faster than it ever has.

The tendency towards bigger ships, bulk-carriers, and containerized
cargoes is pulling the port rapidly down the estuary towards deeper waters.
The men who built the Royal Docks a century ago must have hoped for a
longer life from their investment than seems likely at present. A possible
tendency in the opposite direction is the development of the lighter and
barge traffic to carry containers to their destinations up-river and throughout
the inland waterways. This could rejuvenate the upper port and the canal
system. The shape of the port is entirely prescribed by the pattern of trade.
This is, paradoxically, why the ports of Rotterdam and Hamburg, having
been completely flattened in the last war, have found it easier to adapt to
post-war patterns of trade, by starting again from the foundations. The Port
of London, although heavily bombed, was left with an obsolescent dock
system, and the labour troubles consequential to attempts to reform something that is already in existence and working. However the port develops,
a barrage to keep back the tideway is not likely so long as big ships need to
come up-river above Woolwich Reach.

Even without the barrage, the great pool of estuarine water in the tideway
could be used for some industrial and agricultural purposes, though not for
drinking. Such a use would necessitate a two-tier water supply with two
systems of water mains and pipes. The industrial water would, perhaps, be
coloured to distinguish it dramatically from the domestic drinking water.
Such duplication would be expensive. There would always be the fear that
the wrong water would penetrate the domestic system and poison half
London. This solution to the predicted water shortage is therefore an outsider
among the candidates.

The chief effort at controlling the Thames so far this century has been put
into sewage treatment and cleaning the grossly polluted and putrefying tideway. This activity has had such considerable success over the past decade
that the question is now arising of where does the tideway go from here. A
Government committee in the early 1960s, chaired by Professor A. J. S.
Pippard, concluded that only two conditions of the tideway were worth
aiming for: freedom from offensive smells at all times, or a salmon river. The
first condition has now been reached. Is it worth proceeding further? The
Pippard Committee put the alternative aim: 'Beyond securing this safety
margin (to avoid putrescence even under the worst conditions of low upland
flow and high temperature), it appears to us that there is no worthwhile

stopping point short of improving the estuary sufficiently to enable migratory fish, particularly salmon, to pass through it to and from the upper river.' Is this a realistic objective for a metropolitan river estuary? Would the money needed to restore the London River to the purity of the fresh water river above Teddington be available, justifiable, and politically possible? Will London apprentices ever again complain of being surfeited with repeated salmon?

The answer to these questions is no. The pressing preoccupations of the Thames Water Authority for the rest of this century are other than making the tideway fit for salmon to live in. The main effort of Thames authorities so far this century has been spent in improving the treatment of sewage and ending the centuries of neglect and abuse of the estuarine Thames. Research in these fields will continue. But more effort is now needed to improve sewerage: that is, the old and obsolescent sewers and pipes of London, many of which are more than a century old. Bazalgette's great sewerage system needs to be renovated, its flow improved, its channels rebuilt. Other pressing works are to bring the sewage treatment of the whole Thames valley up to the standard of London; to rationalize the pricing structure for water; and, above all, to ensure that the Thames water cycle does not run out of water and dry up by the end of the century.

The other main controlling authority of the tideway is the Port of London Authority, which is responsible for the conservation of the tidal Thames as well as the control of navigation, the docks, and their traffic. The limits of the Port of London used to be defined by a Treasury minute of 1883 as extending from the high-water mark at Teddington Lock down river to an imaginary straight line drawn from the pilot mark at the entrance of Havengore Creek in Essex to the land's end at Warden Point in the Isle of Sheppey in Kent. The seaward boundary was extended by the Port of London (Extension of Seaward Limit) Act, 1964, in order to allow the port to move farther down the estuary and control shipping approaching the Thames. The seaward limit of the port is now officially defined as imaginary straight lines drawn from Foulness Point in Essex to Gunfleet Old Lighthouse, thence to latitude 51 degrees, 26 minutes, 36 seconds north, longitude 01 degrees, 25 minutes, 30 seconds east, and thence to Warden Point in Kent.

The Port of London has the greatest traffic of any port in Britain. About nine thousand ships, an average of twenty-six a day, use it each year: a net registered tonnage of between twenty and twenty-five million tons. If goods and commodities excluding oil and other fuels are considered, nearly twice as much traffic comes up the Thames as to the next busiest British port, Liverpool. Milford Haven, the great new oil port on the south-west tip of Pembroke, has nearly as much traffic as London, but almost all of it is oil and other fuel pumped ashore from the giant tankers. In 1973 56·5 million tonnes of traffic passed through the Port of London, of which 19·2 million

tonnes were materials and goods other than oil. The comparable figures for
Milford Haven were 53·4 million tonnes, and 20,000 tonnes.

Such great and fundamental changes have taken place in the port in the
past fifty years that only a foolhardy prophet would confidently predict how
it will develop in the next fifty. It is, however, safe to say that goods will
continue to become more 'unitized' (organized in larger standardized
packages); ships will become larger and fewer; and ports will consequently
have to become deeper and more accessible to the main shipping lanes.

As far as the Thames is concerned, these developments point unmistakably
to the construction of a deep water port on Maplin Sands, the most ambitious
port project ever undertaken in Britain. The plan is for a large area of Maplin
Sands by Foulness on the north of the estuary to be reclaimed, using
material dredged from the channels of the estuary. A deep water oil port and
a container port directly associated with industries sited on the reclaimed
land would be built, capable of handling the biggest of the modern container
and bulk-cargo ships and the giant oil-tankers. A new deep water channel
would be dredged from the North Sea to Maplin, large enough to give
passage to ships of eighty-five foot draught and half a million tons displace-
ment, the largest that can navigate the English Channel.

Apart from the obvious advantages of size, speed, concentration of operations, and proximity to the trade routes, there are many incidental advantages
in the port's continuing movement downstream. There is far less risk of
pollution and other damage to the environment in the larger ships discharging at Maplin than in many more smaller ships coming up the Sea Reach
towards London. The removal of the port will give an opportunity for imaginative redevelopment of the East End. Britain has always depended on trade
more than countries with greater natural resources. Her trading future
depends predominantly, as it has always done, on the development and
efficiency of the Port of London.

The Greater London Council, with the riparian Borough Councils, is
responsible for the planning and development on the banks of the Thames
in London. Over the past few years great advances have been made in tidying
and improving the river banks by insisting that every development includes
some gain for the riverside such as a footpath. The Thames Water Authority
is preparing plans to hand over to the Greater London Council responsibility
for the control and promotion of all recreational activities, such as boating,
sailing, and angling, on the tideway. In 1974 the Greater London Council,
which already owned Greenwich Pier, bought from the Port of London
Authority the six other main piers in the London Thames: Richmond, Kew,
Putney, Westminster, Charing Cross, and the downstream half of Tower
Pier. The intention is to build another pier at Woolwich, and to develop
private and perhaps public transport on London's widest and wettest road.
The Council with the Government is subsidizing the experimental com-

muter service on the river by hovercraft from Greenwich to central London.

The Council is also responsible for a development as significant to the river as the movement of the port: the Thames barrier at Woolwich. Work started on the barrier in 1972 and, if it goes according to plan, it will be ready to prevent floods by 1979. The Thames needs a barrier because of the serious and increasing risk of flooding. In 1928 fourteen people were drowned when the Thames overflowed its banks. The high tide of 1953 inundated the east coast and the Thames estuary, killing three hundred people. Analysis of tides shows that the mean high water in south-east England appears to be rising higher in relation to the levels of dry land: in other words, south-east England is slowly sinking. Measured at Southend, mean high water is increasing by one and a quarter feet a century. In addition, the mean tidal range, that is the difference between mean high and mean low water, at London Bridge is increasing by about two and a half feet a century, with mean high water becoming higher, and mean low water becoming lower. The scientific reasons for these changes are not yet clearly established. Probably the movement of the earth's crust is responsible for the gradual subsidence of south-east England. Man-made improvements, or at any rate interference with the Thames and its banks, could explain the increased tidal range in central London. Whatever the reasons, if nothing were done, a catastrophic flood would inevitably sooner or later destroy a large part of London.

Possible defences against such an inundation are: raising the banks along the whole length of the tideway; a movable barrier that can be raised to dam dangerous surges and prevent them flooding upstream; a permanent barrage to halt the tide below London; and a combination of bank raising with either permanent barrage or movable barrier. A permanent barrage, A. P. Herbert's proposal to produce his vision of a tideless London River, although feasible, practical, and splendid for those who like messing about in boats, is ruled out for the foreseeable future because the commercial and industrial uses of the Thames in London are still paramount. All the power stations and big riverside undertakings are supplied by river; all the sewage sludge is carried away from London by river. The barrage would be too great an impediment to such essential traffic.

The movable barrier combined with bank-raising downstream from it was therefore chosen. More than a dozen sites for the barrier were considered from Cannon Street in central London to the Clacton to Margate line in the outer estuary. The farther up river a barrier is installed, the less the interference with shipping, and the greater the cost and complexity of raising the banks down-river from it. Conversely, the farther down the estuary the barrier is installed, the less becomes the problem of raising the banks, and the greater the probable interference with shipping.

The engineering difficulties of building a barrier in the outer estuary,

when considered, proved insurmountable. It would have to have gates large
enough to admit great numbers of big ships that use the estuary, yet exclusive
enough to attenuate a surge tide. Machinery capable of performing both
functions has not yet been invented; and the functions are probably incompatible. So the site for the barrier was chosen in the western half of the
Woolwich Reach at Silvertown. Navigationally this is a suitable place, being
in the middle of a long, straight reach. In any case surveys show that the
number of vessels passing through Woolwich Reach is declining steadily.
In addition, the siltation patterns at Silvertown are more favourable than
in other parts of the river. The Thames has a very complex siltation pattern,
with the net movement of silt apparently being, as is not the case in most
rivers, inwards from the sea. One of the arguments against an outer estuarine
barrier or barrage was that it would disrupt this siltation pattern, and cause
silting in the regular approach channels to the estuary, as well as in the
proposed new dredged approach channel to Maplin. Work started at Silvertown on the barrier and the raising of the banks downstream in 1972.

A structure known as a 'rising sector gate' was chosen as the best type of
gate for the barrier: it gives unlimited headroom and the maximum span
practicable to modern engineering. The gates, shaped like segments of a
great cylinder, are normally housed in recessed concrete troughs in the bed
of the river. When a dangerously high tide is expected they can be rotated
up around the central axis by hydraulic machinery into the defensive
position, blocking the tide. Structural steel can only stand so much pressure;
there is expected to be a large differential head of water between one side of
the gates and the other; so the span of the largest gate has been restricted to
sixty-one metres. There will be four main gates of this size, flanked by a
number of smaller gates. The largest ships using this part of the river, about
15,000-tonners, will be able to pass through the central gates. Each of the
large gates with its counterweights will weigh more than three thousand
tonnes. The hydraulic machinery to operate them will consist of electric
motors to supply oil to very large hydraulic rams, which supply the movement and power to raise and lower the gates through a linkage mechanism.
For maintenance and exercise purposes it will also be possible to close one
gate at a time.

It is estimated that when the barrier is finished in about 1979 it will be
necessary to raise it once or twice a year to prevent floods. But, as the water
level continues to rise, it will be necessary to close the gates about ten times
a year by A.D. 2030. The banks below the barrier are being raised to levels
six feet higher than those reached in the great floods of 1953. Once the barrier
is finished and the banks are raised, the serious and growing danger of
flooding in the Thames estuary will be removed for the foreseeable future.

Another remarkable riparian responsibility of the Greater London Council
is the development of Thamesmead. This unique town within a City in the

Plumstead and Erith marshes, seven miles east of central London, is trans-forming a desolate area beside the river. Work started in 1967 and is sche-duled to take place over fifteen years. By the 1990s about 45,000 people will live in Thamesmead, which is intended to be not a dormitory or a ghost town after working hours, but a complete and self-sufficient community for all seasons, with employment, schools, and communal and recreational facilities as well as houses. The plans make use of the riverside site, with four and a half miles of canals, dykes, and lakes. Shopping by boat will no longer be confined to the Norfolk Broads and Venice. The projected ring road round London is planned to pass through the site and under the Thames in a tunnel.

The Greater London Council is responsible for the overall development plan of London, in which the Thames has a special place as the greatest of all London's natural advantages and idiosyncrasies. The most important part of the development of London and the Thames for the rest of this cen-tury will be the redevelopment of the five thousand acres of dockland, which could solve London's chronic housing problem at a stroke; and, whatever is done, will affect the character of the river and London for many centuries.

The human organization that has been controlling the Thames for the longest continuous time is the Corporation of the City of London, whose interest is almost as old as the port itself. In return for its loyalty and financial support, the City gradually extracted fishing, commercial, and trading rights on the Thames from the early Kings, who owned the country as their inheri-tance. In 1197 Richard I granted a charter to the Mayor, Aldermen, and Commonalty of the City, as Conservators of the River Thames and Port of London. The Lord Mayor of London's title as Admiral of the Port is derived from that charter, and still subsists, though nowadays it is purely honorific. Other important medieval ports, like Southampton and Yarmouth, also had the office of Admiral of the Port.

In 1215 King John gave the City the right to elect its own Lord Mayor, at that time an important step forward towards democratic government in England. A few weeks later Magna Carta confirmed the City's jurisdiction on the Thames: 'And the City of London shall have all its ancient liberties and free customs, both by land and water.'

In those days the Mayor's river Court of Admiralty, known as the Con-servators, dealt with civil cases of freightage, insurance, damage from col-lisions, and similar matters. As Admiral, the Lord Mayor had the right to hold a Court of Admiralty over maritime cases; in practice he exercised the right most often over cases of collisions in the river below bridges. These cases gave him the right to many profitable perquisites called droits of Admiralty, now extinct. In the sixteenth century the increasing volume of these cases as the port became more crowded excited the jealousy of the Lord High Admiral. Elizabeth I desired that maritime cases should be dealt with by her High Court of Admiralty rather than by such local courts as the Lord Mayor's. The Lord Mayor of London has never held a Court of Admiralty since. But a charter of James I confirmed the immemorial rights of the Corporation to the office of Bailiff and Conservator of the Thames.

Of more practical importance than the vestigial title of Admiral of the Port, the Lord Mayor and Corporation are trustees of the Bridge House Estates: the fund built up over many centuries by tolls and rents from London Bridge, and legacies of pious Londoners 'to God and the Bridge'. This fund has grown so large that it has paid for the construction, maintenance, and rebuilding when necessary of the City's four bridges, at no cost to the ratepayer or taxpayer.

London Bridge has just been rebuilt for a second time by the Bridge House Estates.

Blackfriars Bridge was paid for by the fund, designed by Robert Mylne, and opened in 1769. The removal of old London Bridge so aggravated the scour and siltation of the river that this first Blackfriars Bridge had to be strengthened, at very heavy cost. The present bridge, on iron arches between stone piers, was designed by Sir Joseph Cubitt and opened by Queen Victoria in 1869. In 1907–8 its original width of seventy feet was extended to one hundred and five feet, making it the widest bridge over the Thames at that time.

Southwark Bridge was originally a toll bridge built for a private company by the elder Rennie, and opened in 1819. In 1864 the Corporation of London abolished the tolls by making payments out of 'City's Cash', an income derived principally from the surplus from the City's three markets and the properties of the ancient municipality before the modern rating system was introduced. In 1868 the Corporation bought the bridge for £200,000. It was rebuilt by Sir Ernest George and reopened by George V in 1921.

The City's fourth and final bridge financed by the Bridge House Estates joins the Boroughs of Tower Hamlets and Southwark, wholly outside the boundaries of the City. Its bascules are seldom raised for ocean-going vessels today now that the wharves in the Upper Pool are closed, and the old steam machinery is too expensive to operate. New electrical machinery is being installed, and four of the eight hydraulic engines are being preserved as museum pieces of Victorian engineering, together with two steam pumping engines beneath the southern approach to the bridge. The Corporation is examining the possibility of opening the chambers that house the machinery under the towers and the upper walkways between the towers to the public.

If in the future any of these bridges needs to be replaced, or if a new bridge, or more probably a tunnel, needs to be constructed in the City, on precedent there is likely to be enough money in the Bridge House Estates to finance it.

The final responsibility of the City of London for the Thames is as the

Port Health Authority for the Port of London. In 1872 Britain was threatened by an invasion of cholera then raging on the Continent. The Government of the day decided to constitute the Corporation of the City as the Port Sanitary Authority for the Port of London, in order to relieve the Privy Council of some of its responsibilities to prevent epidemic diseases from entering the country. As such the Corporation is responsible for preventing the import and spread of communicable human disease and the import of unwholesome food. It is also responsible for the hygiene of ships in the Port Health District, which extends for nearly ninety miles from Teddington to beyond the mouth of the Thames. It is also responsible for the ordinary public health control of nuisance in all shapes and sizes, such as noise, air pollution, dumping of London's refuse on land by the Thames, and the concomitant rodents and rodent-borne disease.

To police the ten thousand ships that enter the Port of London every year the Corporation's Port Health Authority maintains a quarantine boarding station at Denton Hospital near Gravesend. A quarantine cutter called the *Humphrey Morris* and two older vessels enable medical officers to board ships in all weathers and take suspected infectious cases to the isolation hospital at Denton. The million tons of food that enter the port from all over the world each year are continually inspected to make sure that they are fit for human consumption. The Authority's staff to keep the Thames free from disease includes at present twenty health inspectors. As the port changes and develops, whether it is towards bigger ships farther down the tideway or to lighters lifting containers higher up stream, the Port Health Authority will have to adapt its methods and operations to keep pace with it.

Law and order on the river is enforced by the Thames Division of the Metropolitan Police, which patrols the river in boats for the fifty-four miles from Staines Bridge to the sea. Its principal responsibility is defined as the protection of life and property on ships and barges on the river and on the wharves and waterfront.

The Thames Division has evolved from the semi-private force formed at the end of the eighteenth century by the West India Dock Company to protect its cargoes from pilfering and looting. This scheme for a marine force to police the Thames was introduced in 1798 by Dr Patrick Colquhoun and Jeremy Bentham, the Utilitarian philosopher. The first marine police office was opened on the site of the present Thames Division headquarters at Wapping. The original force had a judicial department with a resident magistrate as well as a police department. It was semi-official, with the Government paying the cost of the magistrate, the clerk, and constables, and the West India merchants providing water police and watchmen. Colquhoun claimed that a third of all men working in the port handling cargoes were known to be either thieves or receivers of stolen property, and that their activities disposed of about half of all cargoes entering the port. The police force was recruited from seamen and watermen and had a dangerous and violent life, often being engaged in pitched naval battle by the plunderers. In those gaudy days the Thames police patrolled in rowing boats and sailing boats.

In 1839 the old Marine Police Force was incorporated in the Metropolitan Police as the Thames Division, and its judicial section became the Thames police court. Motor-boats were introduced in 1910, and today there are thirty-six duty boats, most of which are thirty feet long with a single diesel engine, to maintain a patrol throughout the twenty-four hours of the day. In addition to the duty boats, there are three twin-screw launches used by the Chief Superintendent and his senior officers for supervisory and cere-monial duties. All boats and launches are linked by two-way radio telephones with New Scotland Yard, other police stations, and patrolling police cars.

In the brave old days, when organized gangs of pirates swept the estuary, the marine police force was stationed in hulks in the river. These have been replaced by police stations on dry land, except at Waterloo Pier.

An Underwater Search Unit is stationed at Wapping, consisting of a mobile dragging section and a section of eight frogmen available for work under water. In addition to its patrol and criminal investigation duties, Thames Division is responsible for warning people in vulnerable places near the river when there is a threat of abnormally high tides. Modern equipment and modern crime are vastly more complex than they were in the days of the original river police force. But the principle of preserving law and order and protecting property on the tideway remains the same.

The Company of Watermen and Lightermen of the River Thames is still responsible for licensing people to navigate on the tideway; though there is less traffic than there used to be in the days of John Taylor, the Company's most famous freeman, when forty thousand men earned their living on or about the river. Today the Company has about two thousand, five hundred members, of whom all but two hundred are journeymen. The two hundred are mainly owners of craft on the Thames.

Attempts to license watermen and regulate fares began early in the six-teenth century. They culminated in an Act of 1555 appointing 'Rulers' of all watermen and wherrymen working between Gravesend and Windsor, and so creating the Company. Today the Company apprentices boys who wish to work as watermen and lightermen on the river, and examines them after two years and again at the end of their time. It grants licences to the successful and admits them to the freedom of the Company. The Company performs these licensing functions as agent for the Port of London Authority, and with the Authority tries to ensure that standards of navigation are kept high. There will always be watermen needed on the Thames, and their numbers could increase, if the development of trade by lighters carrying containers up river led to the rejuvenation of the inland waterways system.

The canals of London are the responsibility of the British Waterways Board, which controls about two thousand miles of canal in Britain. The canals were built piecemeal and without coordination early in the industrial revolution, and were rapidly superseded by the railways and motor transport.

About fifty miles of canal come within Greater London, most of them as part of the Grand Union Canal. London's canal system runs north of the Thames and impinges on the London River at Brentford and at the Lea Navigation and the Limehouse Cut, both of which are still commercial waterways. South of the river the Surrey Canal is owned by the Port of London Authority. Traffic by waterway is cheaper than by any other method, and it would be prudent to reopen, develop, and rationalize the waterway system, particularly in view of the ever-rising costs and increasing scarcity of fuel.

The Worshipful Company of Fishmongers is one of the oldest City Guilds, having an unbroken existence of more than seven hundred years. It secured a complete monopoly of the sale of fish in London in the Middle Ages. The Fishmongers, with their own Court of Law (*Leyhalmode*), were the head of what were known as the Victualling Guilds. These were interested in maintaining their monopolies in foodstuffs, but were opposed by the Craft Guilds, who wanted free trade in food, but not in the goods that they manufactured themselves.

The Fishmongers finally lost their monopoly in the fifteenth century, but they retain certain atavistic statutory duties connected with fish. Officials of the Company, called 'Fishmeters', still inspect all fish coming into London, between two and four hundred tons a day, and seize any that fail to pass their tests. The Company can prosecute sellers of bad fish under the Food and Drugs Act, 1955. It also has powers to prosecute offenders against the Salmon and Freshwater Fisheries Acts for illegal methods of fishing and for marketing during the close seasons. So long as London continues to buy fish, the Company of Fishmongers will probably retain its charmingly archaic vestigial functions derived from the medieval guilds.

Many other organizations and individuals have responsibilities for the London River. The Corporation of Trinity House is the lighthouse and pilotage authority. The Board of Trade administers the Coastguard Service. The Thames Rescue Service, an association of Royal Life Saving Society lifeguard clubs, patrols the river from Wallingford to the sea. Riparian local authorities, institutions, and individuals have statutory environmental responsibilities for the river.

But above all Londoners, and to some extent Englishmen generally, regard the Thames proprietorially as their patron river. This regard may be partly inspired by imprecise folk memories of how much of the past greatness of London and Britain has been based on and created by the London River. But the Thames is also an emblem of continuity in a world that is changing at frightening speed. The appearance of London has been altered dramatically for the worse in the past century. The suburbs have covered the river banks with brick boxes, and the geometric office blocks have intruded higher and higher into the familiar old skyline. A cockney Rip Van Winkle, returning home after twenty years' sleep in the Surrey mountains, would find it hard to recognize his greatest of cities. St Paul's, the Houses of Parliament, and the Tower are still themselves, though increasingly masked by the forest of tower blocks. But the most unchanging element of London is the majestic curve of its river, ebbing and flowing in rhythm with the universe.

Babylon has vanished, and Troy, and Thebes of the hundred gates. When Macaulay's New Zealander eventually arrives to gaze at the rubble of London's architecture, the one aspect of the City that he will be able to identify at once from the old maps, paintings, engravings, diaries, and poems will be the London River. Until then the prosperity and beauty of London will continue to depend to a great extent, as they have from the beginning, on the Thames. There are greater opportunities now than there have been for centuries to improve the uses and appearance of the river. As long as the British remain in business and in business as a nation, the Thames will continue to be one of the great rivers of the world.

Bibliography

The Thames

ACKERLEY, C. H. Plan for better security of vessels navigating the river Thames, 1834
ADDISON, W. W. Thames estuary, 1954
BELL, A. Port of London (1909–34), 1934
BELL, A. Said noble river, 1937
BELLOC, HILAIRE. Historic Thames, 1909
BELLOC, HILAIRE. River of London, 1912
BESANT, G. B. London Bridge, 1927
BESANT, SIR WALTER. Fascination of London: the Thames, 1903
BIRD, JAMES. The Geography of the Port of London
BOWN, A. H. and DOVE, C. A. Port operation and administration
BRIGGS, M. S. Down the Thames, 1949
BRITISH TRAVEL ASSOCIATION. London from the river
BROODBANK, J. G. History of the Port of London, 2 vols, 1921
BRYANT, ARTHUR. Liquid history, 1960
BUNJE, J. H. O. Tideless Thames in Future London, 1944
CAPPER, C. I. Port and Trade of London, 1862
COLLIER, WILLIAM. Historic buildings: the historic architecture of the Thames valley, 1973
COLQUHOUN, PATRICK. Treatise on commerce and police of the Thames, 1800
COOK, T. A. and NICKALLS, G. T. Doggett, 1908
CORPORATION OF LONDON. The story of three bridges, 1973
CRACKNELL, BASIL. Portrait of London River: the Tidal Thames from Teddington to the Sea, 1968
DE MARÉ, E. S. Time on the Thames, 1952
DE MARÉ, E. S. London's riverside, past, present and future, 1958
DICKENS, CHARLES. Dictionary of the Thames, 1888
ELLIS, A. 300 Years on London River: Hay's Wharf 1651–1951, 1952
FAGAN, DICK and BURGESS, E. A. Men of the Tideway, 1966
FLETCHER, GEOFFREY. London's River, 1966
GIBBINS, ROBERT J. Sweet Thames run softly, 1940
GIBBINS, ROBERT J. Till I end my song, 1957
GODSAVE, G. E. Pleasures of London's river, Father Thames, 1961
GOODSALL, ROBERT H. The widening Thames, 1965
GREATER LONDON COUNCIL. London's River Thames, 1973
GROSVENOR, J. Port of London
HALL, A. The Thames barrier, 1972
HALL, S. C. and Mrs S. C. The book of the Thames from its rise to its fall
HARDING, DENNIS W. The Iron Age in the Upper Thames basin, 1972
HARRISON, M. London beneath the pavement, 1961
HERBERT, J. Port of London, 1947

HERBERT, A. P. No boats on the river, 1932
HERBERT, SIR ALAN P. The Thames, 1966
HOME, GORDON. Old London Bridge, 1931
HUMPHERUS, H. History of the Company of Watermen, 3 vols, 1887
JACKDAW PUBLICATIONS folder. The Port of London
JACKSON, PETER. London Bridge, 1971
JAMES, G. W. London, western reaches, 1950
JONES, LL. R. Geography of London River, 1931
JONES, S. R. Thames triumphant, 1943
KRAUSSE, A. S. Pictorial history of the Thames, 1889
LAMPE, D. The Tunnel: story of tunnel dug beneath the Thames 1824-42, 1963
LE MARCHANT, H. D. Port of London, 1904
LESLIE, G. D. Our river, 1881
LINNEY, A. G. Peepshow of the Port of London, 1929
LOVELL, JOHN. Stevedores and dockers: a study of trade unionism in the Port of London
    1870-1914, 1969
MACCARTHY, J., PRAED, Mrs C. and MENPES, M. The grey river, 1889
MACKAY, C. Thames and its tributaries, 2 vols, 1840
MAXWELL, G. S. Authors' Thames, 1924
MILLWARD, ROY, and ROBINSON, A. South-East England: Thameside and the Weald, 1971
MORGAN, G. H. Forgotten Thameside, 1951
MORLEY, F. V. River Thames, 1926
MYATT, J. and PAYNE, H. C. Mapping out geography
NICHOLSON'S GUIDE TO THE THAMES
NOËL-HUME, I. Treasure in the Thames, 1956
O'DONNELL, E., Great Thames mysteries, 1930
ORAM, R. B. The story of our ports
ORAM, R. B. and BAKER, C. C. R. The efficient port
ORMSBY, H. London on the Thames, 1924
PEEL, JOHN. Portrait of the Thames from Teddington to the source, 1967
PHILLIPS, H. The Thames about 1750, 1951
PILKINGTON, ROGER. Thames waters, 1956
PILKINGTON, ROGER. Small boat on the Thames, 1966
PUDNEY, JOHN. Crossing London's river: the bridges, ferries, and tunnels crossing the
    Thames tideway in London, 1972
PURTON, ROWLAND W. Ports and sea transport, Blandford Press
RIMBAULT, E. F. Old ballads, great frost 1683-4, 1844
SAVILL, M. Tide of London, 1951
SENIOR, W. Thames, Oxford to Tower, 1891
TAYLOR, JOHN. John Taylor's last voyage (1641), in his works, second collection, 1873
TAYLOR, JOHN. Cause of watermen's suit (1613), 1872
THACKER, FRED S. The Thames highway, 2 vols, 1968
THOMPSON, A. G. The royal Thames, 1937
THOMPSON, A. G. London Bridge and Pool, 1949
THOMPSON, RICHARD. Chronicles of London Bridge, 1827
TOMLINSON, H. C. and H. M. Below London Bridge, 1934
TOMLINSON, H. M. London River, 1921
WARD, LOCK AND CO. Guide to the Thames, 1909
WATERS, B. 13 Rivers to the Thames, 1964
WHEELDON, J. P. Angling resorts near London, 1878
WYLLIE, W. L. and M. A. London to Nore, 1905

WYMER, JOHN. Lower Palaeolithic archaeology in Britain, as represented by the Thames Valley, 1968

London

THE ANNUAL REGISTER
BAKER, THOMAS, Medieval London, 1970
BARTON, N. J. Lost rivers of London, 1962
BEBBINGTON, GILLIAN. London street names, 1972
BEDE, The Venerable. Historia ecclesiastica gentis Anglorum (Loeb edition), 1930
BEDFORD, JOHN. London's burning, 1966
BELL, WALTER G. The Tower of London, 1935
BELLOC, HILAIRE. Wolsey, 1930
BIRCH, J. G. Limehouse through five centuries, 1930
BOOTH, C. J. Labour and life of the people, 2 vols, 1889–91
BOSWELL, JAMES. The life of Samuel Johnson. Ed. Clement Shorter, 1924
BURFORD, EPHRAIM. The orrible synne: a look at London lechery from Roman to Cromwellian times, 1973
BURNELL, R. D. The Oxford and Cambridge Boat Race 1829-1953, 1954
CAMBRIDGE COUNTY GEOGRAPHIES
CAVENDISH, GEORGE. The Life and Death of Thomas Wolsey, 1641
CHAMBERS, R. The Book of Days, 2 vols
CHANCELLOR, EDWIN BERESFORD. Historical Richmond, 1885
CHARLTON, JOHN. The Banqueting House, Whitehall, 1964
COOPER, C. S. The outdoor monuments of London, 1928
DAY, JOHN R. The story of London's underground, 1972
DEARING, VINTON. A walk through London with John Gay and a run with Daniel Defoe, 1971
DICKENS, CHARLES. Dictionary of London, 1879
DICTIONARY OF NATIONAL BIOGRAPHY
DUGDALE, GEORGE S. Whitehall through the centuries, 1950
EHRLICH, BLAKE. London on the Thames, 1968
GREATER LONDON COUNCIL. Greater London services, 1973–74
GRIMES, WILLIAM. The Excavation of Roman and Medieval London, 1968
HALL, PETER G. London 2000, 1969
HAMMERSMITH. History and Antiquities of the Parish of Hammersmith, 1839
HARRIS, JOHN, ORGEL, STEPHEN and STRONG, ROY. The King's Arcadia: Inigo Jones and the Stuart Court, 1973
HARRISON, MICHAEL. London Beneath the Pavement, 1961
HIBBERT, CHRISTOPHER. London: the biography of a city, 1969
HOBHOUSE, HERMIONE. Lost London, 1972
HODGES, C. WALTER. Shakespeare's second globe, 1973
HOLLIS, CHRISTOPHER. Sir Thomas More, 1934
HOWELL, JAMES. London and Westminster, 1657
JACKSON, ALAN. Semi-detached London: suburban development, life, and transport, 1900–39, 1973
JACKSON, PETER. London Bridge, 1971
JACKSON, STANLEY. The Savoy: the romance of a great hotel, 1964
JACKSON, W. ERIC. Achievement: a short history of the LCC, 1965
JENKINS, ALAN. London's City, 1973
JENKINS, SIMON. A City at Risk, 1970
JESSE, J. H. Literary and Historical Memorials, 2 vols, 1901

JESSE, J. H. London and its Celebrities, 3 vols, 1901

KENT, WILLIAM. An Encyclopaedia of London, revised by G. Thompson, 1970

LILLYWHITE, BRYANT. London coffee houses, 1963

LINDSAY, PHILIP. Hampton Court: a history, 1948

MACAULAY, Lord. The History of England from the Accession of James the Second, 1863

MALFATTI, C. V. Two Italian Accounts of Tudor England, 1953

MARSHALL, DOROTHY. Dr Johnson's London, 1968

MARTIN, JOHN. Greater London: an industrial geography, 1966

MAYHEW, HENRY. London Labour and the London Poor: a cyclopaedia of the condition and earnings of those that will work, those that cannot work, and those that will not work, 4 vols, 1851–62,

METCALF, PRISCILLA. Victorian London, 1972

MINNEY, RUBEIGH J. The Tower of London, 1970

MITCHELL, R. J., and LEYS, M. D. R. A history of London life, 1958

MORE, CRESACRE. The Life of Sir Thomas More, ed. Rev. J. Hunter, 1828

MORE, SIR THOMAS. The Utopia of Sir Thomas More, Clarendon Press, 1895

MORE, SIR THOMAS. The Works of Sir Thomas More, Knyght, sometime Lorde Chancellour of England, wrytten by him in the English tonge, 1557

MORTON, EARL OF, in collaboration with Sir Donald Allen. The Chelsea Physic Garden—its history and origin, 1965

NORDEN, JOHN. View of London in 1600, 1961

NOTESTEIN, WALLACE. Four worthies, 1956

OXFORD HISTORY OF ENGLAND. Ed. Sir George Clark

PELLING, HENRY. A History of British Trade Unionism, 1963

PEPYS, SAMUEL. Diary, ed. R. Latham and W. Matthews, 8 vols, 1970–74

PERKINS, JOCELYN. Westminster Abbey, the Empire's Crown, 1937

PEVSNER, NIKOLAUS. The Buildings of England

PLATTS, BERYL. A History of Greenwich, 1973

POLLARD, A. F. Henry VIII, 1919

POLLARD, A. F. Wolsey, revised ed. 1953

PUDNEY, JOHN. Crossing London's River: the bridges, ferries, and tunnels crossing the Thames tideway in London, 1972

RAY, JOHN. The Story of London's Underground, 1972

ROBERTSON, P. The London of Charles Dickens, 1970

ROBSON-SCOTT, W. D. German Travellers in England, 1400–1800, 1953

ROWSE, A. L. The England of Elizabeth, 1950

ROPER, WILLIAM. The Life of Thomas More, ed. S. W. Singer, 1822

ROUTH, E. M. G. Sir Thomas More and his Friends in 1477–1535

RYE, WILLIAM BRENCHLEY. England as seen by foreigners in the days of Elizabeth and James the first, 1865

SAUNDERS, HILARY ST G., Westminster Hall, 1951

SEDGWICK, ROMNEY. History of Parliament: the House of Commons 1714–54, 1970

SURVEY OF LONDON. Ed. F. H. W. Sheppard, 1955–73

STENTON, F. M. Norman London, 1960

SOUTHWORTH, JAMES G. Vauxhall Gardens, 1941

STEPHENSON, HENRY. Shakespeare's London, 1905

STOW, JOHN. A Survey of London. Ed. Charles Kingsford, 1908

SUMMERSON, Sir John. Georgian London, 1970

TACITUS, CAIUS CORNELIUS. Agricola, ed. Maurice Hutton, 1946

TACITUS, CAIUS CORNELIUS. Annales, ed. Henry Furneaux, 1951

TAINE, HIPPOLYTE. Notes on England

TEETGEN, A. B. The Footsteps of Sir Thomas More, 1930

TIMES, the History of the, 1935

TURNER, FRED. History and antiquities of Brentford, 1922

VICTORIA HISTORY OF THE COUNTIES OF ENGLAND

WALL, CECIL, CAMERON, H. CHARLES and UNDERWOOD, F. ASHWORTH. A History of the Worshipful Society of Apothecaries of London

WESTMINSTER ABBEY. Official guide, 1971

WHITTING, PHILIP D. A History of Hammersmith edited for the Hammersmith local history group, 1965

WILDING, NORMAN and LAUNDY, PHILIP. An Encyclopaedia of Parliament, 1958

WILLIAMS, G. GEORGE. Guide to Literary London, 1973

WILLIAMS, NEVILLE. The Royal Residences, 1966

INDEX